Praise for *Research Methods and Applications for Student Affairs*

"Student affairs practitioners are faced with an environment in which they are increasingly challenged to demonstrate that their programs, activities, and learning experiences contribute to student learning and growth through research studies. Patrick Biddix has developed a thorough, comprehensive treatment of how to go about answering this challenge. Whether readers are graduate students or long-time practitioners in student affairs, this volume will provide an excellent foundation for them as they seek to advance their research skills."

—**John H. Schuh**, Distinguished Professor Emeritus, Iowa State University

"*Research Methods for Student Affairs* is an essential resource for student affairs professionals interested in being consumers of and contributors to research in the profession. By using practical language, the book provides a breadth and depth of knowledge that will benefit scholars and practitioners alike."

—**Darby M. Roberts**, Director of Student Life Studies, Texas A&M University

"Applying theory to practice in student affairs is critical to supporting college students and depends on effective implementation and understanding of research. Whether one is a new or seasoned researcher or a practitioner who consumes research, Dr. Biddix's text supplies the essential tools to comprehend and execute research as both a product and process."

—**Gavin Henning**, PhD, Professor of Higher Education and Program Director, New England College; President, Council for the Advancement of Standards in Higher Education

"Patrick Biddix's book is a must-have resource for any student affairs practitioner-scholar trying to better understand the often "unconsumed middle" of research articles—the methods and results/finding sections. This useful guide provides concrete examples on how to read and dissect research articles by discussing concepts and methodological terms often found in them."

—**Matthew R. Wawrzynski**, Associate Professor and Coordinator, Higher, Adult, and Lifelong Education, Michigan State University

"Vice presidents for student affairs/life, assessment and research practitioners, and master's and doctoral students alike will benefit greatly from *Research Methods and Applications for Student Affairs*. The practical and technical approaches to conducting research and applying it to practice is easy to understand and places a finer point on the importance of data-informed decision making."

—Melissa S. Shivers, PhD, Vice President for Student Life,
University of Iowa

"This book fills a large gap in the fields of student affairs and higher education. Patrick Biddix makes the case for why research is critical to the field and at the same time offers excellent advice on how to do research well."

—Robert A. Schwartz, Professor of Higher Education,
Chair, Department of Educational Leadership and Policy Studies,
College of Education, Florida State University

"Patrick Biddix weaves together clear explanations, examples from literature, and perspectives from the field to address not only the *how* of research, but also the *what* and the *why*. Comprehensive, practical, and context-specific, this intentionally structured resource provides both practitioners and students with a guide to understanding, using, and designing research in student affairs."

—Laura Dean, Professor, University of Georgia,
College Student Affairs Administration

"*Research Methods and Applications for Student Affairs* is a clearly written and useful tool for student affairs professionals committed to evidence-based practice. It serves as a perfect supplement in graduate preparation courses, and is also a beneficial book for seasoned professionals."

—Debora L. Liddell, Professor of Higher
Education & Student Affairs, University of Iowa

"In an era when the value of higher education is questioned, demonstrating student affairs contributions to student learning and development has never been more necessary. This is a must-read for student affairs practitioners."

—Tricia A. Seifert, Associate Professor of Adult &
Higher Education at Montana State University

RESEARCH METHODS
AND APPLICATIONS
FOR STUDENT AFFAIRS

RESEARCH METHODS AND APPLICATIONS FOR STUDENT AFFAIRS

J. Patrick Biddix

JB JOSSEY-BASS™

A Wiley Brand

Published by Jossey-Bass
A Wiley Brand
One Montgomery Street, Suite 1000, San Francisco, CA 94104-4594—www.josseybass.com

Jossey-Bass books and products are available through most bookstores. To contact Jossey-Bass directly call our Customer Care Department within the U.S. at 800-956-7739, outside the U.S. at 317-572-3986, or fax 317-572-4002.

Wiley publishes in a variety of print and electronic formats and by print-on-demand. Some material included with standard print versions of this book may not be included in e-books or in print-on-demand. If this book refers to media such as a CD or DVD that is not included in the version you purchased, you may download this material at http://booksupport.wiley.com. For more information about Wiley products, visit www.wiley.com.

Library of Congress Cataloging-in-Publication Data are available

ISBN 978-1-119-29970-7 (Hardcover)

Cover design by Wiley
Cover images: © Decorwithme/Shutterstock; © Exdez/iStockphoto

Printed in the United States of America

FIRST EDITION

HB Printing 10 9 8 7 6 5 4 3 2 1

PB Printing 10 9 8 7 6 5 4 3 2 1

*This book is dedicated to the influences of
Esther Lloyd-Jones and Alexander "Sandy" Astin,
pioneering methodologists in the field of student affairs,
for advancing research as fundamental for practice.*

CONTENTS

FOREWORD

Prospective graduate students often ask us if our respective programs are "research focused" or "practice focused." We view this question as reproducing a false binary in student affairs that sets research (or theory) *versus* practice. Rather, we regard the professional ideal in (at a minimum) a matrix construct, in which we can think, act, and communicate from a stance that is high in both research *and* practice. This practitioner–researcher perspective invites professionals whose full-time work is in administration to pose and answer questions as well as use scholarship to inform their work, and those professionals whose full-time work is in research and teaching to address questions of importance to the practice of student affairs in higher education. The book you are about to read strikes exactly at this crucial nexus. In this context, Patrick Biddix has aimed for outcomes in four frames: understanding, reading, evaluating, and using research in practice.

Student affairs professionals have a responsibility to engage in research-informed practice. Such practice will ensure that the academic community that relies upon leadership from the student affairs professional receives guidance based on rigorous investigation of theories, concepts, and professional practices. This type of leadership will only be possible if the professional has an *understanding* of contemporary research and is able to interpret that research appropriately. The ability to understand research enables professionals to interrogate their own practices and make informed judgments about the direction their institutional efforts should take. It should be a foundational skill for student affairs professionals to be able to make sense of the knowledge generated by researchers. It is especially important that leaders of specific functional areas have the capacity to be discerning about the research that might have direct application to their area(s) of responsibility. At the same time, practitioners should be able to understand research beyond their particular community of practice. A firm understanding of research prepares a practitioner to participate in conversations that are important to the dynamism of the academy—*What important questions are being asked? What are we learning about issues important to our institution? How should research inform our efforts?*

If understanding research should be a foundational skill for student affairs professionals, the ability to *read research* should be considered an essential skill. Research is an activity through which knowledge is generated and disseminated. It is the responsibility of student affairs professionals to be engaged and responsible consumers of that knowledge in the many forms that it is made available—print, electronic, websites, and so forth. Professional accountability and commitment require that practitioners regularly read journals, books, monographs, special reports from professional associations, government agencies, and foundations, as well as other sources, in order to stay contemporary in their knowledge. In addition to keeping up to date, reading research regularly serves to hone the professional's skills as a consumer of research. The more research professionals encounter, the more astute they can become in judging relevance, rigor, and applicability to their own work and institutional context. An essential responsibility of an institutional leader is to be research-literate, having the ability to engage with the research of their field and make informed judgments about whether or how that research is applicable. Reading research should be integrated in every practitioner's professional lifestyle and sharing what one is learning from research should be embedded in the organization's culture.

Student affairs professionals must develop the ability and the habit of *evaluating* the source, quality, and value of research, just as they should with other information. It is common even for experienced professionals holding advanced degrees to encounter results of a study that is out of their area or that uses an unfamiliar research method, but having the confidence and competence to evaluate the underlying quality of the study *(How well were the methods used to collect and analyze data aligned with the research purpose/question? How adequately do they support the findings?)* allows them to place it in context with other evidence. One of the strengths of this book is its ability to help readers evaluate research and its value in developing, improving, and/or discontinuing higher education policy and practice. A smart professional will refer to chapters on specific research methods for guidance in assessing quality of a study and its conclusions.

Of course, a primary reason to understand, read, and evaluate research is to *apply* it in practice. Research findings can inform policy decisions, undergird improvements to procedures and programs, and provide counterevidence to prevailing common knowledge in the field or at an institution. Data that are collected and interpreted systematically form the building blocks of arguments to begin, continue, amend, or end policies and practices in all areas of student affairs. Theories derived from and tested through research form the foundation of good practice, experimentation, and innovation. Knowledge gained through research can be used to challenge prevailing assumptions, illuminate challenges, and increase visibility for understudied populations.

As will become clear to readers of this book, different research approaches allow for exploring different kinds of questions. Likewise, different approaches produce findings that are useful in different applied contexts. Qualitative studies can produce compelling narratives and themes; quantitative studies can produce equally compelling statistics; and mixed methods studies can combine the benefits of methodological approaches to produce findings that are useful in a number of institutional, state, federal, and international contexts for policy and practice.

This publication is an incredible resource for the professional development, vitality, and relevance of student affairs professionals. Unlike other texts that tend to focus on how to be a successful researcher, this book emphasizes skill development in the arenas of reading, understanding, evaluating, and applying research. The author has thoughtfully organized this volume to facilitate deeper understanding of how research is organized and presented and how the consumer of research can navigate the literature to determine its fitness for the reader's professional needs. We are certain that this book will be a significant addition to your library and serve your professional development needs for years to come.

Kristen A. Renn
Professor of Higher, Adult, and Lifelong
Education and Associate Dean of
Undergraduate Studies for Student Success
Research, Michigan State University

Larry D. Roper
Professor and Interim Director, School of
Language, Culture, and Society and
Former Vice Provost for Student Affairs,
Oregon State University

ABOUT THE AUTHOR

Dr. J. Patrick Biddix is Professor of Higher Education and Associate Director of the Postsecondary Education Research Center (PERC) at the University of Tennessee in Knoxville. He teaches graduate courses in research, assessment and evaluation, and special topics in higher education and student affairs. His areas of expertise include research methodology and assessment, college student experiences, and postsecondary outcomes. Prior to coming to UT, he was associate professor and program coordinator for higher education and student affairs at Valdosta State University. He also worked as a student affairs professional at Washington University in St. Louis. He has received three faculty excellence awards for research and teaching (2010, 2011, 2015). In 2015, he was a U.S. Fulbright Scholar at Concordia University in Montreal, Canada.

Dr. Biddix received his doctorate in education with a concentration in higher education from the University of Missouri in St. Louis (2006). He also holds a graduate certificate in Institutional Research from UMSL (2005). He received a master's degree in higher education administration from the University of Mississippi (2003) and a bachelor's degree in classical civilization from the University of Tennessee (2001). His published research has appeared in top-tier student affairs and communication technology journals. He also coauthored the second edition textbook of *Assessment in Student Affairs* (Jossey-Bass, 2016).

Dr. Biddix is an active member of the National Association of Student Personnel Administrators (NASPA) and a frequent presenter at the Annual Conference. He serves on the Student Affairs Assessment Leaders (SAAL) board of directors and the NASPA Assessment, Evaluation, and Research (AER) Knowledge Community

Leadership Team. He is also an editorial board member for the *Journal of College Student Development* (JCSD), the *Journal of Student Affairs Research and Practice* (JSARP), and the *NASPA Journal about Women in Higher Education* (NJAWE), and *Oracle: The Research Journal* of the Association of Fraternity/Sorority Advisors (editor from 2009 to 2013).

Dr. Biddix has an active family of five that includes his wife and three young children. Aside from spending time with them (which includes Legos, music, sports, and the occasional date night), he enjoys hiking, listening to hip-hop music, and playing board games. When you see him in person, ask about the music playlist associated with this book.

ABOUT THIS BOOK

This introductory text provides an overview of the book with details about its features. It includes a statement of purpose, a rationale, details about the structure of the book and organization of chapters, a chapter outline, an explanation of key features, and information on additional support.

Purpose

The purpose of this book is to provide graduate students, faculty, and professionals with a primary textbook and reference guide for understanding, reading, evaluating, and applying research in student affairs. Continued calls for accountability and the ability to demonstrate how programs and practices connect to learning outcomes are no longer outlooks, but are expectations of every professional (Schuh, Biddix, Dean, & Kinzie, 2016). Supporting professionals who are competent with research methods and applications, capable of consuming, critiquing, applying, and creating knowledge based on evidence, is increasingly important. Yet, both new graduates and chief student affairs officers admit to lacking fundamental research proficiencies (Sriram, 2014; Sriram & Oster, 2012). This textbook is intended to addresses these needs by providing an instructional guide as well as a professional reference for research methods and applications.

Rationale

Student affairs professionals often are exposed to research in the field for the first time during an introductory graduate course in research methods. In contrast to applied courses and internships, a research methods course can seem unconnected to practice. Common criticisms include:

"I just don't understand why I need to learn research."

"I am least excited to learn about this topic."

"I came into this program to work as a practitioner, not to be a researcher."

"I don't want to be a faculty member."

"I hate [am terrible at] statistics."

This book was written with those reservations and misperceptions in mind. Specifically, the first chapter incorporates these objections to serve as a convincing argument for the need to learn about research for practice and to appreciate the broader applicability of a research skillset. Learning about research can be challenging, particularly for learners who do not see clear connections between research and practice. Others may find the language of research difficult. Research can be engaging when it is relevant, and intimidating and overwhelming when it is not. Similar to job training, learning about research cannot be accomplished simply by taking one course. Learning about research is an engagement activity that begins with an introduction in formal coursework and extends into practice. The authors of the ASK standards (2006) noted:

> While student affairs graduates are taught basic research and assessment skills in their programs, many more seasoned professionals look to current publications and professional organizations such as ACPA to assist them with the development of the skills and knowledge needed to successfully identify, measure, evaluate and articulate students' co-curricular learning outcomes. (American College Personnel Association, 2006, p. 1)

Research is a broad and complex topic, spanning multiple disciplines, perspectives, and skillsets. Learning to effectively read, evaluate, and apply research can require substantial time and effort. This book is organized to help make learning easier and seeing connections to practice clearer.

Structure of the Book

This book contains 14 chapters. Structurally, the chapters are divided into Frames, Foundations, and Methods chapters. Each section also has a specific organization. An overview follows.

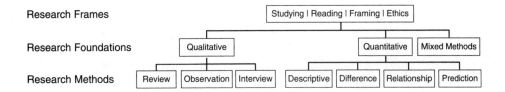

Research Frames chapters introduce rationale, basic terminology and applications, and incorporates guidelines for reading research. Also included are ethical considerations. These chapters comprise the skills needed for a basic understanding of research in student affairs. Each is organized to build knowledge logically from initial concepts to applications.

Research Foundations chapters include core concepts, terminology, and basic applications for the main types of research methods. These chapters are structured in a question-and-answer format designed to address a central question: What essential concepts do student affairs practitioners and researchers need to know to understand (qualitative, quantitative, or mixed) methods? Each of the associated questions are derived from frequently asked questions, misunderstandings, and misconceptions about research. Key concepts are included for reference.

Research Methods chapters present a detailed overview of specific research methods. There are three qualitative-focused and four quantitative-focused chapters. Each is organized into four subsections corresponding to learning outcomes. Each subsection also includes a summary list to help guide the reader. Following is an outline of each subsection and associated summary list:

Understanding > Reasons for Understanding

Reading > Guidelines for Reading

Evaluating > Questions for Evaluating

Applying > Opportunities for Applying

This structure of the book and organization of the chapters was designed to promote usability. A scaffolding approach paired with Bloom's taxonomy was used to build learning sequences. This decision was intended to accomplish two goals:

1. To order content from lower- to higher-ordered understanding.
2. To portion content so that it could be assigned in total or referenced in sections.

The Research Foundations and Methods chapters, in particular, were organized in this way to present an easily accessed, single reference for reading and evaluating research. For example, if a reader needs to learn the difference between a descriptive and an inferential statistic, they could quickly reference that question in text. Or, if a reader simply wants to know how to read regression results, they should be able to review the section labeled Reading Prediction Research along with the accompanying checklist Guidelines for Reading. Each chapter also contains numerous examples from student affairs research to contextualize the content.

Chapter Outline

Chapter 1 (Studying Research) introduces the role of research in student affairs and demonstrates connections between the text and skills, competencies, and intended learning outcomes. Chapter 2 (Reading Research) describes the individual sections that make up a research study and applies concepts by taking apart an article to analyze each section. Chapter 3 (Framing Research) overviews the four core components of methodology and details how they work together to create a study. Chapter 4 (Considering Ethics) provides an overview of ethical considerations in research, including origins and student affairs applications.

Chapter 5 (Learning Qualitative Research) contains the basics of qualitative research methods and emphasizes essential questions such as "How much qualitative data are enough?" and "How do researchers analyze qualitative data?" Chapters 6 (Reviewing Documents), 7 (Observing People and Places), and 8 (Interviewing Individuals and Groups) detail each of the main types of qualitative research methods. Each chapter emphasizes the purpose and rationale for each method, how to differentiate major types, and how to understand, read, evaluate, and apply results.

Chapter 9 (Learning Quantitative Research) contains the basics of quantitative research methods emphasizing essential questions such as "What is a statistic?" and "How are they classified?" Chapters 10 (Describing Trends), 11 (Testing Differences), 12 (Assessing Relationships), and 13 (Making Predictions) detail the main types of quantitative research methods. Each chapter emphasizes the purpose and rationale for each method, how to differentiate major types, and how to understand, read, evaluate, and apply results.

Chapter 14 (Exploring Mixed Methods) contains the basics of mixed methods research emphasizing essential questions such as "What is meant by mixed methods?" and "How are mixed methods results presented?" Fundamental concepts in mixed methods research are introduced, such as diagramming, method prioritization, and integration.

Features of the Book

The book is structured and organized to support formal (classroom) learning, self-directed learning, and referencing. The book also features a glossary of common terms that are also identified in corresponding text sections. Two additional features are highlighted:

- Perspectives From the Field
  Perspectives From the Field are small commentaries solicited from faculty and practitioner experts about specific topics. Some emphasize information already in the text, others offer a different perspective, while others expand or introduce concepts and applications.
- Words Researchers Use
  Most chapters include several Words Researchers Use features. The concepts described typically are not common terms to be considered keywords, but are the source of many questions students and practitioners ask when learning about research methods.

Additional Support

Each chapter ends with a section titled Building Your Research Skillset that includes references and suggestions for expanding the information in each chapter. Additional resources are available online at **www.wiley.com/go/biddix/research**. These include presentation files for each chapter and a list of associated articles. Associated articles are published studies that can be paired with each chapter to enhance learning. Many of the associated articles are already cited in the corresponding chapters. These can be assigned or read alongside chapters. An article analysis worksheet is also included as a prompt for aiding article analysis, with guiding questions intended to promote an understanding of methods as well as considerations for applying results. Associated articles were chosen based on approachability and usability. The content is intentionally broad to include various publication venues, data sources, functional areas, institutional contexts, and student populations.

References

American College Personnel Association. (2006). *ASK standards: Assessment skills and knowledge content standards for student affairs practitioners and scholars.* Retrieved from http://www.myacpa.org/publications

Schuh, J. H., Biddix, J. P., Dean, L. A., & Kinzie, J. (2016). *Assessment in student affairs: A contemporary look* (2nd ed.). San Francisco, CA: Jossey-Bass.

Sriram, R. (2014). The development, validity, and reliability of a psychometric instrument measuring competencies in student affairs. *Journal of Student Affairs Research and Practice, 51*(4), 349–363.

Sriram, R., & Oster, M. (2012). Reclaiming the "scholar" in scholar–practitioner. *Journal of Student Affairs Research and Practice, 49*(4), 377–396.

ACKNOWLEDGMENTS

I love teaching research methods. I try to show my enthusiasm in every class, advising meeting, presentation, and conversation I have related to research. I truly enjoy helping others identify a research problem, specify and operationalize questions, and consider ways to answer those questions. I hope that the lessons I learned while helping others come through in this book.

Writing a textbook about research for a field that does not have one was challenging. Often, I had to make decisions about terminology, practices, and applications that the field has not formally codified. I drew on my familiarity with the existing research base, frequent discussions with colleagues across the country, and literature in the interdisciplinary field of methodology for assistance. In agreement or disagreement, I hope readers appreciate the effort and will engage in continued discussions of how we understand and apply research methods in student affairs.

The list of people to thank for the encouragement, reassurance, and motivation to write this book would take me nearly as many words as it took to finish it. This process spanned two countries, multiple cities and states, countless coffee shops across Montreal, Knoxville, and Johnson City, and hours upon hours of music ranging from trance/house and classical in the beginning to 1980s/yacht club in the middle to hip-hop and symphonic metal during editing. It included innumerable and unquantifiable valuable conversations with colleagues, mentors, and professionals who listened patiently so many times when content strayed from esoteric to minutiae. I cannot begin to name all the names of individuals whose advice shaped this work.

I need to specifically thank several individuals. Norma Mertz, my mentor and friend, gave me the time, space, and pragmatism to write this book. I will miss our conversations as it developed. I wish to thank John Schuh for introducing me to textbook writing and encouraging this one. I also need to thank Laura Dean and Diane Cooper for reassuring me that this book was important. My departmental colleagues, Dorian McCoy, Karen Boyd, and Terry Ishitani, provided invaluable clarification with their expertise when I needed it most. I would not have met any of my deadlines without the editing work of Katie Singer, Jacob Kamer, Wade McGarity, and Melissa Edwards. I also want to thank the contributors to the Perspectives From the Field features, many of whom represent my role models in the field. I am honored to share some page space with each of you. Finally, to all the authors I cited in this work, thank you for contributions to our field.

My final and most important acknowledgments go to my family. Writing a single-author book can be lonely work. It has its ups for sure, but some days are harder to leave to write than others. Mom and Dad, you never told me I couldn't do anything, and that is more important than you'll ever know. Benjamin, thank you for giving up Lego building and Imaginext time. I am looking forward to making some of that up. Clare Bear, thank you for the magic you gave me each night before I got up for a long writing session. Jackson, I see an author in you as well, but I know your work will be a lot funnier than mine. Finally, Erika, you gave me the love (sometimes #toughlove), time, and motivation I needed to get up all those early mornings and stay those extra hours. You are my muse and inspiration, and the person who always has the best advice. Your encouragement and ideas wrote more of this book than I ever did. Truly, thank you.

RESEARCH METHODS
AND APPLICATIONS
FOR STUDENT AFFAIRS

CHAPTER ONE

STUDYING RESEARCH

Learning Outcomes

By the end of this chapter, you should be able to:

- Describe several reasons for the importance of research.
- Identify the historical and contemporary context of research.
- Explain why practitioners need to be researchers.
- Articulate the need for research skills and competencies.
- Relate research skills to student affairs practice skills.

Research is essential to student affairs. It chronicles the history of professional practice, informs contemporary work, and recommends how the field must shift to address future challenges and opportunities. Practitioners who are skilled and proficient research consumers, capable of understanding, reading, evaluating, and applying evidence-based information, are becoming indispensable to the field. The ability to support and to demonstrate how programs and practices connect to educational outcomes is no longer an advantage but an expectation in all functional areas (Schuh, Biddix, Dean, & Kinzie, 2016). Research-based evidence, collected directly or synthesized from existing studies, is progressively the basis for informing and legitimizing decisions in practice. Yet both new professionals and chief student affairs officers admit to lacking fundamental research competencies (Sriram, 2014; Sriram & Oster, 2012).

Practitioners need research skills to be effective. Research skills can be learned through graduate study and professional development, continually on the job, and through practice to accomplish work. Practitioners need research competencies to thrive. Research demonstrates the value of work, forecasts future needs, and validates effective practices. Research skills and competencies are not mutually exclusive. While some skills are precursors to competencies, many serve as foundations for attaining basic, intermediate, and advanced proficiencies.

The purpose of this chapter is to introduce basic research terminology and to articulate the need for competence in student affairs practice. Essential skills and competencies are explained as well as considerations for applying research skills to practice. The chapter begins with an historical overview of how research came to be valued in student affairs practice. Next is context and background for understanding and studying research. This is followed by an overview of concepts and a discussion of research specific to student affairs, which serves as a transition to the contemporary landscape and transitions into recommended skills and competencies.

Understanding Research

Researchers have been directly studying student services and the effects of programs and interventions on students for nearly a century. Staff in the personnel department at Northwestern University, influenced by a research focus brought to the university by President Walter Dill Scott (Biddix & Schwartz, 2012), were among the first to approach college-student problems with empirical data in a systematic way. *Student Personnel Point of View* (SPPOV) lead author Esther Lloyd-Jones, who began her career as a staff member in the personnel department (Certis, 2014), emphasized research as a core component of practice in the foundational document:

> Certain problems involving research are common to instruction and student personnel work. Any investigation which has for its purpose the improvement of instruction is at the same time a research which improves personnel procedures. Similarly, the results of any studies, the aim of which is to improve personnel procedures, should be disseminated throughout the instructional staff. In both cases wherever possible such projects should be carried on as cooperative ventures. (American Council on Education, 1937, p. 6)

The authors closed the report with a set of five research-focused future directions, noting that, "student personnel services will never develop as they should unless extensive and careful research is undertaken" (American Council on Education, 1937, p. 12). This statement was intended as a two-fold proposition: The field needs to identify and define its core functions and practitioners need to engage in or direct research to understand students. The report closed with four areas requiring immediate attention from the field (in other words, practitioners should be engaged in the work): student out-of-class life, faculty–student out-of-class relationships, financial aid to students, and follow-up studies of college students. Much of contemporary research on college students shares these areas of focus (Mayhew et al., 2016).

As student affairs practitioners struggled to identify their place and role in the 1920s, a division between those who saw the field as a calling versus those who saw the need for research to inform practice emerged (Schwartz, 1997). By the 1940s, this dual focus began to merge with a rise of professionalism that extended into the 1970s (Brubacher & Rudy, 1997). By the late 1990s extending into the present, an emphasis on practitioners as scholars developed (Blimling, 2001; Komives, 1997; Sriram & Oster, 2012).

Words Researchers Use—Practitioner–Scholar and Scholar–Practitioner

Educational researchers sometimes refer to practitioners engaged in scholarship as practitioner–scholars or scholar–practitioners. Following are some definitions to help clarify the terms.

Practitioner–Scholar

"An individual who aspires to study problems of practice in a more comprehensive and systematic way, allowing them to better understand the schools, districts, and other educational organizations within which they work. Practitioner–scholarship is *both* about your practice as an educator and your practice as a researcher" (Lochmiller & Lester, 2015, p. 3).

Scholar–Practitioner

"The scholar–practitioner exists in a space where research and practice inform each other and create a synergy: research informing practice, practice informing scholarship, and the many combinations. A scholar–practitioner understands the importance of practice and research informing each other and the need to ground work in theory and evidence and create measurements that demonstrate impact as well as explore phenomena" (Kupo, 2014, p. 96).

Studying Research

For many students, the first exposure to student affairs research is in a student development theory class. Unfortunately, faculty teaching theory or research methods courses seldom discuss how those theories were developed—such as the empirical basis of Astin's initial (1970a, 1970b) conceptualization of involvement or the original sample informing Chickering's (1969) theory.

Beyond graduate school, an increased need for research-competent professionals has become evident with the multifaceted concerns and issues that can affect student success. In addition, legislative scrutiny of higher education has led to questions about how student services directly contribute to academic outcomes. This also is related to increased federal accountability for higher education. Heightened attention on learning outcomes from accrediting agencies is an example. Administrators have recognized that demonstrating the value of student affairs work is critical in this environment, giving rise to a proliferation of full-time assessment professionals.

Developing and continuing to cultivate research skills has professional benefits for work and personal benefits for career development. Research experiences, both directly and as a consumer, improve the ability to formulate and ask good questions, evidence an argument, relate concepts across situations, develop and solve problems, and communicate solutions effectively. Research skills also teach professionals to be skeptical, logical, problem solvers who can adapt approaches to practice across varied situations, settings, and audiences. As professionals gain responsibilities in program development and decision making, being knowledge-able about research and assessment pays dividends for evaluating and demonstrat-ing the value of student services.

Defining Research

Definitions for research are varied, emphasizing research as a process, stressing the importance of research questions and hypotheses, or identifying specific procedures. Different academic fields also have assorted definitions of research, ranging from theory verification and hypothesis testing to theory development and open inquiry. Synthesizing these approaches, Creswell (2012) identified a broadly applicable process-based definition, stressing a comprehensive approach:

> Research is a cyclical process of steps that typically begins with identifying a research problem or issue of study. It then involves reviewing the literature, specifying a purpose for the study, collecting and analyzing data, and forming an interpretation of information. This process culminates in a report, disseminated to audiences, that is evaluated and used in the educational community. (p. 627)

A definition of research suitable for student affairs practice needs to emphasize investigation in educational contexts, be flexible to include multiple ways to study a problem or issues, but be process oriented to emphasize rigor. It should also be able to be differentiated from assessment and evaluation. A general definition for research applicable to student affairs is that *research* **is a systematic approach to learning that involves asking and answering questions**. This definition includes five key concepts: systematic, approach, learning, asking (questions), and answering (questions). Table 1.1 displays the definition with a discussion of each concept.

Table 1.1. Definition of Research and Five Key Concepts

Research is a systematic approach to learning that involves asking and answering questions.

Systematic implies that researchers follow a process when conducting research. This does not mean that the approach is the same for every project. Researchers often adjust their approach based on variable aspects of the study such as data sources, accessibility, feasibility, and efficiency. Systematic also does not mean organized in the sense of orderly, as some researchers prefer an open or less structured approach to conducting a study. Systematic implies that researchers follow a sequence. It is essential that the sequence is documented so that others are able to follow or replicate the study.

Approach encompasses aspects of methodology, ethical considerations, and the use of theory. From a methodological standpoint, research has a perspective, type, design, and methods. Ethical considerations comprise the concern and respect researchers extend to data sources, inclusive of participants, places, and other data forms. Theory can be used to guide all decisions related to research, or it may inform specific aspects such as participant or data selection, integration, or discussion.

Learning suggests an openness to discovery. Researchers need to be receptive to new information while being skeptical of existing knowledge. A holistic focus on learning suggests that not all answers have been found, regardless of existing or related knowledge. It also suggests that while learning is a goal, the process is also a form of teaching. As educators, student affairs professionals emphasize learning as a fundamental goal. Researchers need to be mindful of this purpose by placing it central to their investigative processes and outcomes.

Asking (questions) is the core of research. All research begins with one or more large or big-picture questions. Sometimes, the questions remain unchanged throughout the conduct of a study. Other times, questions shift based on any number of factors. In addition, smaller, related questions are threaded throughout all aspects of research. For example, when a researcher chooses a topic, they ask questions about why the topic is important. Once this is established, questions about prior evidence arise. This is succeeded by innumerable questions about methods, findings, discussion, and implications. Good research answers questions. Better research has rationale to justify all decisions in the research process. Great research leads to more questions. Flawed research begins with an answer.

Answering (questions) is the practice of research. The process of answering questions includes all aspects of conceptualization, research design, data analysis, and effective reporting. Specifically for student affairs research, effective reporting includes recommendations for practice. Each aspect has multiple steps and requires careful consideration. Answering questions effectively and efficiently is listed as the last concept in the definition of research because it requires the most comprehensive understanding. Competent researchers need a varied and deep understanding of research to answer the larger questions framing a study as well as the variety of smaller but equal important questions that guide it.

Recognizing the Purposes of Student Affairs Research

Research has two primary purposes in student affairs: contributing to knowledge and improving practice. Stage and Manning (2016) differentiated research in student affairs as basic or applied (p. 5). The *Journal of Student Affairs Research and Practice* (JSARP) solicits manuscripts based on a related definition: "JSARP seeks to publish practice articles that are firmly grounded in research and literature and research articles that speak to practice" (JSARP, 2017). Following is an overview of the dual purposes of student affairs research. Examples suggest how research focusing on student success might be applied to practice.

The Dual Purposes of Student Affairs Research

Contribute to Knowledge	Improve Practice
Address gaps in knowledge	Enhance services
Expand knowledge	Promote efficiency
Replicate knowledge	Determine best practices
Add voices of individuals	Evaluate initiatives

Research Contributes to Knowledge

The U.S. Department of Health and Human Services (DHHS, 2009) defined research as "systematic investigation, including research development, testing and evaluation, designed to develop or contribute to generalizable knowledge" (45 CFR 46.102). This broad description is intentional. It encompasses interdisciplinary fields from social sciences to technology and provisions for both immediately applicable as well as highly theoretical studies. In summary, the essential function of research, according to the federal definition, is to contribute to knowledge.

Following are some aspects of knowledge contribution from a student affairs perspective, each with an example based on student success. An important feature is to address gaps in what is already empirically evidenced about a topic. While socio-economic status has been identified as a risk factor for college success, multiple unknown or under-researched factors also can affect student achievement. Another general contribution of research is to expand knowledge. Researchers are continuously searching for new ways to increase what is known about factors affecting student persistence. Research also replicates knowledge. Researchers have proposed models for student success revealing contributing factors that can be used to help refine theory.

Finally, research adds voices of individuals. Much of what was known about student success initially was based on specific populations of students. Researchers working with marginalized or underrepresented students have added important perspectives to the study and practice of student academic support. This last aspect is considered by many researchers to be the most important function of student affairs research, because it shares a philosophical perspective with foundational values on individual student success (Boyle, Lowery, & Mueller, 2012).

Research Improves Practice

Research in student affairs is focused on improving practice. As a result, the research is often referred to as applied. The primary venue to distributing research in student affairs is an academic journal. Returning to the JSARP guidelines, manuscripts for the primary section, Innovations in Research and Scholarship, are described with the following definition: "Manuscripts submitted for review in this area may include qualitative and quantitative manuscripts that clearly provide a theory–research–practice connection" (JSARP, 2017). This emphasis on a "theory–research–practice connection" means that research published should directly apply to aspects of work in the field, or include implications for how results might shift or influence practices. Pragmatically, research focused on or intended for practice means that the discussion of results includes specific recommendations that can be implemented for improvement.

Following are some aspects of improving practice, each with an example based on student success. An important feature is to enhance services by suggesting improvements. For example, research might show that a lower ratio of advisors to at-risk students can dramatically improve first-year retention. Another way research improves practice is to promote efficiency. Declining resources or shifting budget priorities may make hiring a new advisor impossible, but examination of the core responsibilities and focus of the proposed position described in research may result in revised job responsibilities for current staff. Research also helps to determine best practices by providing perspectives on how the larger field is responding to trends or handling challenges. For example, student services for returning veterans has been informed by research in the last decade focused on ways to meet the unique needs of this population (Ackerman, DiRamio, & Garza Mitchell, 2009).

Finally, research evaluates initiatives, both directly and indirectly. Direct evaluation includes case studies of new, innovative, or existing programs to determine their effectiveness. Indirect evaluation is less focused on a specific program or service, but more on concepts and grounding as the basis for initiatives. From a research perspective, this may center on a single initiative such as a unique living learning community (LLC) housing first-generation students or may be a synthesis of common LLC features designed to evaluate the effectiveness of specific features.

Perspectives From the Field—Why Practitioners Need to Learn About Research

Professionals engage in practice, meaning that they apply what they have learned from their advanced educational experiences to the work responsibilities that have been assigned to them. Through practical experience and continued study, they should be committed to improving their effectiveness so they can add value to the educational experiences in which students participate. An important aspect of professional development for practitioners is that they be exposed to research, be it through reviewing literature, attending conference-based programs, or working with consultants who share their research so that practitioners can become more efficient in their work and their work becomes more potent. At a minimum, practitioners need to be able to distinguish well-conducted research projects from those that are flawed, and understand how to apply findings to their practice setting. Whether they conduct research projects or not, the ability to learn and grow as practitioners depends to a great extent on their ability to understand research and to apply findings in ways that add value to the students they serve. Professionals who do so will make valuable contributions to the growth and learning of the students they serve. Those who do not will be mired in the mediocre.

John H. Schuh—Distinguished Professor Emeritus, Iowa State University

Differentiating Research and Assessment

Research focused on improving practice is conceptually similar to assessment. Both research for practice and assessment share a focus on program evaluation and/or improvement. Both incorporate rigorous research methods for data collection and effective practices for communicating results. Typically, the scope of the two approaches is a distinguishing factor. The extensive use of assessment in conjunction with research necessitates some clarification.

Assessment is the collection, analysis, and interpretation of context-specific data to inform the effectiveness of programs and services. Suskie (2009) specified that assessment is "disciplined and systematic and uses many of the methodologies of traditional research" (p. 14). Schuh et al. (2016, pp. 7–8) further differentiated research from assessment based on the following points:

- Assessments are guided by theory but research frequently is conducted to test theories.
- Research often is not time bound to the extent that assessments are time bound.

- It is common for assessments to have a public or political dimension to them.
- Assessments typically are funded out of unit or divisional budgets. . . . Research often is financed through special support such as a grant or contract.

A simplified distinction between the two concepts concerns audience and intention:

- Research is meant for an external audience and is intended to generate knowledge.
- Assessment is meant for an internal audience and is intended to inform practice.

A related concept often also used in conjunction with the two terms is evaluation. Schuh et al. (2016) defined evaluation as the use of assessment data to determine effectiveness. Suskie (2009) emphasized that assessment results are intended for guidance and not decision making, should be used to determine alignment between intended and actual outcomes, and are helpful for investigating the quality or worth of a program or project rather than for measuring student learning. Evaluation typically also requires the evaluator to make a judgment, where research and assessment are more focused on sharing findings and offering interpretation or application.

Sriram (2017) related the difference between assessment, research, and evaluation to the accountability movement. According to Sriram, assessment was intended to improve higher education, but has been reframed as "about proving, not improving" (p. 28), calling for practitioners to describe and consider their assessment work as a research activity.

> First, I do not think there is a genuine difference between the terms *assessment* and *research* in practice. Second, I think there is an important difference in the implied meaning of the two terms. *Assessment*— at least in practice—concerns proving that programs that do exist should exist. *Research*, by contrast, aims to discover truth that will alter how we see the world. (Sriram, 2017, p. 29)

Identifying Research Competencies and Skills

Researchers have found that while research skills are among the most valued abilities in terms of importance for practitioners (Herdlein, Riefler, & Mrowka, 2013; Sandeen & Barr, 2006), they are also among the lowest rated in terms of perceived development (Sriram, 2014). Following is an overview of research-based competencies and skills for student affairs practitioners as described in foundational documents related to standards, expectations, and skills for practice.

Perspectives From the Field—Research Skills and Competencies

One challenge with the field of student affairs (and higher education in general) is the use of acronyms. People often confuse the CAS Standards, ASK Standards, and ACPA/NASPA Competencies. The important thing to consider is the focus of the standards/competencies. The CAS Standards, developed by a consortium of 41 higher education associations, define standards of professional practice for student service programs such as residential life and housing, student activities, academic advising, etc. The 10 ACPA/NASPA Competencies center on skills and knowledge that student affairs educators should possess. The Assessment Skills and Knowledge (ASK) Standards also relate to individual competence, but focus solely on assessment-related skills and knowledge student affairs practitioners should possess. They can be used to develop a professional development plan, design a student affairs professional curriculum, or assess individual and department performance. Their applications are versatile and robust. These three sets of standards and competencies provide a framework for individual and program excellence in student affairs.

Gavin Henning—Professor of Higher Education and Director of the Doctorate of Education and the Master of Higher Education administration programs, New England College

CAS

In 2015, the Council for the Advancement of Standards in Higher Education (CAS) released its most recent set of Standards for Master's Level Student Affairs Professional Preparation Programs (CAS, 2015). These standards help frame a larger discussion on the related skills and competencies needed across a career in student affairs. Two areas directly relate to the need for research skills development.

Subpart 5b.2: Student Characteristics and Effects of College on Students

This component of the curriculum must include studies of student characteristics, how such attributes influence student educational and developmental needs, and effects of the college experience and institutional characteristics on student learning and development.

Graduates must be able to demonstrate knowledge of how student learning and learning opportunities are influenced by student characteristics and by collegiate environments so that graduates can design and evaluate learning experiences for students. This area should include studies of the following: effects of college on students, campus climate, satisfaction with the college experience, student involvement in college, student culture, campus environment, and factors that correlate with student persistence and attrition. (p. 11)

The authors identified specific areas that need focus to ensure that the unique needs of all students and subpopulations are accounted for in student services and programs. This includes accounting for student characteristics such as sexual identity, academic ability and preparation, national origin, and developmental status, as well as student populations such as residential, part-time and full-time, student athletes, student group members, international students, and veterans.

Subpart 5b.5 lists expectations of graduate preparation content:

> Subpart 5b.5: Assessment, Evaluation, and Research
>
> This component of the curriculum must include the study of assessment, evaluation, and research. Studies must include both qualitative and quantitative research methodologies, measuring learning processes and outcomes, assessing environments and organizations, measuring program and environment effectiveness, and critiques of published studies.
>
> Graduates must be able to critique a sound study or evaluation and be able to design, conduct, and report on a sound research study, assessment study, or program evaluation, grounded in the appropriate literature. Graduates must be aware of research ethics and legal implications of research, including the necessity of adhering to a human subjects review. (p. 13)

The authors also identified specific methodologies that need cultivation, as well as the abilities practitioners need, including measuring learning processes and outcomes, assessing environments and organizations, measuring program and environment effectiveness, and critiques of published studies. They also add the need to be aware of the ethics and legal implications of research. CAS professional program expectations serve as a guide for faculty in graduate programs for what content should be included for professional preparation. Further, they suggest what content-based skills professionals need to be successful in their work.

A closer look at these standards, as well as others in the complete document, highlight research-based skills that extend beyond research design and data collection. These include the ability to read, evaluate, and use published research; know and incorporate literature from the field in decision making; and understand the need for research ethics.

ACPA/NASPA Joint Statement

American College Personnel Association–College Student Educators International (ACPA) and the National Association of Student Personnel Administrators (NASPA) have emphasized the importance of developing and maintaining research as an essential competency area for student affairs practice. In 2015, the two organizations co-published a joint statement identifying 10 core competency areas for student affairs educators. Assessment, Evaluation, and Research (AER) was among these fundamental concepts. Following is the description of the competency:

> The Assessment, Evaluation, and Research competency area focuses on the ability to design, conduct, critique, and use various AER methodologies and the results obtained from them, to utilize AER processes and their results to inform practice, and to shape the political and ethical climate surrounding AER processes and uses in higher education. (ACPA & NASPA, 2015, p. 12)

Examining the individual parts of the description reveals several areas of emphasis. The ability to design, conduct, critique, and use research comprises the major phases of conducting a study. These four skills can be learned through formal coursework or a self-directed approach. The second part of the description is more challenging—to take those skills and use them to inform practice and to shape the political and ethical climate surrounding their use in higher education. These aspirations require more explanation. Upcraft and Schuh (1996) and, more recently, Schuh et al. (2016) emphasized that it is nearly impossible to separate assessment, and by extension, research, from the political environment in which studies are conducted and used. Research both shapes and is shaped by contemporary context. Recognizing how these aspects affect the conduct and use of research can offer influence and advantage to practitioners who can recognize how to advocate for resources and decisions informed by evidence.

Adjacent to the basic description of the AER competency is a depiction of professional growth.

> Professional growth in this competency area is broadly marked by shifts from understanding to application, and then from smaller scale applications focused on singular programs or studies to larger scale applications that cut across departments or divisions. Many advanced level outcomes involve the leadership of AER efforts. (ACPA & NASPA, 2015, p. 12)

The authors noted that professional development in any competency is not static, but must be ongoing to maintain and advance learning within any area. They divided each competency into three levels—foundational (requisite), intermediate, and advanced, stressing that each should not be considered as a capability level or treated as a checklist of items to be completed. Instead, they should be viewed as goals for progressive development that can be mapped. This perspective lends further emphasis to the importance of continued professional development.

ASK Standards

In 2006, the ACPA Commission for Assessment for Student Development published the ASK Standards, a set of proficiencies intended to communicate areas and degrees of content expertise practitioners need to engage in assessment. The 13 standards include abilities in design, writing learning outcomes, collecting and managing data, analyzing data, benchmarking, program review and evaluation, ethics, effective reporting, the politics of assessment, and assessment education. The authors framed the necessity for learning research-based skills in the need for measurement and reporting competencies for learning outcomes assessment. They noted that many of the constructs such as leadership, citizenship, and appreciation for diversity that represent the hallmarks of work with students present challenging issues for measurement.

> In student affairs, the articulation and assessment of student learning has been especially challenging given the complex psychosocial and cognitive constructs that are the hallmarks of our work with students. . . . The ASK standards seek to articulate the areas of content knowledge, skill and dispositions that student affairs professionals need in order to perform as practitioner–scholars to assess the degree to which students are mastering the learning and development outcomes we intend as professionals. (ACPA, 2006, p. 3)

Each of the 13 standards includes several proficiency areas, written as "ability to" action statements. For example, under content Standard 8: Benchmarking, the authors list "Ability to use benchmarking data for strategic planning purposes" (p. 8). Many of the areas relate specifically to data skills learned in a research methods or assessment course or furthered through either formal (courses, conference presentations) or personal (self-guided courses, books) professional development. Most of the abilities listed are "doing" skills that complement and extend research foundations. Consistent with this, the authors noted, "Proficiency standards complement content standards. Proficiency standards articulate the degree of expertise of the practitioner in a given area of content" (p. 4).

Relating Competencies and Skills to Practice

Developing research skills also improves practice skills applicable in other areas of student affairs practice. Following is a listing and discussion of six skills engaged while learning about research that are relatable to professional practice. The skills can be divided into two groups. The first group relates to critical thinking: communication, reasoning, and skepticism. The second group relates to determination: autonomy, perseverance, and resourcefulness.

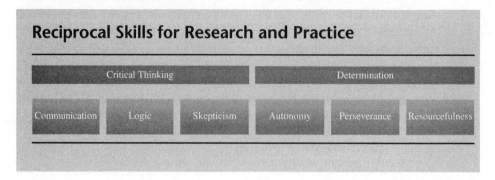

Communication

Communication includes both verbal and written interactions. It includes summarizing and synthesizing research as well as being able to articulate findings for specific audiences. Under the heading of "writing, editing, and more writing" Creswell (2012) noted:

> Researchers cannot escape the ever-present aspect of writing as a key facet of research . . . writing is more than recording ideas on paper or in a computer file. It is also organizing ideas, preparing interview questions, jotting down notes during an observation, and writing for permission to use someone else's questions or articles. Writing exists in all phases of the creative process of planning and in conducting research. (p. 25)

Practitioners engage communication skills continuously. Whether writing reports or developing policy, answering email, or simply delivering information during a meeting, communication skills are pervasive and essential to good practice. Communicating about research results requires being able to deliver a report that is clear, which includes close attention to editing as well as consideration of the logic or arrangement of the content. It also requires being succinct but knowing the essential details to include. Finally, it means being accurate which involves careful reading and knowledge about the content. All of these are valuable skills for learning to communicate to audiences across and beyond campus.

Logic

Logic is the ability to recognize and work through a problem in a purposeful way. While different types of research designs and methods can influence the application of logic, studying the research process to understand how it was initiated, how it developed and progressed, and how it was finalized reveals the researcher's reasoning. Creswell (2012) described this skill as being good at solving puzzles, drawing a parallel between a researcher's ability to see the final picture of a complete project and using a process to complete it.

Practitioners encounter problems every day. One of the attractions of this profession for many is that every day is different. Some issues can be resolved easily and others require a more thoughtful and long-term approach. Often, the time it takes to work through a problem is influenced by prior experience with a similar situation, the expertise of others, and any number of conditions beyond control that need to be accounted for to address an issue.

Skepticism

Skepticism is driven by curiosity, which is a fundamental research ability. Synonyms for skepticism—disbelief, suspicion, and uncertainly—are also accurate characteristics of this skill. Skepticism helps with identifying research problems, which leads to researchable topics. Researchers need to be willing to disbelieve, or to suspend, what is known to consider ways to investigate or revaluate and issue using a different approach.

In practice, skepticism is related to questioning. Practitioners use skepticism to investigate issues and to make decisions related to program revision or development. Being skeptical means thinking beyond how things have always been done to develop innovative solutions to issues or problems. Practitioners also use skepticism reactively. For example, student conduct officers use this skill when gathering facts about an issue. While skepticism can be a valuable way of thinking, too much skepticism is unproductive for both research and practice applications.

Autonomy

Autonomy is the ability to work self-sufficiently. Individuals who conduct research in student affairs rarely are full-time researchers. Research time typically competes with other work responsibilities, whether for faculty with teaching, advising, and service or for practitioners with primary and voluntary tasks. Collaborating with others can help to offset time and expertise limitations; however, research typically still needs an independent component. Further, being a research consumer also requires autonomy and independence as reading and evaluating research, especially as a novice or infrequent consumer, involves a time commitment and focus.

Autonomy is a valuable skill for student affairs work. The need to include multiple points of view and to account for various perspectives can lead to a lot of meetings, particular as decision-making responsibilities increase. As a result, non-meeting time needs to be efficient. Even with delegation, individuals typically need to set aside time to complete their responsibilities.

Perseverance

Perseverance related to research involves the determination to finish a study, as a consumer or producer. Time on task is vital for most research, as studies are time-intensive both in planning and execution. Producing or consuming research can be a solitary activity that requires intrinsic motivation. Creswell (2012) regarded a similar skill as lengthening one's attention span. One example he provided was the ability to read a journal article, which requires patience and focus.

Perseverance as a professional skill is helpful when dealing with the vague nature of student affairs work. It is also beneficial when working within the bureaucracy of higher education.

Resourcefulness

Resourcefulness is a multifaceted research skill. Pragmatically, being resourceful when conducting research means knowing how and when to use available resources to complete work. For example, identifying and obtaining literature to evidence a topic can be time consuming. Access to an academic library or subscriptions to relevant journals can make the process more efficient, but it is not always possible to acquire the resources needed in a timely way. Resourcefulness also means doing more with less. When gathering data through interaction with others, such as with surveys or interviews, being resourceful can mean identifying optimal ways to gain participation in research, such as sending surveys to more targeted samples at particular times or identifying key individuals that can help facilitate participation in interviews.

Resourcefulness is also a useful skill for practitioners. It can involve establishing and using a local network to aid with campus issues or developing a larger professional network for advice with bigger concerns. Resource-sharing partnerships across and beyond campus are invaluable for practitioners, who are often tasked with doing more work with less time, money, or facilities.

Building Your Research Skillset

Learning about research can be overwhelming. One of the most beneficial ways to begin building a research skillset is by talking with others. Ask supervisors and colleagues how they use research, question faculty about their projects, and attend professional development sessions at conferences. When learning independently, choose topics that directly relate to an area of interest or that can contribute to practice to stay engaged. Asking questions about the material while reading can also be valuable. Questions do not have to be confined to new terms and concepts. They might focus on the need for research on the topic, the literature researchers used to frame the problem, methods used to arrive at the findings, or results. When reading landmark, or highly referenced, studies, consider what made them so important. For example, Astin's (1984) "Student Involvement: A Developmental Theory for Higher Education" is among the most highly cited studies in student affairs research. What makes the work significant to the field?

Thinking about applications is also helpful when studying research, such as considering how the findings might be adapted to a specific institutional context. If a study is theory-based, reflect on how (or if) the model or its key tenets might be used in practice. Researchers often describe this as operationalizing theory. A benefit of considering applications while reading is that uses for research do not have to be specific to the topic. For example, results from a national study about academic engagement may highlight student–faculty interactions as critical to fostering learning outcomes. Considering that interactions between faculty and students do not have to be in a classroom might lead to ways those relationships might be facilitated in student affairs.

A final point to keep in mind when learning about research is that mastery will not be accomplished in a single class or even during graduate study. Education on any topic is never complete. For practitioners, formal study in research is inversely related to when they need it. The necessity to interpret research and evidence-based results often increases with decision-making responsibilities. As noted in the review of competencies and skills, professional organizations view learning about research as an ongoing aspect of professional development. Sriram (2017) emphasized this point, stating, "If those of us who work in higher education want to improve college students' learning, we must become better learners ourselves" (p. 30).

References

Ackerman, R., DiRamio, D., & Garza Mitchell, R. L. (Eds.). (2009). *Transitions: Combat veterans as college students* (New Directions for Student Services No. 126). San Francisco, CA: Jossey-Bass.

American College Personnel Association. (2006). *ASK standards: Assessment skills and knowledge content standards for student affairs practitioners and scholars.* Retrieved from http://www.myacpa.org/publications

American College Personnel Association & National Association of Student Personnel Administrators. (2015). *Professional competency areas for student affairs practitioners.* Washington, DC: Authors.

American Council on Education. (1937). The student personnel point of view. *American Council on Education Studies* (Series I, Vol. I, no. 3).

Astin, A. W. (1970a). College influence: A comprehensive view. *Contemporary Psychology, 15*(9), 543–546.

Astin, A. W. (1970b). The methodology of research on college impact. *Sociology of Education, 43,* 223–254.

Biddix, J. P., & Schwartz, R. (2012). Walter Dill Scott and the student personnel movement. *Journal of Student Affairs Research and Practice, 49*(3), 285–298.

Blimling, G. S. (2001). Uniting scholarship and communities of practice in student affairs. *Journal of College Student Development, 42*(4), 381–396.

Boyle, K. M., Lowery, J. W., & Mueller, J. A. (Eds.). (2012). *Reflections on the 75th anniversary of the student personnel point of view.* Washington, DC: ACPA–College Student Educators International.

Brubacher, J. S., & Rudy, W. (1997). *Higher education in transition. A history of American colleges and universities* (4th ed.). New York, NY: Harper & Row.

Certis, H. (2014). The emergence of Esther Lloyd-Jones. *Journal of Student Affairs Research and Practice, 51*(3), 259–269.

Chickering, A. (1969). *Education and identity.* San Francisco, CA: Jossey-Bass.

Council for the Advancement of Standards in Higher Education. (2015). *CAS professional standards for higher education* (9th ed.). Washington, DC: Author.

Creswell, J. W. (2012). *Educational research: Planning, conducting, and evaluating quantitative and qualitative research* (4th ed.). Boston, MA: Pearson.

Department of Health and Human Services. (2009). Human Subjects Research Act, 45 U.S.C.A.

Herdlein, R., Riefler, L., & Mrowka, K. (2013). An integrative literature review of student affairs competencies: A meta-analysis. *Journal of Student Affairs Research and Practice, 50*(3), 250–269.

Journal of Student Affairs Research and Practice. (2017). *Submission guidelines.* Retrieved from https://www .naspa.org/publications/journals/journal-of-student-affairs-research-and-practice/guidelines

Komives, S. R. (1997). Linking student affairs preparation with practice. In N. J. Evans & C. E. Phelps Tobin (Eds.), *The state of the art of preparation and practice in student affairs: Another look* (pp. 177–200). Lanham, MD: American College Personnel Association.

Kupo, V. L. (2014). Becoming a scholar–practitioner. In G. L. Martin & M. S. Hevel (Eds.), *Research-driven practice in student affairs: Implications from the Wabash National Study of Liberal Arts Education* (New Directions for Student Services No. 147, pp. 89–98). San Francisco, CA: Jossey-Bass.

Lochmiller, C. R., & Lester, J. N. (2015). *An introduction to educational research: Connecting methods to practice.* Thousand Oaks, CA: Sage.

Mayhew, M. J., Rockenbach, A. N., Bowman, N. A., Seifert, T. A. D., Wolniak, G. C., Pascarella, E. T., & Terenzini, P. T. (2016). *How college affects students: Vol. 3. 21st century evidence that higher education works.* San Francisco, CA: Jossey-Bass.

Sandeen, A., & Barr, M. J. (2006). *Critical issues for student affairs: Challenges and opportunities.* San Francisco, CA: Jossey-Bass.

Schuh, J. H., Biddix, J. P., Dean, L. A., & Kinzie, J. (2016). *Assessment in student affairs: A contemporary look* (2nd ed.). San Francisco, CA: Jossey-Bass.

Schwartz, R. A. (1997). How deans of women became men. *Review of Higher Education, 20,* 419–436.

Sriram, R. (2014). The development, validity, and reliability of a psychometric instrument measuring competencies in student affairs. *Journal of Student Affairs Research and Practice, 51*(4), 349–363.

Sriram, R. (2017). *Student affairs by the numbers.* Sterling, VA: Stylus.

Sriram, R., & Oster, M. (2012). Reclaiming the "scholar" in scholar–practitioner. *Journal of Student Affairs Research and Practice, 49*(4), 377–396.

Stage, F. K., & Manning, K. (2016). *Research in the college context: Approaches and methods* (2nd ed.). New York, NY: Brunner-Routledge.

Suskie, L. A. (2009). *Assessing student learning: A common sense guide* (2nd ed.). San Francisco, CA: Jossey-Bass.

Upcraft, M. L., & Schuh, J. H. (1996). *Assessment in student affairs.* San Francisco, CA: Jossey-Bass.

CHAPTER TWO

READING RESEARCH

Learning Outcomes

By the end of this chapter, you should be able to:

- Differentiate the main sources of research in student affairs.
- Locate and obtain various sources of research in student affairs.
- Identify the basic format of a published study.
- Articulate the role and importance of the problem statement.

The ability to read research is a foundational student affairs skill. Reading research is a literacy-based expertise that incorporates the capacity to locate, acquire, and comprehend empirical results. Understanding how a research topic becomes a research problem significant to practice is important to learn, since these components inform the purpose and ultimately the research questions researchers use to carry out a study. Although the sources, topics, and methods used in student affairs research can be varied, many of the reporting formats share a standardized structure or format. Learning this structure promotes research literacy by helping readers learn to evaluate research based on the presence or absence of core components.

Student affairs practitioners increasingly are tasked with providing evidence for existing programs and new initiatives, either directly through assessment or in a summary from existing sources (Schuh, Biddix, Dean, & Kinzie, 2016). Chapter 1 established why it is important for practitioners to study research. This chapter uses a pragmatic approach to teaching research literacy. The content includes a review of research sources in student affairs and higher education, information on how to find and acquire the sources, and a detailed overview of the main components of a published study using excerpts from a journal article.

Identifying Research

Reading research begins with identifying sources and understanding differences between types of data, audience, and uses. When referring to research, researchers typically are describing empirical studies published in peer-reviewed journal articles. *Empirical* means that data were collected from primary sources (direct interaction such as survey or interview) or secondary sources (existing datasets). Publications that fit into this category include journal articles, research reports, reviews of literature, dissertations and theses, and books and monographs. An indicator of a study being empirical is the presence of key characteristics including research questions, identification of a population and/or data sources, and a description of the data collection and analysis processes including sampling, instruments, and analysis techniques.

Sources of Published Research

Research is published in various different formats. There are several common types of publications research in student affairs and higher education. Table 2.1 is an overview each format with a quick description including the review level (peer, editorial, faculty, none).

Journal articles are the most common venues for published, empirical research. An important characteristic of journals is peer review. *Peer review* means that a group of experts have made a determination about the research before it could be published, critiquing both the methodology and data sources, as well as its potential contribution to a specific aspect of the field. Journals are distributed in print and online formats. Several times a year, ACPA publishes the *Journal of College Student Development* and NASPA publishes the *Journal of Student Affairs Research and Practice* (formerly known as the *NASPA Journal*). These are the two most prominent journals specific to the student affairs field based on the reputation of the editorial and peer review boards, acceptance rates (e.g., the number of articles accepted for publication relative to the number of submissions), and distribution.

Table 2.1. Common Publication Formats in Student Affairs

Format	Description
Journal Article	A published study typically conducted using the five-part research format (introduction, literature review, methods, results, discussion). Data sources are most often empirical. Often rigorously reviewed by an editorial board of expert peer reviewers.
Newsletter or Magazine	A collection of highlighted results or commentary based on practice. Data sources are seldom empirical. Often reviewed by an editor.
Research Report	A study published by a researcher or organization highlighting findings. Often, a report does not include a review of literature. Methods, if included, are often referenced in another document or included in an appendix. Data sources are most often empirical. Reports generally are not peer-reviewed.
Review of Literature	A comprehensive study of literature published as a synthesis of research on a topic. A review may be published in a journal. Data are most often not empirical, but derived from empirical sources. May be peer-reviewed.
Thesis or Dissertation	A study conducted using the five-part research format (introduction, literature review, methods, results, discussion). Typically, it is available online through a university repository. Data sources are most often empirical. Reviewed by a faculty or advising committee.
Book, Book Chapter, or Monograph	A publication that can include various formats, such as empirical study, highlighted results, or commentary based on practice. Data sources may or may not be empirical. Reviewed by an editorial staff and may also be peer-reviewed.

Other journal publishers include regional professional organizations (SACSA—*College Student Affairs Journal*), professional associations (AFA—*Oracle: Research Journal of the Association of Fraternity/Sorority Advisors*), and research/resource centers (The National Resource Center for the First-Year Experience and Students in Transition—*Journal of The First-Year Experience and Students in Transition*). Journals also have emerged based on interest in specific topics (Student Affairs Assessment Leaders [SAAL]—*Journal of Student Affairs Inquiry*).

Perspectives From the Field—The Importance of Peer Review

To be an informed consumer of research, one should ask critical questions not only about the rigor of its methods and soundness of its framework, but also how it came to be published in the first place. Is it self-published? Has it been developed with the assistance of an editor or publisher? Is it peer reviewed? If it is reviewed, is it a masked or blind review?

Scholarship that is peer reviewed and doubled blinded (where neither the reviewer nor the author know the identity of the other) is rigorous scholarship. Peer review gives the reader confidence that the manuscript was carefully scrutinized. In fact, peer reviews matter so much that institutions typically use this as a criterion for evaluating faculty productivity.

Masked (or anonymous) reviews help ensure the ethical responsibility we have to avoid dual relationships and conflicts of interest. As reviewers, if we do not know whose work we are critiquing, we are more likely to exercise objective judgment. This adds value and credibility to the review.

While submitting one's work for others to evaluate can be intimidating, most reviewers will approach this task with humility and see it as an opportunity to help make the work better. Indeed, our academic journals are only as good as our reviewers—reviewers may provide content and methodological expertise, as well as a diverse perspective that can improve one's work. Peer reviewers help us safeguard the quality of the research in our field, and submitting one's work to such scrutiny is an ethical responsibility of every professional.

Deborah L. Liddell—Professor at the University of Iowa and editor of the *Journal of College Student Development*

Newsletters or magazines are generally published by professional associations. They may include reviews of research, reports of best practices, discussion of current events, or dialogue related to a specific topic. Some include empirical research. Formats can vary from magazine-length articles to columns, published in print or online, and delivered on a daily, weekly, or monthly schedule. Examples include *About Campus, Diversity Issues in Higher Education, Inside Higher Education,* and *Women in Higher Education.* Information published in newsletters or magazines are excellent sources for researchers developing context or establishing the need for a study, but typically are not cited as research.

Research reports typically are published by research centers and focus on findings related to large-scale surveys or ongoing projects. An example is the annual report on *The American Freshman: National Norms,* published by the Higher Education

Research Institute (HERI) at UCLA. Other examples include reports from organizations such as The New Media Consortium (NMC) and EDUCAUSE Learning Initiative's (ELI) annual *Horizon Report* focusing on the current and projected role of technology in higher education. Similarly, *The Chronicle of Higher Education* publishes an annual *Almanac of Higher Education* that includes summary analyses of data related to faculty and students in all 50 states. Information published in research reports are used to establish context and often cited as research.

A review of literature is a synthesis of research on a topic. Examples are Kuh's (2009) review of literature on student engagement, Finley's (2011) review of research on civic engagement in higher education, and Biddix's (2016) review of issues associated with fraternity involvement. A large-scale example is Mayhew et al.'s third edition of Pascarella and Terenzini's *How College Affects Students* (Mayhew et al., 2016). In addition to serving as a research-based, in-depth overview of a topic, a review of literature often points out strengths and weaknesses in the existing knowledge base as well as suggesting best practices and areas for continued research. One type of review of literature is a meta-analysis, which is a statistical comparison of results from multiple studies (although the term is sometimes used to mean simply a large-scale comparison of literature). A variation is an annotated bibliography, which is a summary listing of studies and citations on a topic without a review. Reviews of literature are useful to researchers as comprehensive studies as well as to practitioners as research-based evidence.

Words Researchers Use—Published Literature Review Versus Literature Review Section

A published review of literature can be differentiated from a literature review section appearing in a journal article by the size and focus of the content. In an article, the review serves as a grounding and argument for a study. A published review of literature is typically a much larger and in-depth synthesis that generally includes a summary and recommendations.

A thesis or dissertation is a large scale, in-depth study of an issue completed as a graduate school requirement. In most cases, a thesis is associated with a master's degree while a dissertation is associated with a doctorate. Often, both are published in library databases and made available online. Theses and dissertations tend to follow the same format as journal articles, but include substantially more detail in each section. For example, while the literature review for journal article may be only a few paragraphs or pages long, a thesis or dissertation review can be a 20- to 30-page chapter. Theses and dissertations can yield journal articles, depending on the researcher's ability to condense or separate findings. Information published in theses or dissertations are often cited as empirical research.

Books, book chapters, and monographs are sometimes sources of published research. They are not generally structured like journal articles, instead taking a narrative or review approach to an issue. An example of a research book focused on student affairs practice is *College Students in the United States: Characteristics, Experiences, and Outcomes* (Renn & Reason, 2012). Another category of book is an edited volume, which is a collection of similar topics organized by an editor with expertise. A prominent example is the *New Directions in Student Affairs* series. Books or book chapters may or may not include empirical research or involve peer review. A monograph is an academically focused, in-depth review of literature on a single topic or issue. It is typically written by one or more authors (not edited) and generally does not include empirical research. An example is the *ASHE Higher Education Monograph Series*, considered to be among the most rigorously peer-reviewed publications in higher education. Information published in books, book chapters, and monographs can be used for context, background, theory-based analysis, and literature reviews, though they are not often cited as empirical research.

Finding Published Research

Published research is found in print and electronic journals, research databases, or websites. Journals are typically sponsored, administered, maintained, and endorsed by professional associations, academic programs, or research-based centers. Some fields distinguish academic and practitioner journals. An academic journal typically is intended for a research audience and features empirical studies and theory intended to generate knowledge. A practitioner journal typically is intended for a practitioner audience and includes a more direct emphasis on informing practice. Student affairs researchers and practitioners tend to use the terms journal article or scholarly article or even research article interchangeably when referring to studies published in both academic and practitioner journals.

Research databases are collections of journal articles and other sources, organized around a theme. Some databases focus primarily on one field, such as ERIC for education, while others are more interdisciplinary, such as EBSCO. Databases are a convenient and efficient way to locate and access research on a topic. They typically contain the most recent publications and archives from thousands of journals and other scholar sources. One limitation to using databases is that they can be cost prohibitive. College and university libraries subscribe to databases, which are then made freely available to students, faculty, and staff; however, funding can restrict which databases are offered. This can be problematic in cases where a particular journal is not part of the available databases. Another limitation is the nonintuitive search features of some databases that rely on an understanding of specific terminology to effectively locate and access articles.

Published research, including journal articles and empirical reports, is increasingly available online. Researchers have made their work available on sites such as Google Scholar and Research Gate, either for download or by contacting the researchers directly. One limitation is that copyright restrictions can make some articles unavailable publically. Online searching is increasingly an effective way to locate published research. It promotes the ability to follow citations or to locate articles that cite other works. For example, a researcher using Astin's (1984) Theory of Involvement can search for the original publication and then view links to articles citing that original source to see other applications of the theory in published research.

Reading Research

Most types of published research feature a common format that includes five sections: introduction, literature review, methodology, results, and discussion. Researchers have some flexibility in the sections they choose to include. Some journals also have specific guidelines about the sections they want included in articles. For example, most articles do not include the word introduction, instead beginning with the title and implying that the text that follows is the introduction. The review of literature can be listed as the review of literature or as the review of related research. Several sections also often contain subheadings to separate major points. For example, a review of literature generally includes subheadings specific to the topics the researcher reviewed. Table 2.2 lists the five major sections of published research with common headings. Parentheses indicate that the section may not be included or specified. The first three sections (introduction, literature review, and methodology) are considered the research proposal.

Table 2.2. The Five Major Sections of a Research Publication

	(Introduction)
	Background/Context Problem Statement Purpose of the Study Significance of the Study (Theoretical/Conceptual Framework)
	Literature Review
	Review Subheading 1 Review Subheading 2 (Review Subheading 3) Review Summary
	Methodology
	Research Questions Research Design (Type and Perspective) Research Methods Procedures (Data Sources, Data Collection, Instrumentation) Data Analysis (Dependability and Trustworthiness or Validity and Reliability) Limitations Ethical Considerations
	Results
	Descriptive Report Results Subheading 1 Results Subheading 2 (Results Subheading 3) Results Summary
	Discussion and Implications
	Discussion and Implications Subheading 1 Discussion and Implications Subheading 2 (Discussion and Implications Subheading 3) Conclusion (Future Research)

(Left vertical label spanning the Introduction, Literature Review, and Methodology rows: **Research Proposal**)

Following are details about the contents of each major section of a study. Included are excerpts from a published article to show specific elements in context along with researcher commentary related to the profiled section. The section begins with a brief summary of the article.

Excerpt From a Published Study

Pittman, E. C., & Foubert, J. D. (2016). Predictors of professional identity development for student affairs professionals. *Journal of Student Affairs Research and Practice, 53*(1), 13–25.

Researcher Commentary (Ed Pittman)

This article began with an interest in the topic of professional identity. I was trying to decide on a thesis topic during my graduate program and was always fascinated with the concepts of social identity and career development. Because social identity and career development were such broad topics, I needed to find a way to bridge the two concepts together, which led me to professional identity development. Through my research, I discovered that a multitude of studies existed in the fields of medicine, nursing, teaching, and law regarding professional identity. However, there seemed to be very few studies in the field of student affairs related to professional identity development. Throughout my research, it became apparent there was a divide between the schools of thought on whether student affairs was a profession or a field. Upon further research, it became clear that the purpose of the study was not to determine whether student affairs could be validated as a profession, but what factors actually contributed to developing an identity as a student affairs professional.

A study generally begins with a topic. The researcher has a general interest in a topic that is refined by asking questions, reviewing prior research, and/or considering its potential importance. Sometimes this process is deductive, meaning that initial decisions work from general to specific (i.e., a top-down approach). Often, the topic is a theoretical explanation for something that needs testing or evaluating, so the research process moves from broad to testable. Conversely, the process can be inductive, where the researcher moves from specific to general (i.e., a bottom-up approach). In this way, the study starts with a hypothesis or specific observation and moves to a broader theory with the intent of making generalizations. Inductive reasoning is more exploratory initially, where deductive reasoning is more narrow and concerned with testing or confirming hypotheses. Consider the topic of college student retention, defined as remaining enrolled from the freshmen to sophomore year. A deductive approach starts with the broad problem of trying to address retention and looks for potential solutions, such as reasons students do (or do not) return. An inductive approach might start with a reason students generally stay, such as involvement in a student organization, and evaluates the extent to which that reason may be accurate. The researcher then moves to the step of identifying and defining the problem.

Introduction

Published research often begins with an interesting story, fact, or insight. Creswell (2012) referred to this as a narrative hook and described its function as drawing the reader into a study. He elaborated that good narrative hooks cause the reader to pay attention, elicit emotional or attitudinal responses, spark interest, and encourage the reader to continue reading. Researchers also include contextual information in the introduction to familiarize the reader with the topic. This may be references to recent events, citations from other studies, or an overview of the topic. The background or context often serves as the narrative hook but may appear anywhere in the introduction. Following is the first paragraph of a study establishing the background.

Excerpt From the Introduction

During the 20th century, college student life evolved into much more than learning inside the classroom. The concepts of educating the whole student and connecting academics to extracurricular activities provide the basis for the student personnel movement. By the 1960s, college student personnel had become a professional field (Dungy & Gordon, 2011). Subsequent movements within the profession shifted emphasis from student conduct to learning and development. Given the recent historical emergence and shifting focus of the profession, student affairs professionals need to have a clear understanding of and a deep commitment to their professional work. (Pittman & Foubert, 2016, p. 13)

Researcher Commentary (Ed Pittman)

In this first section, we wanted to provide a concise and pointed history of the student affairs profession. While this was not the focus or topic of the study, it was necessary to provide this historical context to frame the study within the current environment. Not only does the introduction provide context, it also sets the stage leading up to the problem statement. This way, the reader understands why there is a problem that deservers studying. Before we could even address the problem statement (or what is not known), we had to address specifically what we knew already. One of the challenges we faced was not to dive too deep into the argument of whether or not student affairs was considered a profession or a field, as that was not the true focus of the study. The historical context that we provided was pointed, concise, and solely directed to our problem statement.

Problem Statement. Ary, Jacobs, and Razavieh (1996) described systematic research as originating with a problem. The authors evoked Dewey's (1933) observation that the first step in the scientific method is the recognition of a felt difficulty, an obstacle, or problem that puzzles the researcher. Merriam (2009) admonished that "It would be a fruitless undertaking to embark on a research journey without first identifying a research problem" (p. 58). For Creswell (2015), research is intended to address problems; it is often easier to write about what is being done rather than what needs to be done. He observed that many problems are framed in "what exists" rather than "what needs to be fixed" (p. 13). In most cases, the research problem is derived from a deficiency, or gap, in the knowledge base about a topic. Problems may arise from issues, difficulties, and current practices. Lochmiller and Lester (2015) noted that a research problem is not simply a statement that "this study is about . . ." rather, it formulates the topic in a way that conveys *why* the research is needed and *what* the research will accomplish.

When specifically identified in a study, research problems in published research may be labeled as the problem, the statement of the problem, or the problem statement. Unfortunately, research problems are seldom easy to identify. For example, despite being called a statement, the problem statement is generally not a single sentence. It is a collection of components that make up the entirety of a statement. In a dissertation or larger study, it may be comprised of several paragraphs. Typically, it will be included within the first few paragraphs of an article or chapter. The *problem statement* specifies the need and value of a study by answering three questions:

1. What is known about the topic?
2. What is not known about the topic?
3. Why do we need to know what is not known about the topic?

What is known about the topic is a brief statement of current research or prior findings. It adds context to the research topic and demonstrates that the researcher is familiar with the existing work on the topic. What is not known about the topic suggests what information, experiences, or other findings are missing from the current knowledge base. Why do we need to know what is not known about the topic is the argument for the study. It should answer the "So what?" question about the need for a study, including the need for research on the topic and its potential contribution. Table 2.3 is an excerpt from Pittman and Foubert (2016, p. 13) showing how to identify the three questions of a problem statement. The statement was not labeled in text, but appeared as the second paragraph in the article.

Table 2.3. Identifying the Problem Statement

What Is Known (about professional identity)	Research on professional identity development within higher education has mostly focused on theories, pedagogies, and learning strategies (Trede, Macklin, & Bridges, 2011).
What Is Not Known (about professional identity)	A gap in the literature exists regarding the impact of education, workplace learning, and mentoring on professional identity (Trede, Macklin, & Bridges, 2011).
Why We Need to Know What Is Not Known (about professional identity)	Studying the relationships among these processes is important to help professional associations best meet the needs of newer members (Crim, 2006), to address attrition from the profession (Renn & Jessup-Anger, 2008; Tull, 2006), and to help graduate programs meet their students' needs (Gardner & Barnes, 2007; Renn & Jessup-Anger, 2008; Tull, 2006).

Source: From Pittman and Foubert (2016).

Significance of the Study. The problem statement informs the *significance of the study*, which Marshall and Rossman (1995) identified as how the research contributes to what is known by either refining or expanding theory or framing the problem as a resource cost (time or money) that affects policy and practice. The significance is the importance of the study. The significance can be multifaceted and have implications to various stakeholders, in different contexts, and at different time periods. For example, Pittman and Foubert (2016) summarized the significance of their study as how "congruence between an individual's professional identity and chosen career is important for job satisfaction and effectiveness (Holland, 1985)" (p. 14). They followed this statement with details about various audiences that could be impacted by the results of the study.

Purpose of the Study. The *purpose of a study* is the reason for conducting the research. For Creswell (2014), the purpose statement "is the most important statement in the entire study, and it needs to be clear, specific, and informative . . . readers will be lost unless it is carefully drafted" (p. 123). The purpose is a formulaic statement that is easy to identify, as many researchers begin the sentence with "The purpose of this study is _____." Pittman and Foubert (2016) added the purpose to the end of the problem statement:

> This study examines the degree to which having a graduate degree in student affairs or a related field, role of mentors, the level of professional involvement, and the supervision style of supervisors are related to the professional identity development of graduate students and new professionals in student affairs. (p. 13)

The authors restated the purpose at the end of the review of literature by rewording the statement and using the identifiable clause:

> The purpose of this study is to examine each of these factors and their relationship to the professional identity of student affairs professionals to determine whether there is overlap in the predictive effects of these constructs or whether they contribute unique elements to the formation of professional identity. (p. 16)

Research Questions. *Research questions* direct the study, guiding how the problem will be researched and addressed. Research questions sometimes reveal the data sources (such as variables or people), methods, and analysis. Data sources are often directly listed in research questions, generally in the order they are researched. Keywords such as describe, difference, relate, or predict in statistical analyses, or explore, learn, or experience in qualitative research are frequently used to signify the method and analysis. Pittman and Foubert (2016, pp. 16–17) described their intent to examine the influence and extent (keywords for prediction) of factors (variables) as well as consider group differences:

1. Do certain factors (i.e., role of mentors, supervision style received, and professional involvement) influence the professional identity development of student affairs professionals?
2. To what extent do certain factors influence the professional identity development of student affairs professionals?
3. Do certain factors of professional identity development differ between graduate students and new professionals?

Research questions play a central role in a study as the initial guide, a constant when questions arise during data collection, a direction for analysis, and a prompt for discussion and results. Stage and Manning (2016) regarded identification of the research question as the most important decision of the research process. Research questions determine the literature to be used, identify methodology, and guide the study. However, they noted that "rarely is a research question as clear in the beginning of the study as it is at the end" (p. 8).

Theoretical/Conceptual Framework (optional). Researchers sometimes also include a theoretical or conceptual framework in the introduction. A *theoretical framework* is one or more theories a researcher uses to guide aspects of the study, ranging from selection of literature to review to design considerations such as data sources or instruments. Researchers may also revisit theory when developing the discussion and implications to compare and contrast results to existing theory. A *conceptual framework* is an initial framework the researcher develops from existing theory. For example, in a study of why student leaders remain involved their senior year, a researcher might view only the moving out concept of Schlossberg's (1981) Transition Theory as applicable alongside Komives, Longerbeam, Owen, Mainella, and Osteen's (2005) concept of generativity (stage 5 of the Leadership Identity Model). The researcher would not be using both theories in their entirety in the study, but considering how aspects of each relate to the topic.

Literature Review

A *literature review* is synthesis of research on a topic. Synthesis implies that the review is not simply a summary of sources, but an informative, detailed, critical analysis of research. A well-written literature review incorporates multiple related and divergent sources and is presented as a logical argument. When incorporated into an empirical research project, it helps to substantiate the need for a study, demonstrates that the researcher is aware of existing research, and positions the proposed study in what is already known about a topic. Depending on the topic, a literature review can be a highly focused and in-depth review of studies on a single subject or it may be a broad overview of research on several subjects related to a topic. For example, a literature review about service learning may focus on a particular aspect, such as community volunteerism, or broader considerations such as class-based projects, alternative breaks trips, and student groups.

Visually, a literature review is a separate section, often subdivided into related subjects, that typically has numerous in-text citations to reference research. The review section may begin with a listing of the general topics that will be covered as well as rationale for those that will not. It should be an organized, cohesive section with transitions that closes with a summary of findings from the literature. The summary can act as a transition to research questions to show that they were derived from existing studies. One common method to organize a review is to identify two or three main topics related to the main issue of the study as subsections and review research separately in each section. Another common method resembles a funnel that starts with a broad topic and works to the narrower focus of a study. For example, in their study of sense of community and belonging related to living learning communities (LLCs), Spanierman et al. (2013) reviewed the broad literature on factors associated with sense of community and sense of belonging, narrowed to the role of residence halls in sense of community and belonging, then ended the review with a focused section relating the potential contributions of LLCs.

A common misinterpretation about a literature review stems from its name. The word review is not an accurate description of its purpose. Often, a review is thought of as an overview, or summary. Some literature reviews are written this way. However, a literature review should be more of an in-depth study of literature, or more precisely, a critical analysis of sources arranged as a synthesis. Mongan-Rollis (2014) differentiated a review from a summary:

> While a summary of the what [sic] you have read is contained within the literature review, it goes
> well beyond merely summarizing professional literature. It focuses on a specific topic of interest to

you and includes a critical analysis of the relationship among different works, and relating this research to your work.

A synthesis is a blending of sources. Works are compared and contrasted and the analysis is presented in a clear and cohesive argument. One way to differentiate a literature review from a summary or annotated bibliography is to look at the structure of the content. With few exceptions, single citation paragraphs indicate a collection of summaries rather than a synthesis. Following is an excerpt showing how research is described and presented in text using synthesis.

Excerpt From the Literature Review

Role of Mentors

Mentoring includes support, challenge, knowledge and skill development, career development, advising, role modeling, and leadership (Schmidt & Wolfe, 2009; Tull, 2009). Professional identity development is dependent upon the existence of mentors to help new professionals establish their appropriate identity (Adams, Hean, Sturgis, & Clark, 2006). Mentors may exert influence on the cognitive and behavioral stages of professional socialization, allowing for the development of professional identity. While mentor relationships can form haphazardly or intentionally, the relationships must be authentic and goal oriented, while maintaining a personal and professional balance (Tull, 2009).

Mentors can provide a social support system to those experiencing role conflicts to help prevent attrition from the profession (Tull, 2009). In student affairs, mentors often influence an individual to become involved in a professional association, which could provide another means of social support and influence graduate students' professional development (Gardner & Barnes, 2007). (Pittman & Foubert, 2016, p. 15)

Researcher Commentary (Ed Pittman)

Here, we wanted to provide a holistic synthesis of each independent variable we were studying. Throughout our research, we pulled numerous sources from multiple channels, including peer-reviewed research articles, research reports, and books. We were careful to look at sources across multiple professions, as well. While a multitude of studies exists on the role of mentorship in student affairs, the role of mentors did not originate within the profession of student affairs. Therefore, it was necessary to explore research in the social sciences to determine the meaning of a mentor and how that role is defined. We then compared that historical literature to what we know about mentors in student affairs. For example, historically mentors hold the role of social support. Having that historical knowledge of a mentor, we then provided insight as to how that role was supported in the student affairs literature. This approach allowed us to synthesize multiple studies across multiple professions, without having to provide a summary of each individual article studied.

Material included in a literature review is generally from peer-reviewed articles, research reports, and dissertations or theses. Books sometimes also are included, but typically only when relating empirical research. Researchers cite recent materials (5 years or less) when available, but some cited studies may be older when there is a good reason, such as a landmark or foundational study or theory or when there is no directly related research on the topic. Materials cited tend to be from student affairs or higher education journals; however, research on college students appears in many academic fields, so it is common to see research reviewed from communication, counseling, psychology, sociology, or other interdisciplinary fields.

When writing about research, authors focus on several different aspects of studies they review to support their argument. For example, if they are making the case for expanding research on an issue using a different methodology, such as interviews when prior research has been surveys, they might highlight methodological differences in the review. Alternately, the researchers might be using a different definition for the issue they are studying and focus the review on the different ways the term has been defined or operationalized. When landmark or important studies are included, researchers may summarize the study and results, then point out specific aspects. The purpose of a literature review is not to provide an exhaustive analysis of a topic (that is a review of literature), but a reasoned argument leading to the need for the present study.

Methodology

The methodology section of a study details the procedures and measures used to identify, collect, and analyze data. While there is no standard format for this section, researchers should provide enough details that a reader could replicate the study with access to the same data. Common elements of the methodology include the research questions, design, methods, procedures inclusive of data sources, data collection, instrumentation, data analysis, and limitations. Researchers also generally include information about the trustworthiness or validity of the instruments or measures, depending on the type of study. Ethical considerations such as approval by an institutional review board (IRB) as well as human subjects and data protections researchers implemented (for example, anonymizing data or using pseudonyms) may have its own section or be listed with data collection.

Research questions are derived from the problem statement and purpose of the study. They reveal how the researcher will complete the study and should suggest the data sources and methods used. Keywords are often used to identify the methods. For example, Pittman and Foubert's (2016) first research question was:

> Do certain factors (i.e., role of mentors, supervision style received, and professional involvement) influence the professional identity development of student affairs professionals? (p. 16)

This specifies one of the outcomes of interest in the study (professional identity development) and the variables studied (role of mentors, supervision style received, and professional involvement). The word influence also suggests a quantitative study that uses prediction as the analysis method. Using a qualitative example, McCoy and Winkle-Wagner (2015) wrote:

> How do summer institutes influence underrepresented students' identity as graduate students/ scholars? (p. 429)

This question also specifies the outcome of interest (identity as graduate students/scholars), the sample (underrepresented students), and the setting (summer institutes). The word influence also could suggest a quantitative study, but the next two sentences specify that the question "was posed to understand" and that the "focus remained on the students and their experiences," which are concepts associated with qualitative methods.

Quantitative research and in particular studies involving inferential statistical tests such as t-tests and ANOVA rely on hypothesis testing. Hypotheses are seldom listed in published student affairs research, but they are still being tested. Reporting them is less customary in the field, particularly for studies with multiple individual variables. Instead, researchers include the research question and let the reader infer hypotheses.

Immediately preceding or following the research questions is research design including type and perspective. In this section, researchers describe the basic methodological approach of the study, cite other authors who are considered experts in the method, and, when possible, reference related studies that used similar methods. The next chapter provides a detailed discussion about these elements of a study, considered to be the methodological framework of a study.

Next are the details about data sources in the study, including site, sample, and population, as well as information about the data collection procedures and instrumentation. Data sources can include people, places, events, and/or records. Researchers often provide details about the population in general (for example, first-year college students) then about the sample they collected data on (first-year college students enrolled in Fall 2017 at a Midwestern university in the Southeast). Details about data collection reveal how the researchers identified sources and the data collection procedures, such as how they accessed a quantitative dataset or recruited focus group participants. Information about the instrumentation may be included in this section or as its own section afterward. This includes information about any instruments used, how they were developed or accessed if they were existing instruments, and how they were administered. This section is also sometimes labeled as measures. Following is a section from a methodology section describing the measures in general followed by one of the surveys the researchers used.

Excerpt From the Data Collection

The online survey consisted of five questionnaires. The first construct measured was the dependent variable, professional identity. Following the dependent variable, questionnaires measuring demographic information, role of mentors, supervision style received, and professional involvement were presented. Information regarding the questionnaires are outlined next.

Professional Identity Scale. The professional identity scale, created by Brown, Condor, Matthews, Wade, and Williams (1986), and adapted by Adams et al. (2006), was selected to measure the dependent variable, professional identity. Adams and colleagues conducted an exploratory factor analysis on the pool of items to assess whether they formed a unidimensional scale. A nine-item, single-factor solution was produced with an internal reliability of .70 (Cronbach's alpha). The alpha in the present study produced a reliability of .867 with an overall M = 38.39 and a SD = 5.039. (Pittman & Foubert, 2016, p. 17)

Researcher Commentary (Ed Pittman)

We began this section by providing an overview of every variable we were studying. Due to the large number of variables in the study, we had to find a scale for all five. We outlined the origin of every single scale as well as the reliability. All of our scales held internal reliability, which means we knew they were measuring what they were supposed to be measuring. In other words, we knew that the individual scale for professional identity was actually measuring professional identity and not something else. While lengthy, this section of the paper was necessary to provide validity to the study. As a result of measuring five constructs, the survey itself was quite lengthy (over 500 items).

After data collection, researchers describe the data analysis procedures. This is a listing of how data were examined. It should include any changes or manipulations the researcher made, such as how outliers or extreme data were handled in survey data. Any software or programs used to analyze data are typically also listed in this section. Following data analysis, researchers (should) provide details about the rigor of the study related to data collection, instrument, and/or data analysis procedures. Qualitative researchers describe features of the study that enhance dependability and trustworthiness. Quantitative researchers list validity and reliability measures. Some researchers devote considerable time to these sections to convince the reader of the rigor of the study based on methodology. This is especially the case when the researcher develops a new instrument. Methods sections typically end with a discussion of limitations. Here, the researcher acknowledges ways the study is imperfect based on the methodology. In many cases, researchers list a potential issue then follow it with rationale. For example, Pittman and Foubert (2016, pp. 17–18) included several paragraphs of limitations. Following is an excerpt showing a limitation they acknowledged related to survey data as well as their justification.

> The reliance on self-reporting of data in an uncontrolled environment is an important facet to consider. Because surveys were distributed online, there was no way for participants to complete the questionnaires in a controlled environment, which could have allowed for environmental influences to occur during data collection or resulted in misleading or false information. When studying identity development, however, self-reported data is crucial in order to learn the participants' experiences, while conducting the research in an ethical manner. (p. 17)

A limitations section typically appears at the end of methodology; however, it is sometimes included at the end of the study along with directions for future research.

Introduction + Literature Review + Methodology = Proposal

Together, the introduction, literature review, and methodology sections are considered the research proposal. A *research proposal* is a convincing argument for conducting a study, based on identification of a clear problem statement, well-evidenced literature review, viable research questions, accessible data sources, and feasibility of data collection and analysis. In dissertation or thesis studies, a researcher proposes research in this format to a faculty committee before gaining approval to collect data.

Results

The results section reveals the findings from data analysis. Often, it begins with a descriptive report, such as information about interview participants or demographic data about the site or sample. In qualitative studies, researchers sometimes also provide a summary table of themes from data analysis. Results sections frequently begin with contextual information about the research site or setting.

Researchers have considerable flexibility in terms of overall structure when reporting results, although findings are commonly organized by subheadings. A common format is to list results by research questions. Qualitative studies often include subheadings for major themes and incorporate representative quotations from participants or data sources, or detailed descriptions of settings for observation reports. Quantitative results are listed in both graphic (tables and/or figures) and narrative format, following established conventions for statistical reporting. Results sections generally do not include references to other studies (citations), focusing instead only on the results of the present study. They also tend to not include rationale or discussion, but may provide some factual statements such as which values were highest or lowest, or which themes were most or least prevalent.

Pittman and Foubert (2016) began their results section with a two-paragraph demographic report, listing descriptive details about the sample. Next, they organized results by research questions and included both tables and text. Following is an excerpt from a section with the subheading "Primary Analyses of Research Questions 1 and 2."

Excerpt From the Results

Using data from both graduate students and new professionals, all three independent variables emerged as significant predictors of professional identity development in a regression equation, $F(3, 381) = 27.352$, $p < .01$ (Table 1). The three predictor variables together significantly predicted the professional identity of all participants with an $R^2 = .17$, $F(3, 381) = 27.352$, $p < .01$. Partial correlations revealed that professional involvement ($sr = 0.196$) showed the lowest predictive power. Role of mentors ($sr = 0.213$) followed by supervision style received ($sr = 0.253$) showed the highest predictive power on professional identity. (Pittman & Foubert, 2016, p. 19)

Researcher Commentary (Ed Pittman)

In this section, we wanted to provide an analysis of our pure results. Our study consisted of three research questions. We combined the analysis of research questions one and two because the first question was posed to determine if certain factors influence professional identity and the second question was posed to determine to what extent do those factors influence professional identity. The results of our study indicated that certain factors do, in fact, influence professional identity. The above excerpt outlines which factors hold the most influence. It was important for us to communicate the results in an extremely clear and unbiased manner. This section does not include any sort of discussion, thought, or implication. It is a pure analysis of the results we found within our study. It provides the foundation and evidence to then draw upon for conclusions, discussion, and future implications.

Discussion and Implications

Discussion and implications is the final section of a study. Sometimes, these are written separately, with discussion focusing on how the findings relate to existing research or theory and implications suggesting how the results could be used to inform practice. Structurally, researchers often use subheadings to highlight specific points. There are many ways to discuss results, though typically researchers begin by highlighting findings that confirm or oppose existing research. They also may note surprising results and suggest the need for further research. The discussion should also tie directly back to the prior literature reviewed, which means citations are included. For this reason, the literature review and discussion are sometimes described as linked or parallel. Implications for practice can be written specifically for a program or service if that is the focus of a study, or more broadly to apply to multiple settings and/or situations. The section typically closes with a conclusion that connects back to the problem statement and suggests directions for further research. Pittman and Foubert (2016) separated their discussion and implications. Following are excerpts from both sections.

Excerpts From the Discussion and Implications

Discussion

Supervision style was the only significant predictor of professional identity development for new professionals. This might be because new professionals rely heavily upon their supervisor when they first enter the field. Research asserts supervisory relationships hold great potential to influence positive self-image, orient new professionals, and increase role awareness (Shupp & Arminio, 2012; Tull, 2006, 2009). (Pittman & Foubert, 2016, p. 23)

Implications and Recommendations for Future Research

Faculty members and senior student affairs officers should have intentional conversations with graduate students and new professionals about career goals, aspirations, and experiences. Opportunities for graduate students and new professionals to interact in an informal atmosphere may provide a way to break down access barriers and feelings of intimidation. Both parties should formally recognize the mentor relationship and hold discussions about expectations and potential benefits. (Pittman & Foubert, 2016, p. 24)

Researcher Commentary (Ed Pittman)

In the discussion section of our paper, we wanted to be very thoughtful in providing implications for practice and research. The discussion section was our opportunity to communicate the meaning of our results. We found it important to clearly state our thought process behind some of the significant results we reviewed, then aligning that point with evidence from prior research. Once we thoroughly discussed the significance of our results, we then wanted to provide reasoning as to why this is important. In my opinion, the implications and recommendations section is the most practical and valuable section of a study. This is the section that learners will reference to enhance their practice and research. We made sure that we covered implications to meet every audience—student affairs practitioners as well as student affairs researchers. This allowed us to provide practical recommendations for the practitioners as well as the researchers of our profession.

Building Your Research Skillset

Finding, acquiring, and evaluating empirical studies are foundational research literacy skills. Identifying the structure of a study, knowing the importance of each component, and recognizing how the individual components function together is critical for learning to read, evaluate, and apply research. Learners motivated to understand more about their functional area, the profession, student outcomes, or related topics can find can valuable sources in published studies or books, professional reports, and published dissertations or theses. Other media such as periodicals and newsletters often include results from studies that can be applied to practice. Formal coursework can provide skills in finding and evaluating sources. Attending presentations and workshops at professional conferences, engaging in association or group discussions (online and/or in person), and networking with colleagues across and beyond campus about research-based applications are valuable opportunities for learning how to apply research to practice.

References

Adams, K., Hean, S., Sturgis, P., & Clark, J. M. (2006). Investigating the factors influencing professional identity of first-year health and social care students. *Learning in Health and Social Care, 5*(2), 55–68.

Ary, D., Jacobs, L.C., & Razavieh, A. (1996). *Introduction to research in education* (5th ed.). Fort Worth, TX: Harcourt Brace College Publishers.

Astin, A. W. (1984). Student involvement: A developmental theory for higher education. *Journal of College Student Personnel, 25*, 297–308.

Biddix, J. P. (2016). Moving beyond alcohol: Other issues associated with fraternity membership with implications for practice and research. *Journal of College Student Development, 57*(7), 793–809.

Brown, R., Condor, S., Matthews, A., Wade, G., & Williams, J. (1986). Explaining intergroup differentiation in an industrial organization. *Journal of Occupational Psychology, 59*(4), 273–286.

Creswell, J. W. (2012). *Educational research: Planning, conducting, and evaluating quantitative and qualitative research* (4th ed.). Boston, MA: Pearson.

Creswell, J. W. (2014). *Research design: Qualitative, quantitative, and mixed methods approaches* (4th ed.). Thousand Oaks, CA: Sage.

Creswell, J. W. (2015). *Educational research: Planning, conducting, and evaluating quantitative and qualitative research* (5th ed.). Boston, MA: Pearson.

Crim, E. J. (2006). *The development of professional identity in student affairs administrators* (Unpublished doctoral dissertation). Pennsylvania State University, University Park, PA.

Dewey, J. (1933). *How we think.* New York: D. C. Heath.

Dungy, G., & Gordon, S. A. (2011). The development of student affairs. In J. H. Schuh, S. R. Jones, S. R. Harper, & Associates (Eds.), *Student services: A handbook for the profession* (5th ed., pp. 61–79). San Francisco, CA: Jossey-Bass.

Finley, A. (2011). *Civic learning and democratic engagements: A review of the literature on civic engagement in post-secondary education.* Paper prepared for the U.S. Department of Education as part of contract ED-OPE-10-C-0078.

Gardner, S. K., & Barnes, B. J. (2007). Graduate student involvement: Socialization for the professional role. *Journal of College Student Development, 48*(4), 369–387.

Holland, J. H. (1985). *Making vocational choices: A theory of vocational personalities and work environments* (2nd ed.). Englewood Cliffs, NJ: Prentice-Hall.

Komives, S. R., Longerbeam, S., Owen, J. O., Mainella, F. C., & Osteen, L. (2005). A leadership identity development model: Applications from a grounded theory. *Journal of College Student Development, 47*(4), 401–418.

Kuh, G. D. (2009). What student affairs professionals need to know about student engagement. *Journal of College Student Development, 50*(6), 683–706.

Lochmiller, C. R., & Lester, J. N. (2015). *An introduction to educational research: Connecting methods to practice.* Thousand Oaks, CA: Sage.

Marshall, C., & Rossman, G. B. (1995). *Designing qualitative research.* Thousand Oaks, CA: Sage.

Mayhew, M. J., Rockenbach, A. N., Bowman, N. A., Seifert, T. A. D., Wolniak, G. C., Pascarella, E. T., & Terenzini, P. T. (2016). *How college affects students: 21st century evidence that higher education works* (Vol. 3). San Francisco, CA: Jossey-Bass.

Merriam, S. B. (2009). *Qualitative research: A guide to design and implementation.* San Francisco, CA: Jossey-Bass.

McCoy, D. L., & Winkle-Wagner, R. (2015). Bridging the divide: Developing a scholarly habitus for aspiring graduate students through summer bridge programs participation. *Journal of College Student Development, 56*(5), 423–439.

Mongan-Rollis, H. (2014). *Guidelines for writing a literature review.* Retrieved from http://www.duluth.umn.edu/~hrallis/guides/researching/litreview.html

Pittman, E. C., & Foubert, J. D. (2016). Predictors of professional identity development for student affairs professionals. *Journal of Student Affairs Research and Practice, 53*(1), 13–25.

Renn, K. A., & Jessup-Anger, E. R. (2008). Preparing new professionals: Lessons for graduate preparation programs from the national study of new professionals in student affairs. *Journal of College Student Development, 49*(4), 319–335.

Renn, K. A., & Reason, R. D. (2012). *College students in the United States: Characteristics, experiences, and outcomes.* San Francisco, CA: Jossey-Bass.

Schlossberg, N. K. (1981). A model for analyzing human adaptation to transition. *The Counseling Psychologist, 9*(2), 2–18.

Schmidt, J. A., & Wolfe, J. S. (2009). The mentorship partnership: Discovery of professionalism. *NASPA Journal, 46*(3), 371–381.

Schuh, J. H., Biddix, J. P., Dean, L. A., & Kinzie, J. (2016). *Assessment in student affairs: A contemporary look* (2nd ed.). San Francisco, CA: Jossey-Bass.

Shupp, M. R., & Arminio, J. L. (2012). Synergistic supervision: A confirmed key to retaining entry-level student affairs professionals. *Journal of Student Affairs Research and Practice, 49*(2), 157–174.

Spanierman, L. B., Soble, J. R., Mayfield, J. B., Neville, H. A., Aber, M., Khuri, L., & De La Rosa, B. (2013). Living learning communities and students' sense of community and belonging. *Journal of Student Affairs Research and Practice, 50*(3), 308–325.

Stage, F. K., & Manning, K. (2016). *Research in the college context: Approaches and methods* (2nd ed.). New York, NY: Brunner-Routledge.

Trede, F., Macklin, R., & Bridges, D. (2011). Professional identity development: A review of the higher education literature. *Studies in Higher Education, 37*(3), 365–384.

Tull, A. (2006). Synergistic supervision, job satisfaction, and intention to turnover of new professionals in student affairs. *Journal of College Student Development, 47*(4), 465–480.

Tull, A. (2009). Supervision and mentorship in the socialization process. In A. Tull, J. B. Hirt, & S. A. Saunders (Eds.), *Becoming socialized in student affairs administration: A guide for new professionals and their supervisors* (pp. 129–151). Sterling, VA: Stylus.

CHAPTER THREE

FRAMING RESEARCH

Learning Outcomes

By the end of this chapter, you should be able to:

- Define perspective as related to research.
- Identify the major types of research.
- Differentiate the major research designs in student affairs.
- Associate research methods with types and designs.

Understanding, reading, evaluating, and applying research in student affairs requires knowledge of the basic characteristics of methodology and how it functions in a study. *Methodology* is the research plan that serves initially as scaffolding and later as a framework for a study. Developing a methodology begins with consideration of perspective, or a view about the study that will influence how the research is conducted. This is followed by specifying a research type, which generally informs how data will be collected. Design is next, which identifies the research procedures and suggests how data will be collected. The design also includes considerations about the ethical conduct of research. The last aspect of methodology is the methods, or the techniques researchers use to analyze data.

This chapter focuses on how research is framed using the four core components of methodology: perspective, type, design, and method. The information is intended to be both an initial introduction and a review or reference chapter that can be revisited as new concepts are learned.

Table 3.1. Four Core Components of Methodology

Perspective	>	Type	>	Design	>	Method
Constructivism		Qualitative		Qualitative + Basic Qualitative + Case Study + Grounded Theory + Phenomenology + Narrative		Qualitative + Document Review + Observation + Interviews
Postpositivism		Quantitative		Quantitative + Nonexperiment + Quasi-experimental		Quantitative + Description + Difference + Relationship + Prediction
Pragmatism		Mixed Methods		Mixed + Concurrent + Sequential + Embedded		Mixed + Multiple

Research Methodology

Research methodology is characterized by four components: Perspective > Type > Design > Method. Table 3.1 shows the relationships between each component. Viewed from left to right, the graphic appears to be sequential; however, the arrows are indirect to suggest that while each feature informs the next, it is not essential to specify all features in sequence. Method is the exception, as it requires identification of perspective and type. Basic characteristics of the three perspectives, three types, ten designs, and seven methods are described in this chapter. Details on each method are provided in subsequent chapters focusing on those methods.

Research Perspectives

A *perspective* is a lens for how a person sees and makes sense of the surrounding world. Researchers use a perspective when designing, conducting, and reporting studies. It can be helpful to think about perspective as a series of reflective questions, such as the following:

Think about how you see the world. What is knowledge? What are the conditions of knowing? How do we arrive at those conclusions? How confident are we in them?

Perspectives From the Field —A Methodology Is Not an Identity

Research exists, in essence, to answer questions . . . or at least to add insight into our understanding of things. Do living-learning programs increase retention? How are we helping our first-gen students to succeed? What's it like to be an international student on this campus? The research methods we use to find answers or understand phenomena must, logically, be driven by the questions themselves. The answers to some questions lie in discovering what is true for large groups of students, while insight into others can best be gained from deeply understanding the experiences of a few. It is crucial, therefore, for practitioners to be literate in all forms of research—quantitative, qualitative, and mixed methods—so that they can choose and use the method that will best address the question.

A methodology is not an identity; while practitioners may be more comfortable with or drawn to one kind of method or another, claiming and using only one (e.g., "I'm a quant person") is tantamount to saying, ". . . and I'm not interested in those other questions." Good practice calls us to ask good, and sometimes hard, questions, and to develop the skills to explore them by whatever method best fits.

Laura A. Dean—Professor, College Student Affairs Administration (CSAA), program coordinator, CSAA-M.Ed., University of Georgia

Perspectives are commonly shaped by the researcher's background (unrelated to research), influential faculty and/or advisors, and past experiences as a research consumer or producer. These beliefs often lead researchers to prefer quantitative or qualitative designs. Table 3.2 is a comparison of the three major perspectives common to student affairs research based on key characteristics. Notes based on each comparison follow. Examples of how perspectives are used in research appear in subsequent chapters.

Table 3.2. Comparison of Research Perspectives by Key Characteristics

	Constructivism	Postpositivism	Pragmatism
Knowledge	Understanding	Truth	Situational
Evidence	Multiple meanings	Reductionism	Holistic
Researcher	Subjective	Objective	Both
Theory	Development	Verification	Either or both

Knowledge

Constructivism: Knowledge is based on the view that reality or truth is understood. In this way, knowledge is defined as situational, depending on the views and experiences of an individual. A goal is to understand knowledge from the individual's viewpoint.

Postpositivism: Knowledge is a discoverable truth. There are singular answers to a problem that can be revealed.

Pragmatism: Knowledge is situational. Understanding or truth might be a goal, depending on the question and the needed solution to the problem.

Evidence

Constructivism: Evidence is based on individual interpretations, which can create multiple meanings accounting for culture, context, and other factors that affect an individual's reality. Data is presented to preserve the richness and complexity of the findings.

Postpositivism: Evidence is systematically collecting according to standardized procedures. Data is reduced to the least possible number of variables, factors, or causes that affect outcomes.

Pragmatism: Evidence is drawn from qualitative sources to explore meaning and quantitative data to explain it.

Researcher

Constructivism: The researcher is acknowledged as having a subjective influence on all aspects of the study. Researchers sometimes are viewed as co-creating knowledge with participants and data sources to acknowledge their role in and effect on the research process.

Postpositivism: The researcher is thought to take an objective view in the study. Standardized data collection and analysis procedures are verifiable and data are interpreted simply based on calculated results.

Pragmatism: The researcher may view data collection using either perspective, depending on which fits the overall goal of addressing the problem by providing a solution.

Theory

Constructivism: Theory is often generated (or emerges) as part of the research process to explain individual and situational behaviors and viewpoints.

Postpositivism: Theory is often tested and verified (or rejected) as part of analysis.

Pragmatism: Theory can be generated and then verified as part of the same study.

Emphasizing the importance of perspective in research, Broido and Manning (2002) noted that "research cannot be conducted without the conscious or unconscious use of underlying theoretical perspectives. These perspectives inform methodology, guiding theory, questions pursued, and conclusions drawn" (p. 434). Some researchers refer to perspective as an approach to signify how they conceptualize their work during all phases of a study. Perspective is typically not a conscious or obvious choice. In other words, the choices a researcher makes when working on study reveal their perspective, even if the researcher never explicitly states it.

Words Researchers Use—Synonyms for Perspective

When researchers write about perspective, they use several words synonymously. Following is a listing of the most commonly used words, along with some minor distinctions worth noting.

Perspective
A specific viewpoint, usually described as held by or coming from an individual or group.

Worldview
A general orientation about the world and the nature of research a researcher holds.

Approach
A way to describe the point of view of the research and how it influenced the study.

Paradigm
A (usually) qualitative categorization of research perspectives. Paradigms often dictate, with varying degrees, the design of a research investigation. Denzin and Lincoln (2011) referred to paradigm as a continuum, "with rigorous design principles on one end and emergent, less well-structured directives on the other" (p. 45).

Orientation
A researcher's preconceived notions or beliefs about a phenomenon that influenced the study.

Epistemology
The study of knowledge comprised of perspectives, assumptions, and/or worldviews.

Knowing the perspective, or how a researcher approached a problem, clarifies the decisions that informed a study. It also suggests alternative ways of understanding a research problem, if considered from a related or opposing perspective. For example, a study focused on student retention will be fundamentally and operationally different based on the framing perspective. A constructivism-based study might seek to understand how institutional policies and practices affect retention for underserved or marginalized students using focus group interviews along with analysis of institutional documents. A postpositivism-based study might start with retention theory to identify characteristics of nonretained students from a large-scale or longitudinal dataset. A pragmatism-based study may start with the large dataset, and then follow up with interviews and document analysis informed by the dataset findings. Each perspective will lead the researcher to different data sources, analysis, and interpretation.

Words Researchers Use—Other Perspectives

Constructivism might be thought of as an umbrella perspective, covering several distinct subperspectives that share its key features. One commonly used subperspective in student affairs research is the transformative view. Conversely, postpositivism has few subperspectives, but was derived from positivism. A brief overview of each follows.

Transformative
The transformative perspective is also referred to as advocacy or participatory. Key concepts include a change-oriented agenda, a focus on empowering individuals, and a collaborative approach with research participants. The requirement for a change-oriented, advocacy-based agenda differentiates it from a broader constructivist perspective. Often, feminist perspectives, radicalized discourses, critical theory, queer theory, and disability theory are considered transformative.

Positivism
Positivism holds the notion that truth is absolute. The goal of research is to hypothesize and test theory with the overall goal of discovering truth and affirming knowledge. This is accomplished through empirical measurement using the scientific method. Postpositivism relaxes this more rigid belief to suggest that it is not possible to be certain about claims of knowledge when studying the behavior and actions of humans.

Research Types

There are three basic research types, qualitative, quantitative, and mixed methods. The root words of each term provide insight to their definitions.

Qualitative Research. Qualitative is related to quality, suggesting that the research is focused on understanding and exploring the qualities of a person, place, process, or phenomenon. Qualitative research seeks to explore and represent reality as it exists in context and to enlighten the ways in which individuals experience that reality.

Quantitative Research. Quantitative is related to quantity, suggesting that the research is focused on understanding and explaining the quantities related to a person, place, process, or phenomenon. Quantitative research seeks to identify and explain reality as it exists.

Mixed Methods Research. Mixed is related to mix, suggesting the research is focused on understanding, exploring, and explaining both the qualities and quantities of a person, place, process, or phenomenon. *Mixed methods* integrate multiple, different methods in the same study to explain, explore, or inform a research topic.

Misperceptions and Myths About Research Types. A common misperception is that quantitative research, and in particular statistics, is more difficult than qualitative research. This consideration can be related to a general sentiment that qualitative research is more approachable. Reading quantitative data seems to require memorizing formulas or symbols, or learning to read text and tables with sophisticated calculations. Conversely, qualitative research seems more approachable because it, generally, can be read and understood without prerequisite knowledge. As a result, novice researchers often incline toward qualitative methods. Researchers collecting qualitative data or working with qualitative results for the first time find the mistake in this misperception. While qualitative research may seem more approachable, conducting it well can be extremely difficult. The opposite might be observed about quantitative research. For researchers unfamiliar with or averse to statistics, quantitative research can be extremely intimidating; however, data collection, common analytical approaches, and generally standardized formatting, once learned, can make quantitative research much less difficult. Figure 3.1 is a display of this conceptualization.

There are numerous common misconceptions about quantitative and qualitative research rigor. Table 3.3 highlights some common myths about bias in qualitative research stemming from subjectivity. While it is true that the researcher is considered an integral part of qualitative inquiry, and in some cases, is regarded as a coconstructor of reality or findings, quantitative research shares similar characteristics. The following considerations primarily relate to collecting qualitative data through interviews and quantitative data through survey research.

FIGURE 3.1. QUANTITATIVE–QUALITATIVE CONCEPTUALIZATION

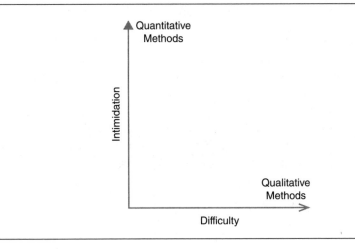

Table 3.3. Common Quantitative and Qualitative Myths

Qualitative Myth	Quantitative Myth	Reality
Instruments are created.	Instruments are standardized.	Instruments are selected.
Data collection is biased.	Data collection is standardized.	Data and samples are selected.
Data analysis is subjective.	Data analysis is standardized.	Analysis methods are selected. Data are cleaned/manipulated.
Results are selected.	Results are displayed in consistent formats.	Results are emphasized, highlighted, or not reported.

Instrument-Related Myths   An *instrument* is the tool researchers use to collect data. Even when using a standardized guide, form, or questionnaire, many qualitative researchers regard themselves as the instrument. A criticism is because qualitative researchers write their own questions, they introduce bias, or partiality toward a particular belief—especially in cases where the questions are not prewritten or standardized. In quantitative research and surveys in particular, researchers may create or use an existing instrument. The questions are standardized to create consistency in the data collection. Despite this standardization, quantitative researchers must select the questions or instrument, which also introduces bias to the research.

Data Collection-Related Myths   Philosophically, many qualitative researchers consider themselves as part of the research because of their role in data collection and interpretation. Further, qualitative samples tend to be smaller and selected intentionally to represent certain criteria or to explore a particular perspective. When qualitative researchers collect data, they often ask questions—either directly to participants or indirectly while working with existing data or making observations. Quantitative methods tend to be indirect—even survey distribution in person can involve little interaction. However, despite the indirect interaction during data collection, researchers also select the sample and instrument. For example, a researcher studying political orientation on campus may select a conservative views instrument and distribute the survey on a traditionally more liberal campus or to a less conservative student group.

Data Analysis-Related Myths   Qualitative data analysis typically involves reviewing transcript data and developing themes, or commonalities in the text. While researchers may describe their data analysis process in detail, the nature (and philosophy) of qualitative inquiry means that exact replication by another researcher, even with the same data, would be difficult. Conversely, quantitative data analysis involves standardized formulas matched to data. There is some personal choice in data analysis techniques, however. For example, many researchers treat Likert scale items (for example, 1–5 strongly disagree . . . strongly agree) as scale, while others consider Likert data to be nominal. This has significant implications for which statistical tests can be used. Further, quantitative datasets rarely are completely ready for analysis. Frequently, datasets have missing data, outliers, or other issues that must be corrected or manipulated prior to analysis.

Results-Related Myths   Qualitative researchers do not have a standardized format for reporting or writing about findings. A common approach is to list and describe themes from data analysis and include excerpts or sample quotations. Others highlight individual stories using a narrative format that includes more or longer quotations. Researchers using observation or document data may include a contextual section while emphasizing themes. Conversely, quantitative researchers tend to follow standard and consistent reporting formats for statistics in texts and tables. There is some variation based on the details of what to include with some statistical analyses; however, statistical results can be emphasized, highlighted, or not reported. Researchers tend to emphasize results that address their research questions more directly.

These choices introduce bias that is seldom discussed. Further, combining data or changing the scales or data in graphs and tables is another way statisticians can present data in alternate ways.

Despite these misconceptions and myths, the most important consideration is that the research type should align with the research problem, purpose, and questions. Further, regardless of the type selected, researchers should acknowledge the limitations of their selected approach and offer considerations for further research based on alternative ways to study the problem.

Research Design

Design is the foundational framework of a study that influences decisions researchers make before, during, and after data collection. Numerous textbooks have been written about research design—ranging from overviews (Mills & Gay, 2015) to works dedicated to specific methodologies (Strauss & Corbin, 1998; Tabachnick & Fidell, 2012). It is not possible to adequately cover the breadth of research designs with an overview approach. Readers interested in advanced coverage of design should consult the texts cited in the following sections. A brief overview of 10 common designs in student affairs research follows.

Qualitative Designs

Prominent qualitative methodologist Michael Quinn Patton (1990) wrote that "qualitative inquiry seems to work best for people with a high tolerance for ambiguity. (And we're still only discussing design. It gets worse when we get to analysis)" (p. 183). One of the major challenges when learning about qualitative designs is the "broad specificity" of the concepts and terminology. While there are consistent and frequently used designs and associated concepts, the nature and the philosophical tenets of constructivism resulted in the development of multiple theoretical positions, data collection forms, and types of data analysis that can be daunting and confusing. Denzin and Lincoln (2011) regarded this issue as a barrier to qualitative methodology, identifying two limiting issues: (1) a resistance to impose a single structure due to its open-ended nature (pp. xiii) and (2) a debate over complex terms, concepts, and assumptions (pp. 3–4). An overview of five qualitative designs common to student affairs research (Figure 3.2) follows.

FIGURE 3.2. COMMON QUALITATIVE RESEARCH DESIGNS

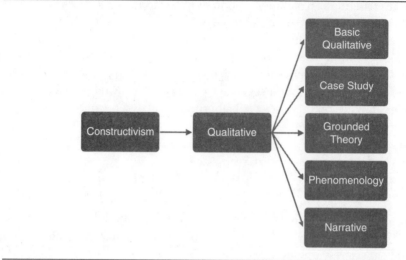

Basic Qualitative Design. *Basic qualitative design* involves using primary methods for data collection and a generalized approach to data analysis. Merriam (2009) differentiated this approach as a basic or fundamental procedure for qualitative research that does not fit into a specific design. Key tenets of this approach include eliciting understanding and meaning, the researcher as the primary data collection instrument, use of different field methods, inductive data analysis, and reporting results using rich description. Unless the researcher specifies an alternative method, basic qualitative research typically is the default design for studies incorporating qualitative methods.

Case Study. *Case study* is a form of qualitative research that involves the collection and analysis of multiple forms of data to build understanding about an individual, site, or process. Cases are typically located within a larger context. An important consideration with case study research is bounding, which refers to the parameters researchers set. Boundaries might be thought of delimitations; researchers delimit, or restrict, data collection, analysis, and interpretation based on set criteria. Stake (1995) and Yin (2013) are two major authors researchers cite when following a case-study design. An example case study is Biddix, Somers, and Polman's (2009) research on Internet use in activism during a living wage protest at Washington University in St. Louis.

Grounded Theory. *Grounded theory* is a systematic procedure used to create theory that explains a process, issue, or action. A primary characteristic of grounded theory design is a focus on emergent findings (Corbin & Strauss, 2014). This means that a working theory or explanation about a research problem is developed from the data, following a systematic process of data analysis, rather than from analysis of existing research or theory. Differences in grounded theory have to do with the data analysis, or coding, and research process (Charmez, 2014; Glaser & Strauss, 1967). Examples include systematic design (Komives, Longerbeam, Owen, Mainella, & Osteen, 2005), emergent design (Waldron & Dieser, 2010), and constructivist design (Edwards & Jones, 2009).

Phenomenology. *Phenomenology* is concerned with how individuals experience, conceptualize, perceive, and/or understand (or make meaning of) phenomena. Rands and Gansemer-Topf (2016) described phenomenology simply as exploring variation in experiences. Central to phenomenological design is the concept of essence or how participants describe their meaning of an experience. Essence is typically considered an intersubject concept, meaning that even though each individual experience is recognized and explored, the goal is to identify the core (or essence) of the shared (or lived) experience. Phenomenology can be one of the more difficult designs for novice researchers to understand, due to the new terminology coupled with a less formulaic approach to data collection and analysis. Typically, the length necessary for phenomenological studies make them more common in dissertations and theses or books. An example of phenomenology is Rhoads's (2000) study of activism and cultural diversity.

Narrative Design. *Narrative design* uses descriptions or accounts of events to enlighten experiences and perspectives. Researchers collect stories from participants with the goal of contextualizing and describing their experiences. The focus tends to be on a single person or small group of individuals. Key features of the design include an emphasis on the history of an event or experience as told by the participant, the creation of the narrative or story through the researcher/participation interaction, a time-structured or chronologically arranged retelling, and emphasis on contextual details (such as conflict, predicament, time, and place). Examples of narrative studies include Wolf-Wendall, Twombly, Tuttle, Ward, and Gaston's (2004) research on experiences of student affairs professionals during the Civil Rights Movement and Petchauer's (2010) study of sampling practices and social spaces.

Other Qualitative Designs. Two notable but less used qualitative designs in student affairs are ethnography and historical research. Ethnography describes, analyzes, and interprets shared, or group-based, understandings about an experience, a phenomenon, or a process. A student affairs study example is Nathan's (2006) *My Freshman*

Year. As implied, historical research focuses on past events. Some historical researchers use case study methods to bind the study to a person, event, or time frame. An example of historical research in student affairs is Biddix and Schwartz's (2012) study of the influence of Walter Dill Scott in the development and codification of the profession.

Quantitative Designs

Quantitative research design is differentiated by the purpose of the study and the sampling method. The classic quantitative design, sometimes referred to as the gold standard, is experimental. The purpose of experimental design is to evaluate the use of a proposed treatment or intervention within a population or group. The basic format for an experimental study is taking two randomly sampled groups and testing a treatment condition with one group versus a control condition (no treatment) with the other. Variations of this design include using more than one group or varying the data collection periods; however, the requirement of having randomly assigned treatment and control groups is essential. The random assignment minimizes additional influences and potential variation that could bias or confound the study.

This basic format presents several problems for educational research. Primarily, true random assignment is nearly impossible within educational structures. For example, researchers wanting to study the effects of a new instructional method on the classroom or leadership experiences of students in particular groups typically cannot randomly assign participants. Secondly, treatments or interventions can rarely be delivered to multiple groups. These limitations led to alternative experimental designs, which are more commonly used in student affairs. An overview of two quantitative designs common to student affairs research (Figure 3.3) follows.

FIGURE 3.3. COMMON QUANTITATIVE RESEARCH DESIGNS

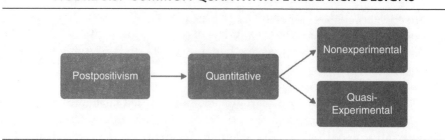

Nonexperimental Design. *Nonexperimental design* typically involves a treatment or condition that has not been manipulated, such as distributing a survey to a sample or population. All participants are given the same instrument or test and there is no group separation based on a researcher-specified condition. Sampling may be random or not, depending on the goals of the analysis. For example, if the goal is to describe the characteristics of a group and to understand their attitudes, perceptions, or beliefs, a random sample is not needed. Conversely, if the goal is to make representative, or inferential, statements about a population from sample data, then a random sample is required. Most quantitative designs in student affairs are nonexperimental.

Quasi-Experimental Design. *Quasi-experimental design* typically involves a pre/post measure that evaluates a treatment, condition, or effect of time. Characteristics of this design are a matched sample (the same participants who take the pretest also take the posttest and their results are compared) and a treatment condition such as the implementation of a program, involvement in an organization, or simply the passage of time. The design is called quasi-experiment because it involves a treatment, but does not include true random assignment or a control group (Padgett, Keup, & Pascarella, 2013). Procedurally, the researcher administers a pretest assessment or survey, then follows with one or more posttests after a specified period of time. The interval from pre- to posttest, as well as the number of follow-ups, depends on the goals of the study. For example, Grandzol, Perlis, and Draina (2010) asked varsity team captains and team members about their leadership characteristics pre- and postseason to examine their leadership development during a season. Another example of this approach is longitudinal surveys. The Cooperative Institutional Research Program (CIRP) uses The Freshman Survey (TFS) in the summer prior to college, then Your First College Year (YFCY) after the first year, then the College Senior Survey (CSS) as an exit survey for graduating seniors.

Mixed Methods Designs

Mixed methods combines or mixes qualitative and quantitative methods. Some rationale for using mixed methods includes the ability to both explain and interpret results, develop and test an instrument, complement the strengths or offset the weaknesses of a single design, and to address a question or theoretical perspective at multiple levels and from varied data sources (Creswell, 2015). The time required to complete mixed methods studies can be limiting, since both forms are fully complete methods. Resolving discrepancies between methods can also be problematic, especially when the data collected are not equally weighted or prioritized.

FIGURE 3.4. COMMON MIXED METHODS RESEARCH DESIGNS

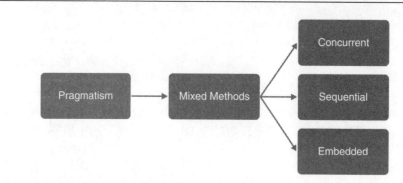

There are three basic mixed methods designs: concurrent, sequential (exploratory and explanatory), and embedded. Because mixed methods design is a relatively new field, researchers are still deciding on commonly agreed terminology. For example, some researchers refer to a concurrent design as parallel or convergent, while embedded may be called nested or intervention. Mixed methods design is not prevalent in published student affairs research, although researchers are beginning to use mixed designs in dissertations and some articles. A brief overview of three basic mixed methods designs (Figure 3.4) follows.

Concurrent Mixed Methods. *Concurrent mixed methods* involves collecting both qualitative and quantitative data simultaneously. The methods are equally prioritized and are kept separate during data collection and analyses. Typically, the data converge, or are integrated, during interpretation. Some advantages to this approach include that it considers a problem from multiple and equally prioritized perspectives. This also allows the methods to validate each other. Seifert, Goodman, King, and Baxter Magolda (2010) used a concurrent design to study student expectations and development during their first year of college. The researchers collected survey data and assessments at the same time as interview data, which they noted, "allowed [them] to construct an enriched and deeper understanding of the practices and conditions that contribute to students' development of liberal arts outcomes" (p. 251).

Sequential Mixed Methods. *Sequential mixed methods* involves collecting data in distinct, sequenced phases. Morgan (1998) referred to this design as a follow-up approach. The general procedure is to collect and analyze data from the first method and then to collect and analyze data from the second. The first data collection phase typically informs the second phase. For example, a researcher could conduct focus groups in the first phase, analyze data, then use the results to develop a survey to administer in a second phase. A significant limitation to this approach is time. The researcher essentially is conducting two full studies and interpreting two sets of data to complete the study. There are two variations to sequential design: explanatory and exploratory.

Explanatory Sequential Design. *Explanatory sequential design* begins with quantitative data collection and analysis. Next, the researcher collects qualitative data to *explain* the quantitative findings. This design works well when a goal for the study is to assess trends and relationships while including explanations or adding voices to the data. Deciding which data need further explanation can be a challenge, which affects participant or data selection for the qualitative phase. For example, Gasiewski, Eagan, Garcia, Hurtado, and Chang (2012) collected survey data from 73 introductory STEM courses across 15 colleges and universities and followed up with focus groups at eight institutions to determine learning strategies and pedagogical practices related to self-reported academic engagement scores.

Exploratory Sequential Design. *Exploratory sequential design* begins with qualitative data collection and analysis. Next, the researcher collects quantitative data to *explore* the qualitative findings. This design works well when the researcher does not know which factors are important in a study and wants to be able to generalize, assess, or test results. This design has two variants, theory development (emphasis is on the qualitative phase) and instrument design (emphasis is on the quantitative phase). For example, Reynolds and Chris (2008) collected focused group data from counseling staff members to develop a survey focused on improving counseling practice (instrument design).

Embedded Design. *Embedded design* involves using one type of data to answer a secondary research question within a predominant method. Other terms for this approach are nested or intervention design, although an informal name is "in the middle of" design. Collection and analysis of data of the secondary data may occur before, during, or after implementation of the primary method. Some considerations for using the approach concern the priority and timing of the second method. Creswell (2015) noted that the intent is not to merge two different datasets to answer the same question, distinguishing embedded from concurrent design. For example, in a study of why faculty leave, O'Meara, Lounder, and Campbell (2014) conducted qualitative interviews with faculty who left and analyzed surveys of faculty who intended to leave along with data from administrators in their departments. They noted, "the quantitative data provided an important baseline sense of faculty explanations of departure; however, the qualitative data better illuminated operating metaphors, narrative, and institutional scripts of departure, as well as why individuals perceived departure as they did" (p. 612).

Research Methods

Research methods are the tools and techniques researchers use to carry out research designs. Seven major approaches can be identified in student affairs research. Qualitative methods include reviewing documents, observing people and places, and interviewing individuals and groups. Quantitative methods include describing trends, testing differences, assessing relationships, and making predictions. Mixed research methods can include any combination of these methods. Subsequent chapters provide details on each method, including how to understand, read, evaluate, and apply results. Tables 3.4 (qualitative) and 3.5 (quantitative) list each method with summary descriptions.

Table 3.4. Qualitative Research Methods

Reviewing Documents	Observing People and Places	Interviewing Individuals and Groups
Involves the discovery, examination, and evaluation of existing information	Involves selecting a person or group, or a time and location, and recording data about people, places, and/or events	Involves interacting with individual and groups to understand perspectives
Main types include document analysis and visual analysis	Main types include location, time-and-location, and person	Main types include individual and focus groups

Table 3.5. Quantitative Research Methods

Describing Trends	Testing Differences	Assessing Relationships	Making Predictions
Involves condensing individual units of information into interpretable, manageable, and useful summaries	Allows researchers to make evidenced guesses about a population, to differentiate groups, and to track changes over time	Lets researchers evaluate associations between two or more data points, or variables	Permits estimates of the influence of one or more measures on an outcome
Main types include frequency, central tendency, and variability	Main types include t-test, ANOVA, and chi-square	Main types include Pearson correlation and Spearman Rho	Main types include multiple regression and logistic regression

Research Perspective > Type > Design > Method

The four core components work together to form the methodology of a research project. The following examples illustrate how each can be mapped in published studies.

Example 1

Broido, Brown, Stygles, and Bronkema (2015) explored changes in the experiences of women who worked at one university for 25–40 years. Data sources included interviews with 28 classified, administrative, and faculty women and documents related to aspects of their gendered experiences such as employee handbooks and policies. Findings focused on how gender manifested in the institution and how participants responded.

> Perspective > Constructivism (Feminist Epistemology)
>
> Type > Qualitative
>
> Design > Case Study
>
> Methods > Interviews and Document Analysis

Example 2

Mayhew, Seifert, Pascarella, Nelson Laird, and Blaich (2012) sought to understand how institutional type affected moral reason and development of first-year students. Data sources were responses to a survey given to first-year college students ($n = 3,081$) at 19 four-year colleges and universities from across the United States in the fall and spring of their first year. Findings suggested moral development was associated (but not conditional) with specific institution types and that researchers should explore other institutional variables when examining moral reasoning.

> Perspective > Positivism
>
> Type > Quantitative
>
> Design > Quasi-experimental (Pre/post-design)
>
> Methods > Difference (ANOVA) and prediction (multilevel modeling)

Example 3

Barnhardt (2015) studied the relationship between student capacity for democratic participation and the organizational context of collective action. Data sources included national data from a random sample of 149 postsecondary institutions followed by a content analysis of 683 newspaper articles. Findings suggested that distinctive institutional characteristics, including required diversity courses and enrolling large numbers of students in area studies degree programs, exercised a supportive role in fostering student collective action.

Perspective > Pragmatism

Type > Mixed Methods

Design > Embedded Sequential

Methods > Prediction and Document Analysis

Perspectives From the Field—Being Literate in All Types of Research

Even for a researcher early in a career, it is useful and important to know how quantitative, qualitative, and mixed methods work and can, in fact, complement each other. Quantitative data collection and analysis is assumed to be faster than qualitative research. As researcher, you create a survey or work with existing data, do your analysis, determine the results and you are done! Qualitative research is time-consuming as you must do a case study, conduct interviews, or at the least, gather observations—all of which take time. Recently, using mixed methods, or combining quantitative and qualitative data methods, has emerged as a useful middle ground but it does require skills in all three areas to be successful.

Consider carefully what it is you want to know or understand. Doing a survey is useful. You will gather some information from a large group but you may miss the subtleties and differences between respondents. Qualitative interviews give you a deep understanding but only for a limited sample. Doing mixed may offer results on both sides but requires knowledge and appreciation for both quantitative and qualitative data gathering and interpretation. Think carefully about what questions or issues you want to address and then proceed carefully.

Robert A. Schwartz—Department Chair/Professor in Higher Education and Student Affairs, Florida State University

Building Your Research Skillset

Formal coursework in research design or specialized courses in methods can help build an understanding of research methodology. There are also numerous and specific texts related to research design and methods researchers typically use when conducting specific studies, referenced in subsequent chapters. A less formal way to build skills in research methodology is deconstructing a study by identifying the four core components of methodology. This reveals the decisions a researcher made throughout the research process and can help develop reading and evaluation skills. Looking up unfamiliar terminology when reading is also a useful practice.

References

Barnhardt, C. L. (2015). Campus educational contexts and civic participation: Organizational links to community action. *The Journal of Higher Education, 86*(1), 38–70.

Biddix, J. P., & Schwartz, R. (2012). Walter Dill Scott and the student personnel movement. *Journal of Student Affairs Research and Practice, 49*(3), 285–298.

Biddix, J. P., Somers, P. A., & Polman, J. L. (2009). Protest reconsidered: Activism's role as civic engagement educator. *Innovative Higher Education, 34*(3), 133–147.

Broido, E. M., Brown, K. R., Stygles, K. N., & Bronkema, R. H. (2015). Responding to gendered dynamics: Experiences of women working over 25 years at one university. *The Journal of Higher Education, 86*(4), 595–627.

Broido, E. M., & Manning, K. (2002). Philosophical foundations and current theoretical perspectives in qualitative research. *Journal of College Student Development, 43*(4), 434–445.

Charmez, K. (2014). *Constructing grounded theory* (2nd ed.). Thousand Oaks, CA: Sage.

Corbin, J., & Strauss, A. (2014). *Basics of qualitative research: Techniques and procedures for developing grounded theory* (4th ed.). Thousand Oaks, CA: Sage.

Creswell, J. W. (2015). *Educational research: Planning, conducting, and evaluating quantitative and qualitative research* (5th ed.). Boston, MA: Pearson.

Denzin, N. K., & Lincoln, Y. S. (Eds.). (2011). *The SAGE handbook of qualitative research.* Thousand Oaks, CA: Sage.

Edwards, K. E., & Jones, S. R. (2009). "Putting my man face on": A grounded theory of college men's gender identity development. *Journal of College Student Development, 50*(2), 210–228.

Gasiewski, J. A., Eagan, M. K., Garcia, G. A., Hurtado, S., & Chang, M. J. (2012). From gatekeeping to engagement: A multicontextual, mixed method study of student academic engagement in introductory STEM courses. *Research in Higher Education, 53*(2), 229–261.

Glaser, B., & Strauss, A. L. (1967). *The discovery of grounded theory: Strategies for qualitative research.* Chicago, IL: Aldine.

Grandzol, C., Perlis, S., & Draina, L. (2010). Leadership development of team captains in collegiate varsity athletics. *Journal of College Student Development, 51*(4), 403–418.

Komives, S. R., Longerbeam, S., Owen, J. O., Mainella, F. C., & Osteen, L. (2005). A leadership identity development model: Applications from a grounded theory. *Journal of College Student Development, 47*(4), 401–418.

Mayhew, M. J., Seifert, T. A., Pascarella, E. T., Nelson Laird, T. F., & Blaich, C. F. (2012). Going deep into mechanisms for moral reasoning growth: How deep learning approaches affect moral reasoning development for first-year students. *Research in Higher Education, 53*, 26–46.

Merriam, S. B. (2009). *Qualitative research: A guide to design and implementation.* San Francisco, CA: Jossey-Bass.

Mills, G. E., & Gay, L. R. (2015). *Educational research: Competencies for analysis and applications* (11th ed.). Upper Saddle River, NJ: Pearson.

Morgan, D. (1998). Practical strategies for combining qualitative and quantitative methods: Applications to health research. *Qualitative Health Research, 8*, 362–376.

Nathan, R. (2006). *My freshman year: What a professor learned by becoming a student.* Ithaca, NY: Cornell University Press.

O'Meara, K., Lounder, A., & Campbell, C. M. (2014). To heaven or hell: Sensemaking about why faculty leave. *The Journal of Higher Education, 85*(5), 603–632.

Padgett, R. D., Keup, J. R., & Pascarella, E. T. (2013). The impact of first-year seminars on college students' life-long learning orientations. *Journal of Student Affairs Research and Practice, 50*(2), 133–151.

Patton, M. Q. (1990). *Qualitative evaluation and research methods* (2nd ed.). Thousand Oaks, CA: Sage.

Petchauer, E. (2010). Sampling practices and social spaces: Exploring a hip-hop approach to higher education. *Journal of College Student Development, 51*(4), 359–372.

Rands, M., & Gansemer-Topf, A. M. (2016). Phenomenography: A methodological approach for assessment in student affairs. *Journal of Student Affairs Inquiry 1*(2), 1–22.

Reynolds, A., & Chris, S. (2008). Improving practice through outcomes based planning and assessment: A counseling center case study. *Journal of College Student Development, 49*(4), 374–387.

Rhoads, R. A. (2000). *Freedom's web: Student activism in an age of cultural diversity.* Baltimore, MD: Johns Hopkins University Press.

Seifert, T. A., Goodman, K., King, P. M., & Baxter Magolda, M. B. (2010). Using mixed methods to study first-year college impact on liberal arts learning outcomes. *Journal of Mixed Methods Research, 4*(3), 248–267.

Stake, R. E. (1995). *The art of case study research.* Thousand Oaks, CA: Sage.

Strauss, A. S., & Corbin, J. (1998). *Basics of qualitative research: Techniques and procedures for developing grounded theory* (2nd ed.). Thousand Oaks, CA: Sage.

Tabachnick, B. G., & Fidell, L. S. (2012). *Using multivariate statistics* (5th ed.). Upper Saddle River, NJ: Pearson.

Waldron, J. J., & Dieser, R. B. (2010). Perspectives of fitness and health in college men and women. *Journal of College Student Development, 51*(1), 65–78.

Wolf-Wendel, L., Twombly, S., Tuttle, K., Ward, K., & Gaston, J. (2004). *Reflecting back, looking forward: Civil rights and student affairs.* Washington, DC: National Association of Student Personnel Administrators.

Yin, R. (2013). *Case study research: Design and methods* (5th ed.). Thousand Oaks, CA: Sage.

CHAPTER FOUR

CONSIDERING ETHICS

Learning Outcomes

By the end of this chapter, you should be able to:

- Know a brief history of research ethics.
- Distinguish the three basic ethical principles.
- Recognize minimal risk and the need for informed consent.
- Acknowledge the role of ethics in student affairs research.

Researchers have an obligation to ensure the safety and privacy of study participants. *Research ethics* are concerned with the responsible treatment of individuals and their data. Ethics encompass the responsibilities researchers have to participants and their data before, during, and after a study. An ethically aware researcher considers how the study may affect others—either during participation or afterward when results are published. This brief chapter provides an historical overview of ethics in research to frame a discussion of how research ethics apply directly to research in student affairs. Included is an overview of key documents, concepts, and considerations for qualitative, quantitative, and mixed methods studies. The chapter closes with a discussion of why practitioners need to know how to evaluate research based on ethical principles, both as consumers of research and gatekeepers to potential study participants.

Understanding Ethics in Research

Prior to collecting data, researchers develop a plan for their research. If a study involves an individual or their records, either directly (survey or interview) or indirectly (observation, document or record review), the research plan must be reviewed prior to conducting the research activity. An *Institutional Review Board (IRB)* is a committee comprised of faculty, staff, and community members who review ethical considerations of research. The basic review process depends on a determination of risk, inclusive of characteristics of the individuals involved, how individuals or records are recruited or accessed, the conduct of the study including how individuals or records are treated, and any associated risks and/or benefits. Researchers should always include a statement about the ethical considerations of their work, whether the study was approved by an IRB, and how potential risks for participants were minimized.

In the following example, Rhoads (1995) discussed an ethical dilemma he faced when conducting research on fraternity culture. The excerpt enlightens considerations researchers face during and after a study has been conducted.

> In the end, I was faced with one of those ethical decisions that ethnographic and qualitative researchers rarely seem to discuss: Should I out of obligation to my research participants ignore the serious implications of their interactions with women and focus on other cultural issues (and there were many), or should I put a concern for advancing understanding of fraternity exploitation of women first? The choice was difficult, but I chose to do the latter. (p. 312)

A Brief History of Research Ethics

The Belmont Report is a document detailing the basic rights and provisions for the protection of human participants in research (U.S. Department of Health, Education, and Welfare, 1979). The report was informed by the mistreatment, exploitation, and/or neglect of individuals in research-based trials, referencing those perpetuated in Nazi Germany (see discussion of the Nuremberg Trials), as well as the Tuskegee Syphilis Experiment and also referencing Milgram's (1965) work on the psychology of authority and Zimbardo's (1973) Stanford Prison Experiment. In 1981, multiple federal agencies adopted the three basic ethical principles outlined in the Belmont Report, which included respect for persons, beneficence, and justice. In 1991, the U.S. Department of Health and Human Services (DHHS) as part of its Code of Federal Regulations (CFR) developed 45 CFR 46, a federal policy defining the Common Rule that added requirements including Institutional Review Boards (IRBs), basic elements for obtaining and documenting informed consent, and additional details about research compliance. Two revisions, one in 2009 and another in 2017, expanded and refined provisions for research participants and updated the review process.

Perspectives From the Field—Why Practitioners Need to Understand Research Ethics

Consideration of ethical behavior and conduct should be ongoing aspects in any research activity. In fact, every decision made throughout the process should include reflecting about how that decision could impact the participants, community, institution, or reflect professionally on the researcher. We have ethical standards through our professional organizations we need to know and follow. Finally, as we work toward more equity and socially just campus environments, we need to conduct our research in such a way that we follow procedures to be inclusive of all possible participants for our study.

In student affairs, we benefit from working with our Institutional Review Board for ethics checkups as we design and conduct our studies. Formal IRB approval means we have completed the process required of the Federal Policy for the Protection of Human Subjects or the recently revised Common Rule (Menikoff, Kaneshiro, & Pritchard, 2017). IRB provides the external review of our proposed research to ensure we have considered our study participants' safety, gotten informed consent, and are giving additional safeguards to identified, protected groups of individuals.

Diane L. Cooper—Professor, Department of Counseling & Human Development Services, University of Georgia

Classifying Research

The federal government defines human subjects research as a systematic investigation, including research development, testing, and evaluation designed to develop or contribute to generalizable knowledge (45 CFR 46.102d). Human subjects refer to individuals who participate in research or research-based studies. This includes direct interaction with people as well as indirect access to their records. Translated to practice on college campuses, the IRB typically uses a three-part test to determine whether a proposed study qualifies as research and needs to be reviewed. If a project meets any of the following it must be reviewed:

- Intended as a contribution to general knowledge
- Portrayed (explicitly or implicitly) as research or an experiment
- Intended to fulfill research requirements for a master's thesis, doctoral dissertation, or other institutional-related project

The following projects may not be classified as research based on an IRB's interpretation of the federal definition and therefore would not require review and approval:

- Internal data collection for departmental or other university purposes such as teaching, student and/or staff evaluations
- Program evaluation carried out for external organizations that are intended for internal purposes such as personnel and staff effectiveness studies, cost benefit analysis, or treatment effectiveness

Three Basic Ethical Principles

Table 4.1 provides an overview of the three basic principles from the Belmont Report that researchers consider and adhere to prior to conducting a study. A brief description of each principle with an example is included after the table.

Table 4.1. Overview of Basic Ethical Principles and Their Provisions

	Respect for Persons	Beneficence	Justice
Definition	Individuals should be provided with enough information to make informed decisions about participating in research, including activities and/or potential adverse effects.[2]	Individuals should not be put into harmful situations including physical and psychological risks, particularly due to negligence.	Individuals have the right to be treated fairly and equally with regard to recruitment in the conduct of the study.
Provisions[1]	Researchers must provide sufficient information for individuals to make a choice and provide the right to privacy or confidentiality.	Researchers must: ensure respect for participant decisions, make efforts to protect participants from harm, and make efforts to secure participant well-being.	Researchers must not: conceal information about a study,[2] exploit participants or their data, or misrepresent the data or findings.

[1] Partially derived from Kitchener (1985) and Schuh, Biddix, Dean, and Kinzie (2016).
[2] An exception is deception research, which is subject to additional provisions.

Respect for Persons. Respect for persons is concerned with choice. Individuals should have enough information about a study to be able to act as free agents and have freedom of thought or choice. The Belmont Report authors considered this provision as affording autonomy. Even individuals unable to make an informed decision, either by mental capacity or other situation such as being a vulnerable population (for example, minors, prisoners), must be afforded this protection. A second facet of this principle is the right to privacy or confidentiality related to participation in research. Individuals should be made aware whether or not their identity will be revealed in any way and if so, what risks knowledge of their participation in the study may pose. Finally, this principle is the basis for informed consent, literally meaning that individuals who are able to give their consent to participate in a study have been adequately informed of its procedures. One way student affairs researchers meet this guideline is by providing details about the storage and use of the data they collect from individuals, including any provisions for confidentiality or anonymity.

Beneficence. Beneficence has two aspects, do no harm and maximize potential benefits. The concept of do no harm relates to both intentional actions and negligence, or placing an individual in a harmful situation though carelessness or inattention. The second provision has to do with evaluating the risk of participating versus the potential benefits of the study. Researchers should make potential risks and benefits clear, even if benefits may not apply to the individual directly but more broadly to society. One way student affairs researchers meet this guideline is by detailing specific risks associated with the study, including risk if their participation in the study is known or in some way identified such as their standing with the university, peers, or an employer.

Justice. Justice in relation to research is concerned with fairness and equal treatment. One application of this relates to participant selection, which provisions that participants should be recruited and selected without regard to bias toward any trait or characteristic unless the study has a specific reason for the restriction. Kitchener (1985) explained this consideration as being just (impartial, equal, and reciprocal in the treatment of all individuals) and faithful (not denying access to information) in research. Schuh and Associates (2009) noted that participants invest their time, experiences, and perceptions in a study and as a result should be made aware of all potential benefits and outcomes. One way student affairs researchers meet this guideline is by explaining to participants exactly how their involvement is beneficial, even if that benefit is indirect such as potential improvement for retention-related programs and services.

Minimal Risk and Informed Consent

Two concepts important to know related to research ethics are minimal risk and informed consent. *Minimal risk* is the least possible harm that a researcher anticipates could result from involvement in a study. It is generally thought of as being not greater than risk encountered in ordinary circumstances or situations in daily life or during participation in routine physical or physiological tests. *Informed consent* is the process of gaining an individual's approval for participation in a study. In most cases, autonomous individuals (those with the capacity to make a decision) must be made fully aware of the study procedures and anticipated risks allowing them to make an informed decision about their participation. Translated to practice, the researchers request that individuals sign an informed consent document that outlines the study, procedures, and potential risks prior to beginning a study.

Words Researchers Use—Deception and Incentives

Deception is a special case of research when participants may not be made aware of all activities and risks at the beginning of a study. Deception, sometimes referred to as incomplete disclosure, typically requires full IRB approval and includes provisions for participant welfare, details about debriefing once participation is completed, and full consideration of risks and benefits associated with the deception. When reviewing deception-based studies, an IRB determines whether there is sufficient rationale for not revealing information about the study and whether or not the consent and debriefing processes are adequate and justified.

Incentives in research is a common practice for encouraging participation. They are used widely in survey research to increase return rates as well as with individual and focus groups interviews as a way to ensure participants attend sessions. Examples of incentives include cash or gift cards, entry into prize drawings, or extra credit for a course. From an ethical standpoint, an incentive should not be enticing enough that the choice to participate tempts individuals against their better judgment (respect for persons, beneficence). Further, the incentive should not be enough to constitute coercion (justice) (Grant & Sugarman, 2004).

Ethics in Qualitative Research

Researchers collecting qualitative data also should be mindful of additional considerations when interacting directly with participants. Because qualitative research methods can vary significantly in terms of participant recruitment, context, and content, risk assessment should not utilize a routine and standard approach.

Interviews, conducted in person or mediated with technology, offer researchers the capability of tailoring questions to the conversation, using follow-up questions and probes to learn more about a topic. While the exact nature of the questions cannot be anticipated, the description of the research focus should be detailed enough in the informed consent form that participants can determine potential psychological risk triggered by the questions. Interview research also has significant risks for breach of confidentiality, especially with small sample research. When researchers report data, they need to be careful not to provide too much demographic or characteristic information that could unknowingly reveal a participant's identity. Review data can raise concerns when the data reveal details about the history or context of a situation that could be damaging to current participants (by affecting their standing with the institution, for example). Finally, observation research adds additional potential risk depending on how the researcher records data and reveals findings about participants, locations, and/or the activities that occur. Following is an excerpt of ethical considerations from a published qualitative study about women's gendered experiences.

Ethical Considerations

Ethical conflicts are common in qualitative research (Magolda & Weems, 2002). We attempted to balance participants' needs for and our promises of confidentiality with ethical obligations to address incidents of sexual harassment and inequitable policies. In cases where we could identify perpetrators of sexual harassment, the alleged perpetrators had retired from or left the university. In all cases, we felt there was no on-going harm to current students or employees. In cases where identities were not shared with us, we reminded participants of reporting options. We identified one state-level policy with clear disparate impact on women and are in the process of reporting that to state human rights agencies. (Broido, Brown, Stygles, & Bronkema, 2015, p. 607)

Ethics in Quantitative Research

Researchers using quantitative methods should take special care to ensure participants clearly understand how their data will be used in a study. Recall that an informed consent document describes the focus and purpose of the research and details potential risks and benefits in enough detail that the participant can make a knowledgeable decision about participating. The prevalence of online survey data collection has altered the informed consent process. Rather than requiring a signature, researchers using online data collection methods typically use an information sheet describing the study that a participant has to agree to prior to answering questions. The information specifies that participants may stop at any time by closing the survey. If the questions are sensitive in nature or could be construed as harmful, researchers should include a resources page, such as contact information for counseling services. Another consideration is confidentiality when collecting, storing, or reporting survey or database research. Many researchers use laptops or online storage for datasets that could result in a breach of confidentiality in the case of stolen information or hardware. Researchers should take care to store information without linking identifiers and use adequate password protection. Following is an excerpt of ethical considerations from a published quantitative study about career paths to the Senior Student Affairs Officer (SSAO) position.

> E-mails were sent to the total population ($N = 2,871$) of SSAOs listed in the 2008 Higher Education Directory (Burke, 2008). Potential participants received an IRB-approved description of the study and were asked to send a current electronic resume and to identify gender and race and ethnicity. (Biddix, 2011, p. 446)

Ethics in Mixed Methods

Researchers using mixed methods share ethical responsibilities associated with both qualitative and quantitative methods. Whether they collect data directly (interviews) or indirectly (surveys), they need to acknowledge and provision for potential risk in all aspects of their research. Often, because mixed methods is conducted in sequence, researchers may not know the secondary data sources or instrument until the first method is complete. For example, a researcher using a sequential explanatory method (quantitative followed by qualitative) may not know which participants to interview until after the survey or dataset analysis is complete. Typically, the researcher would seek initial IRB approval for the quantitative study, then submit a modification for the qualitative study that would include consideration of risk and provisions for informed consent. This supplemental review is necessary since the conditions for determining risk (recruiting and interacting with a new sample with new instruments) have changed. In a mixed methods study about motivations and choices for service among college students, Chesbrough (2011, pp. 692–693) noted ethical considerations in three phases of data collection:

> Focus Groups: "Participant must complete an informed consent form and agree to participate in recorded (video and audio) focus group interviews."
>
> Individual Interviews: "Participant must complete an informed consent form and agree to participate in recorded (audio) individual interviews."
>
> Surveys: "Invitations to participate included informed consent disclosures and advisories, as well as a clear statement of the voluntary nature of survey completion."

Ethical Considerations for Student Affairs

In addition to recognizing ethical concerns as a research consumer or anticipating potential issues as a research producer, student affairs professionals often serve as gatekeepers to research participants and data. Each role carries an ethical obligation to safeguard the well-being of others. Knowing that research should be reviewed by an IRB is one consideration, but understanding the rights and protections afforded to research participants is a professional obligation (Kitchener, 1985). ACPA–College Student Educators International provided a more detailed discussion of research ethics in its *Statement of Ethical Principles and Standards* (ACPA, 2006). Under the Student Learning and Development heading (pp. 3–4), the authors detailed numerous provisions affirming ethical research conduct including requirements for professional research training, the treatment of students as research participants, the conduct of research including IRB or related approval and oversight, acknowledgement and citation of others' work, and indirect references to the three basic ethical principles, such as the following:

> 2.8 Inform students about the purpose of assessment and research; make explicit the planned use of results prior to assessment requesting participation in either.
>
> 2.27 Communicate the results of any research judged to be of value to other professionals and not withhold results reflecting unfavorably on specific institutions, programs, services, or prevailing opinion.

More recently, ACPA and NASPA endorsed awareness of research ethics in their professional competencies. In Assessment, Evaluation, and Research (AER) competency, the authors detailed the following Foundational Outcome: "Explain the necessity to follow institutional and divisional procedures and policies (e.g., IRB approval, informed consent) with regard to ethical assessment, evaluation, and other research activities" (p. 20).

Building Your Research Skillset

Few academic courses focus exclusively on ethical research considerations. However, most research-engaged institutions have an IRB or equivalent committee that likely offers consultation or training. One common way researchers build proficiency in the ethical conduct of research is through an elective (or required) ethics certification. For example, the Collaborative Institutional Training Initiative (CITI) offers basic certifications and advanced courses in research ethics.

References

American College Personnel Association. (2006). *Statement of ethical principles and standards.* Retrieved from http://www.myacpa.org/docs/ethicalprinciplesstandards.pdf

Biddix, J. P. (2011). "Stepping stones": Career paths to the SSAO for men and women at four-year institutions. *Journal of Student Affairs Research and Practice, 48*(4), 443–461.

Broido, E. M., Brown, K. R., Stygles, K. N., & Bronkema, R. H. (2015). Responding to gendered dynamics: Experiences of women working over 25 years at one university. *The Journal of Higher Education, 86*(4), 595–627.

Burke, J. M. (2008). *2008 higher education directory.* Falls Church, VA: Higher Education.

Chesbrough, R. D. (2011). College students and service: A mixed methods exploration of motivations, choices, and learning outcomes. *Journal of College Student Development, 52*(6), 687–705.

Grant, R. W., & Sugarman, J. (2004). Ethics in human subjects research: Do incentives matter? *Journal of Medicine and Philosophy, 29*(6), 717–738.

Kitchener, K. (1985). Ethical principles and ethical decisions in student affairs. In H. Canon & R. Brown (Eds.), *Applied ethics in student services* (New Directions in Student Services, no. 30), pp. 17–30. San Francisco, CA: Jossey-Bass.

Magolda, P., & Weems, L. (2002). Doing harm: An unintended consequence of qualitative inquiry? *Journal of College Student Development, 43*, 490–507.

Menikoff, J., Kaneshiro, J., & Pritchard, I. (2017). The Common Rule, updated. *New England Journal of Medicine, 376*, 613–615.

Milgram, S. (1965). Some conditions of obedience and disobedience to authority. *Human Relations, 18*, 57–75.

Rhoads, R. A. (1995). Whales tales, dog piles, and beer goggles: An ethnographic case study of fraternity life. *Anthropology and Education Quarterly, 26*(3), 306–323.

Schuh, J. H., & Associates. (2009). *Assessment methods for student affairs.* San Francisco, CA: Jossey-Bass.

Schuh, J. H., Biddix, J. P., Dean, L. A., & Kinzie, J. (2016). *Assessment in student affairs: A contemporary look* (2nd ed.). San Francisco, CA: Jossey-Bass.

U.S. Department of Health, Education, and Welfare. (1979, April 18). *The Belmont Report.* Washington, DC: U.S. Department of Health and Human Services. Retrieved from http://www.hhs.gov/ohrp/humansubjects/guidance/belmont.html

U.S. Department of Health and Human Services. (2009). Human Subjects Research Act, 45 U.S.C.A.

Zimbardo, P. G. (1973). On the ethics of intervention in human psychological research: With special reference to the Stanford prison experiment. *Cognition, 2*, 243–256.

CHAPTER FIVE

LEARNING QUALITATIVE RESEARCH

Learning Outcomes

By the end of this chapter, you should be able to:

- Understand the purpose and role of qualitative methods in research.
- Differentiate between the major types of qualitative methods.
- Know answers to basic questions about qualitative methods in research.
- Apply basic qualitative terminology.
- Relate qualitative research to student affairs practice.

Qualitative research is used extensively in student affairs to enlighten and inform student success, recommend best practices for programs and services, map learning environments, and identify areas of concern. Interviews are the most prominently used method and are generally used as a primary form of analysis. Document analysis and observation are used more often in a supplemental role to support findings or provide contextual information about the participants and/or setting. Reading qualitative research typically is not challenging. Most results are narrative-based, organized by categories of findings (or themes), and incorporate excerpts such as quotations or notes from observation. Evaluating qualitative research can be difficult because it is dependent on how much detail the researcher provides.

The purpose of the chapter is to serve as an introduction and reference guide for understanding, reading, evaluating, and applying qualitative research. It was written with a single question in mind:

What essential concepts do student affairs practitioners and researchers need to know to understand qualitative methods?

The question is addressed with a series of questions and answers, derived from common challenges and difficulties for new and returning learners to qualitative research. Concepts are explained from a student affairs perspective with applicable examples from published research and reports. The chapter overviews key terms in qualitative research to provide a foundational understanding of methods, data sources, instrumentation, concepts, analysis techniques, and validity and rigor concerns. The chapter begins with some considerations for learning about qualitative research and closes with suggestions for developing foundational skills.

Understanding Qualitative Research

Qualitative research seeks to explore and represent reality as it exists in context and to enlighten the ways in which individuals experience that reality. Qualitative methods answer "how" and "why" questions by focusing on understanding and exploring the qualities of a person, place, process, or phenomenon. Qualities and meanings are not easily measured. The purpose of collecting qualitative data is not to get answers to questions or to record exactly what occurred in a setting, but to learn how something is experienced or perceived (Merriam, 2009). Because experience and perception can be complex concepts, researchers often use multiple data collection methods.

Qualitative research is generally associated with a constructivist perspective. *Constructivism* is a philosophical perspective that seeks to understand reality from individual interpretations (multiple meanings), accounting for culture, context, or other factors that affect those realities. Following this perspective, qualitative research can be characterized as "concerned with meaning, researcher–respondent rapport, co-construction of the research findings by the researcher and respondents, practical application of research findings, and the reciprocity between and among researchers and respondents" (Stage & Manning, 2016, p. 22). As Denzin and Lincoln (2011) noted, however, discerning and representing a distinct reality can be difficult. Patton (2011) added that demonstrating uniqueness while offering useful suggestions to enhance or improve practice is challenging. The philosophical focus on meaning and reality can be very difficult concepts for novice researchers to comprehend.

Qualitative researchers often identify their own interpretations for aspects of their research, which Denzin and Lincoln (2017) described as creating a broad specificity in the terminology. This can make reading qualitative research challenging for new learners. Morse, Barrett, Mayan, Olsen, and Spiers (2002) similarly regarded the terminology for quality and rigor in qualitative research as including "a plethora of terms and criteria introduced for minute variations and situations" (p. 15). While this ambiguity is a feature of the qualitative tradition, the added complexity can make learning about qualitative designs and methods difficult for new researchers.

Overview of Qualitative Research

Perspective: Constructivism
- Understanding: Reality is understood from the point of view the person(s) experiencing it.
- Multiple meanings: There is no single answer, but there are multiple meanings.
- (Sometimes) Theory generation: Depending on goals of the study, design can be used to offer a theory or an explanation.

Type: Qualitative Methods
- Emphasis on understanding and exploring meaning: Seeks to understand and represent meaning for individuals.
- Focus on experiences: Methods explore how something is experienced, rather than what occurred.
- Importance of context: Recognizes and explores contextual influences.
- Goal is not to generalize, but to represent: Intended to create rich, specific explanations that are transferable but not generalizable.

Design: Basic, Case Study, Grounded Theory, Phenomenology, Narrative
- Basic qualitative: Use of primary methods for data collection and generalized coding.
- Case study: A focus on an individual, site, or process.
- Grounded theory: Building theory to explain a process, issue, or action.
- Phenomenology: Exploring meaning and how it is made.
- Narrative: Collecting stories to describe experiences.

Methods: Review, Observation, Interview
- Review: Analyzing documents, including text and visuals.
- Observation: Observing people and places.
- Interview: Interviewing individuals and groups.

Qualitative Methods in Student Affairs Research

Manning (1992) noted that qualitative research "reflects and parallels the complexity and richness of the student affairs field itself" (p. 135). Qualitative methods have been among the most prominently used research techniques in student affairs for the past several decades. Interviews in particular are abundant in published research, dissertations and theses, books, and professional publications. Philosophically, qualitative methods are more directly aligned with the primary student affairs focus on individual and group success. From a student affairs perspective, qualitative research enlightens missing or marginalized perspectives, reveals processes or contextual effects, and adds a more holistic understanding and rationale to practice.

Historically, student affairs work has centered on the human dimension of student success. Policies and practices focused on individuals and groups, along with (at first generalized, then later specialized) personnel to facilitate student success, trace the development of the field from its codification at Northwestern University (Biddix & Schwartz, 2012) to its focus on holistic student development with the publication and reaffirmations of the *Student Personnel Point of View* (American Council on Education, 1937, 1949; National Association of Student Personnel Administrators, 1987). Published research in the field did not mirror this focus until the later 1980s and 1990s, when expanded enrollment policies and an emphasis on underrepresented and marginalized perspectives (Levine & Cureton, 1998; Rhoads, 2000) contributed to a need for and interest in transferable, rather than generalizable, research to inform practice.

Qualitative methods serve several important functions in student affairs practice. These can be categorized broadly as promoting success for all students and staff, informing programs and services, and identifying contextual and environmental effects. Applying recommendations from published qualitative research to programs and services for practice in another context may seem contrary to the nature of constructivist research. Despite a focus on specific individuals, groups, or contexts, qualitative findings often are relatable to similar circumstances. This concept is called *transferability*, or the extent to which research findings are relatable to a similar context. Table 5.1 shows several functions of qualitative research transferable to student affairs practice.

Table 5.1 Functions of Qualitative Research in Student Affairs

Function	Application and Explanation
Add individual perspectives.	Qualitative research adds overlooked, missing, or marginalized perspectives to research and practice. Understanding and accounting for diverse experiences, meanings, and shared behaviors of individuals or groups help to identify ways to promote success for all students. Qualitative data also can aid in investigating student motives and rationales.
Reveal experiences.	Qualitative research enlightens individual experiences, which can reveal additional information about experiences missing from aggregated data.
Explore issues.	Qualitative research takes a more personal and affective approach to problems and issues, which allows for deeper understanding.
Reveal processes.	Qualitative research can help to identify processes that act to support or to inhibit student and professional success.
Trace policy development.	Qualitative research can reveal the context, significant events and personnel, and cultural influences behind existing policies and practices.
Project successes and challenges.	Qualitative research provides new insights by allowing a closer look at the why behind successes and failures of programs, services, and initiatives.
Describe context.	Qualitative research can promote an understanding of the historical and contemporary context influencing actions, attitudes, behaviors, and perceptions. This helps to ensure successful implementation and continuation of programs and services.
Map learning environments.	Qualitative research can be used to reveal where and how learning is promoted and/or inhibited in various environments.
Uncover historical influences.	Qualitative research can reconstruct the development of policy, practice, and individual contributions to reveal successes or challenges.
Examine complex issues.	Qualitative research can help unravel complex issues by considering problems from multiple angles and perspectives.

Perspectives From the Field—Applying Qualitative Research to Practice

Like other student affairs practitioners, I am continuously asked to provide insight and perspectives on the college student experience. I am also fully vested in enhancing student development, while improving student retention, graduation, satisfaction, and learning. Quantitative research, such as assessments and evaluations, are helpful with descriptive and inferential statistics; however, they limit viewpoints and they negate marginalized populations as there is a regression toward the mean. Qualitative research, such as focus groups and case studies, serve as a critical method to convey the lived perspectives of students. As a result, I continuously, seek out, request, and integrate qualitative data to guide my operations and structures. For example, recently a survey was used to collect thoughts on dining services. From that assessment, sums and means indicated a wide array of opinions with a resultant bell curve. The qualitative data, particularly international students and those with dietary restrictions, was much more informative and it helped to guide significant changes to enhance operations and expand selection. Most recently, student satisfaction focus groups indicated there was a strong desire for low-cost housing and on-campus living options. Knowing that affordable housing was not being sought by current students, a campaign was developed to educate the campus about the availability of low-cost, on-campus living and to inform about options to downgrade from existing, more expensive on-campus leases.

Eric Norman—Associate Vice Chancellor and Dean of Students, Indiana University–Purdue University Fort Wayne

Essential Concepts in Qualitative Methods

The terminology and applications of qualitative research can be challenging for novice research consumers. Table 5.2 is a summary list of key questions along with associated concepts that comprise the primary features of qualitative research encountered when reading or evaluating research. Each question and associated concept is examined in subsequent sections.

Table 5.2. Key Questions and Associated Essential Concepts

Key Question	Essential Concepts
What are the main qualitative methods?	Review, observation, interview
Where do qualitative data come from?	Documents, places, people
How do researchers choose qualitative data sources?	Criterion sampling, snowball sampling
What instruments do qualitative researchers use?	Guide, form, questionnaire
How much qualitative data are enough?	Saturation
How do researchers analyze qualitative data?	Coding, themes, approaches
How is qualitative research evaluated?	Rigor, trustworthiness

What Are the Main Qualitative Methods?

There are three main categories of qualitative methods: review, observation, and interview. Following is a broad description of each.

1. Review methods involve examining existing information, inclusive of documents, records, or artifacts in text, visual, or mixed formats such as websites. Three general data sources of campus records are used in student affairs research: institutional, general, and personal. Review methods are typically noninteractive, meaning they do not involve direct contact with data sources.
2. Observation methods involve recording behavior, changes, and other data about people, locations, or events. Data collection may involve one or more individuals or locations and can take place at one time or repeatedly during different days and/or times. Observation methods can be completely noninteractive or involve direct interaction with individuals.
3. Interview methods involve collecting the perspectives of individuals or groups. Interviewing is the most prevalent qualitative research method used in student affairs and higher education research (Ortiz, 2016). Data collection can include one or multiple individuals or groups. Interviews typically are highly interactive.

Many qualitative studies involve more than one form of data collection either to provide context or as a validation strategy to verify findings. Qualitative techniques tend to be mutually reinforcing (Patton, 2015) and together enhance and enrich other forms of qualitative data (Stage & Manning, 2003). Choosing from among the three basic methods of qualitative data collection does not have to be a decision of one over another. Utilizing more than one technique lets researchers explore data more holistically, establishing confirmable results and adding to legitimacy.

Where Do Qualitative Data Come From?

Researchers collect qualitative data from documents, places, and people. Documents are comprised of existing records. Places encompass specific locations and the activities and interactions that take place during various times. People include individuals and groups. Each can be differentiated by both the format and the degree of interaction required to collect data. The instruments used to collect data are also specific to each method. Following is an overview of the main data sources and how they are used in student affairs research.

Reviewing Documents. Reviewing documents involves the discovery, examination, and evaluation of existing information. Uses in student affairs research include: showing how information developed and changed, establishing connections between sources and/or key individuals, and locating background information that may not be discernable otherwise. The two main categories are document analysis (concerned with text) and visual analysis (concerned with images). While review methods are often thought of as materials found in archives, sources are considerably broader. They include institutional (official), general (public), and personal (generally private) documents ranging from policy manuals and student group bylaws to meeting records and training manuals as well as emails and personal photographs from events. Locating, accessing, and analyzing documents can be a highly exploratory and investigative process. An example published study is Saichiei and Morphew's (2014) examination of marketing text and images on institutional websites.

Observing People and Places. Observing people and places involves selecting a person or group, or a time and location, and recording data about people, places, and/or events. Uses in student affairs research include: understanding how people affect places (and vice versa), revealing how learning environments are used (or underused), and suggesting key individuals or events for a more focused study. The three main types include location, time and location, and person. Researchers may collect data unobtrusively or may interact directly with participants. Observations also can include simply taking notes about what is witnessed or casual interviews. The focus can be on individuals and/or groups or one or more locations. When the focus is on locations, the data collection may include multiple and varied times, such as observing a dining facility during typical meal hours, in-between meal service, and after hours. Observation can be extremely rewarding, but it is also very difficult due to distraction, boredom, and fatigue. An example study is Birnbaum's (2013) observation of student behaviors on social media.

Interviewing Individuals and Groups. Interviewing individuals and groups involves working with individuals and groups to understand perspectives through direct interaction. Uses in student affairs research include: revealing insights about programs and services, understanding common and conflicting experiences, adding overlooked, missing, or marginalized perspectives, and examining complex issues. The two main types include individual and focus groups. Researchers typically identify participants based on criteria (such as meeting a certain demographic, offering a specific perspective, or sharing a particular experience) and collect data by asking questions and recording responses. An example study is Hornak, Ozaki, and Lunceford's (2016) semistructured focus group interviews to understand socialization of new and mid-level student affairs professionals at two-year institutions.

Perspectives From the Field—Engaging With and Interviewing Diverse Participants

Trust is essential to engaging with and interviewing participants whose multiple intersecting identities differ from the researcher's identities. How do qualitative researchers develop rapport and trust with diverse participants? This is a critical step in the research process. As the researcher, how do you ensure that your interpretation and analysis appropriately represent the experiences and stories of diverse study participants?

One essential step for doing so is for qualitative researchers to engage in reflexivity. Reflect on the ways your identities and experiences inform how you engage with diverse study participants. This engagement begins with development of the interview questions and continues through data collection and analysis, interpretation, engaging in trustworthiness techniques/methods, and presentation of the finding. When interviewing diverse participants, ask yourself, "What biases do I possess?" "How do my experiences inform this study?" "How did I develop the interview questions?" and "How am I asking the interview questions?" And when engaging in data analysis and interpretation, ask yourself, "Does my interpretation and analysis appropriately represent the participants' experiences?"

Dorian L. McCoy—Associate Professor in Higher Education, CSP program coordinator, University of Tennessee, Knoxville

---

How Do Researchers Choose Qualitative Data Sources?

Sampling is the process of selecting data sources for research. Data sources collected through sampling create the sample for a study. Qualitative researchers have identified and defined numerous ways to choose data sources. Coyne (1997) concluded that most qualitative sampling methods are purposeful in nature, meaning that they are nonrandom, and chosen based on a set of guidelines according to the needs of the study. Patton (2002) noted that "qualitative inquiry typically focuses in depth on relatively small samples, even single cases, selected purposefully" (p. 230). Maxwell (2005) reiterated that purposeful sampling involves deliberate selection of settings, persons, or events. Some sampling methods are more specific to certain methods. For example, time, person, and time and location are more common with observation studies.

Sample selection is influenced by a variety of factors, including knowledge about the data sources, access, availability, and time constraints. The primary criteria for choosing a sample are rationale and credibility. Using these criteria, researchers consider whether the justification for the sample is sound and logical (rationale) and that the procedures and sources are reliable and believable (credibility). Qualitative sampling is often a difficult balance between richness and quantity. A single data source can be extremely content rich, but low on quantity. Conversely, an interview with 40 participants may be content poor in terms of generating few common themes related to the issues(s) being studied. An optimal goal is to obtain rich data sources, which can include voluminous data with multiple observation notes, documents, or informants, or a few highly informative files, cases, or participants. Researchers should be able to defend the choice of a sample based on these considerations.

To choose data sources, student affairs researchers typically use criterion or snowball sampling strategies. Following is a brief description of each. Convenience sampling, or selecting a sample based on availability, is not discussed as a sampling strategy. Despite its efficiency, this strategy involves the poorest rationale and lowest credibility (Patton, 2015).

Criterion Sampling. *Criterion sampling* involves specifying a phenomenon, experience, or event and locating participants that meet the criteria. Locating these sources typically begins with criteria influenced by the goals of the study. These criteria might also be thought of as delimiters, or boundaries. Identifying the sample involves specifying the traits of interest within a population or dataset, sorting potential sources based on these requirements, and negotiating access. In a study of the experiences of Latino students enrolled at historically Black colleges and universities (HBCU), Allen (2016) described a criterion sampling process for both the site and selection of participants:

> After identifying eight four-year HBCUs in Texas, Texas Metropolitan University (TMU) was intentionally selected because it was an HBCU that met the following criteria: (a) it demonstrated outreach and recruitment efforts to the Latino community, (b) its campus leaders have publicly

supported Latino student enrollment, and (c) its Latino enrollment was increasing. These unique institutional characteristics provided a setting that could offer rich, thick descriptions in response to the study's research questions (Patton, 2002). (p. 466)

Snowball Sampling. *Snowball sampling* involves locating information-rich sources based on source recommendations. The process continues, or snowballs, until the researcher is satisfied with the richness of the data (or until saturation is reached). This form of sampling is common with interviews, as participant interaction can lead to recommendations for other participants. Documents also can suggest additional materials that can be followed in a snowball method. In a study of attrition from student affairs, Marshall, Gardner, Hughes, and Lowery (2016) described their sampling procedure as follows:

> Guided by purposeful sampling (Jones, Torres, & Arminio, 2014; Patton, 2002), we sought participants who left full-time employment within the student affairs field within the past 10 years. Snowball sampling, or purposeful sampling, focused on finding information-rich participants and enabled the collection of potential participant names and contact information (Creswell, 2007; Patton, 2002). Patton (2002) described this sampling process as one that begins with the questions, "Who knows a lot about _?" "Whom should I talk to?" (p. 237). Asking for suggestions from others regarding whom to ask to participate in a study results in the "snowball" getting bigger and bigger as people make more and more suggestions for participants who may have experienced the phenomena studied. (p. 149)

Researchers describe two aspects of snowball sampling: initial and continued. The initial aspect involves identifying one or more initial sources and following their recommendations. Often, subsequent sources also recommend or lead to others, hence the characterization of a snowball. Researchers follow these individual snowballs until the suggestions for data converge as key sources are repeatedly recommended.

What Instruments Do Qualitative Researchers Use?

Qualitative researchers collect data with review guides, observation forms, and interview questionnaires, broadly categorized as instruments. An *instrument* is a guide for recording data. An instrument can be a highly structured checklist of questions or a loose collection of prompts with standardized elements, such as space for recording time, place, and participants. Advantages to using a standardized instrument are consistency across data sources and reliability when multiple researchers are involved. An advantage to using a semi- or unstructured instrument is the flexibility to adapt as new or unanticipated opportunities or data emerge.

A physical instrument (guide, form, or questionnaire) is only as good as the conceptual instrument (the researcher). Researchers decide the content to record and emphasize. As a result, qualitative researchers are often also considered instruments due to their direct involvement in data collection. Following is an overview of the three main types of qualitative instruments.

Review Guide. Review guides typically are associated with document analysis. They often are highly standardized to identify and record links between data sources. Data are usually collected using a form to standardize the known and observable facts about a document, including uniform questions about the material, origin, author, or contextual details that can be observed or derived. Saunders and Cooper (2009) reflected that guides provide consistency and continuity across the different forms of data used in document analysis.

Observation Form. Observation forms feature a high degree of standardization and include basic elements such as time, location, and details (such as the number of people in a setting). A common approach is to complete an initial open observation by simply taking basic notes, then developing a more formalized form that includes prompts for specific foci such as behaviors. Using a form for data collection helps observers maintain focus during data collection (Webb, Campbell, Schwartz, & Sechrest, 2000). Too much structure, however, can be problematic. Recording data into set categories can lead to a tendency to reduce data collection to a counting activity (Emerson, Fretz, & Shaw, 2011).

Interview Questionnaire. Interview questionnaires are sets of questions developed prior to data collection, which can range from structured (standardized, set questions), to semistructured (moderate standardization, some set questions and prompts), to unstructured (loose standardization, prompts or no questions). The preference of rigidity versus flexibility is influenced by the researcher's experience and skill, the participants, or the general focus of a study. Questionnaires often include some combination of background/demographics, experiences and behaviors, opinion/values, feelings, knowledge or factual information, and sensory questions. The most common type of questionnaire used in student affairs research is semistructured.

Perspectives From the Field—What Does Researcher as Instrument Mean?

In the context of qualitative research, the researcher is an integral part of the research project. Just as with any research design, the qualitative researcher determines the appropriate research design, approach for data collection, and plans for data analysis. Unlike other approaches, the qualitative researcher acts as the data collection instrument, as well as the data analysis device. In most qualitative approaches, the researcher is collecting data by speaking with people, whether through individual interviews or focus groups. Using a semistructured protocol, the researcher asks the same base questions of all participants, but also utilizes active and reflective listening to ask follow-up and probing questions. Through data analysis, the qualitative researcher reads through all of the transcribed data, making determinations of what is significant, which yields codes, and how things are connected, which yields themes. The qualitative researcher, as instrument, openly acknowledges their biases that are informed, in part, by their positionalities. Their individual subjectivities become a part of the research project, permanently embedding the researcher as instrument in the research project.

Brian Bourke—Assistant Professor and Program Coordinator, Murray State University

How Much Qualitative Data Are Enough?

Researchers must make intentional decisions about when to stop collecting data. Qualitative researchers tend to exchange the breadth of larger scale data for the depth of richer perspectives. In quantitative studies, researchers have general guidelines or tools (such as power analysis) for how much data is needed to determine adequate sample size for achieving statistical significance. In qualitative studies, sufficient data can be a difficult consideration and often is not determinable at the beginning of a study. Data collection and analysis often are linked in qualitative research because analysis can inform the need for further information. A common question researchers consider is "How much data are enough?" This can be a sensitive (and sometimes defensive) question for qualitative researchers, especially when framed as applicability or a perceived rigor argument. Sandelowski (1995) noted the following:

> Determining an adequate sample size in qualitative research is ultimately a matter of judgment and experience in evaluating the quality of the information collected against the uses to which it will be put, the particular research method and sampling strategy employed, and the research product intended . . . A good principle to follow is: An adequate sample size in qualitative research is one that permits—by virtue of not being too large—the deep, case-oriented analysis that is a hallmark of all

qualitative inquiry, and that results in—by virtue of not being too small—a new and richly textured understanding of experience. (p. 183)

Echoing this consideration, Mason (2010) stated that "the sample size becomes irrelevant as the quality of data is the measurement of its value" (p. 10).

Saturation is the point in data collection and analysis in which no new information is discovered. It has been described as the point of informational redundancy (Sandelowski, 1995), diminishing return (Mason, 2010), or counterproductivity (Strauss & Corbin, 1998). A major barrier to the concept of saturation as a defensible rationale for sample size is the inability to verify it. Bowen (2008) noted that researchers have a tendency to claim reaching saturation but do not describe what they mean or how it was achieved. Mason (2010) examined the concept of saturation in a study of sample sizes used in PhD studies ($n = 560$) with interviews as the primary data collection method. He found samples ranging from 1 (a life history) to 95 (a case study) with a median of 28 and mean of 31 (standard deviation of 18.1). The most common sample sizes were 20 and 30, followed by 40, 10, and 25. Mason's synthesis of literature led him to conclude that saturation seems to be reached at comparatively low level and is perceived to exist in multiples of 10. This led him to conclude that "new data (especially if theoretically sampled) will always add something new, but there are diminishing returns, and the cut off between adding to emerging findings and not adding, might be considered inevitably arbitrary" (p. 11).

How Do Researchers Analyze Qualitative Data?

Coding is a process of data analysis that involves identifying patterns and themes in qualitative data to represent findings. Miles, Huberman, and Saldana (2015) defined the qualitative data analysis process as a "continuous, interactive enterprise" (p. 14) with three broad tasks (pp. 12–14):

1. **Data Condensation**
   Selecting, focusing, simplifying, abstracting, and/or transforming the data that appear in data sources. Most often, this process involves "coding" data.
2. **Data Display**
   Creating an organized, compressed assembly of information that allows conclusion drawing and action.
3. **Drawing and Verifying Conclusions**
   Interpreting meaning but maintaining openness and skepticism until conclusions are increasingly explicit and grounded (meaning that they are represented in the context).

A *code* is a category or unit of analysis used to describe a singular aspect of data. Merriam and Tisdell (2015) referred to codes as concept notes representing "recurring regularities" (or patterns) in the data. According to Saldana (2015),

FIGURE 5.1. DERIVING CODES, CATEGORIES, AND THEMES FROM A DATA SOURCE

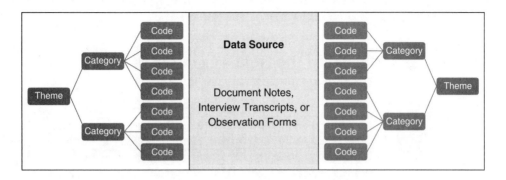

"A code in qualitative inquiry is more often a word or short phrase that symbolically assigns a summative, salient, essence-capturing, and/or evocative attribute to a portion of language-based or visual data" (p. 4). Figure 5.1 is a general illustration of the coding process that consists of reviewing a data source, making notes that become codes, classifying codes into categories, (sometimes) reading again for accuracy across the data, describing categories as themes (and subthemes), and connecting the themes to study goals. A *theme* is a central classification of codes. Themes are generally presented in the results section of a study with explanations and illustrative excerpts from the data.

There are multiple different coding approaches. Three commonly used in student affairs research are basic, *a priori*, and constant comparative. Following are brief descriptions of each approach.

Basic coding, also referred to as descriptive coding, involves reviewing data, searching for interesting aspects and recurring regularities, marking those as codes, categorizing the codes, and creating themes from categories. Boyatzis (1998) described this approach as theoretical, or inductive. Basic coding is represented in Figure 5.1 by reading from the data source out to themes (inside to outside). An extension of basic coding is *in vivo* coding, which labels the data with words or phrases from the participants.

A priori coding begins with the themes or categories (usually from a theory) and works toward verifying them with codes (Crabtree & Miller, 1999). It might be thought of as the opposite approach to basic coding. *A priori* coding is represented in Figure 5.1 by reading from the themes to the data source (outside to inside).

Constant comparative coding involves coding an initial data source to create tentative categories, then comparing those categories to a second source until a set of themes can be developed. Constant comparative coding is related to basic coding and is derived from the grounded theory method (Corbin & Strauss, 2014; Glaser & Strauss, 1967).

Perspectives From the Field—Example of Qualitative Coding

Coding qualitative data, whether from an interview, an open-response item on a survey, field notes, or some other source of text, is a sense-making process of breaking down the data and then looking for patterns, commonalities, and differences. For interview transcripts, I typically start with a hard copy of three or four interviews, formatted to divide the page in half vertically. On the left is the transcript text; the right side is blank. As I read I make notes on the right, depending on the theoretical approach I am taking to the study. In this example of initial coding from an interview of a mixed-race (Asian and White) college student, I made notes about friends, peers, and sense of belonging. The fourth code, in quotes, is an in vivo code, meaning that it is taken directly from the data.

Data	Initial Code
I've always been around Asian people pretty much, but in fact all my friends are Asian and stuff, but it's not really so much an issue	Homogeneous friendships
once I get to know the people, but in the beginning people are really, it's almost something that sticks out, and I guess it's	Aware of others' responses
always been in my mind that I'm not like everyone else, I guess. And for other	Feeling different
minorities you always have something to fall back into, but with mixed people you're kind of out there, you know?	"Out there"

After I have coded three or four transcripts by hand I make a list of codes and align terms. This student said "out there" and I used that in vivo code, which may align conceptually with another student saying "on my own." I might keep "out there" as the term for this concept and use it to code other transcripts. My code "homogeneous friendships" may end up a child code combined into a parent code with data from the other initial, hand-coded transcripts about the composition of students' friendship groups. When I have a sense of the codes I am developing and using, I move to an online platform (my research team uses Dedoose) and begin coding there.

Kristen A. Renn—Professor of Higher, Adult, and Lifelong Education, Michigan State University

How Is Qualitative Research Evaluated?

Quantitative researchers rely on the concepts of validity and reliability to authenticate their work, and often include measures that can be replicated with access to their data. Many qualitative researchers oppose these notions, regarding them as aligned with the postpositivist tradition of attempting to discover singular explanations or an objective reality (Morse et al., 2002; Shenton, 2004). As a result, qualitative researchers use different standards for judging quality and methodological rigor (Lincoln & Guba, 1985). Morse et al. (2002) traced the development of rigor in qualitative research to Lincoln & Gubas's (1985) concept of "trustworthiness." *Trustworthiness* is the extent to which qualitative data and analysis are credible, transferable, dependable, and confirmable. In a fundamental meta-analysis of two decades of research and writing about qualitative methods, Shenton (2004, p. 73) offered the strategies listed in Table 5.3 for ensuring trustworthiness in qualitative research.

Table 5.3. Strategies for Evaluating Qualitative Research

Quality Criterion	Possible Provision Made by Researcher
Credibility	Adoption of appropriate, well-recognized research methods
	Development of early familiarity with culture of participating organizations
	Random sampling of individuals serving as informants
	Triangulation via use of different methods, different types of informants, and different sites
	Tactics to help ensure honesty in informants. Iterative questioning in data collection dialogues. Negative case analysis.
	Debriefing sessions between researcher and superiors
	Peer scrutiny of project
	Use of "reflective commentary"
	Description of background, qualifications, and experience of the researcher. Member checks of data collected and interpretations/theories formed. Thick description of phenomenon under scrutiny.
	Examination of previous research to frame findings
Transferability	Provision of background data to establish context of study and detailed description of phenomenon in question to allow comparisons to be made
Dependability	Employment of "overlapping methods"
	In-depth methodological description to allow study to be repeated
Confirmability	Triangulation to reduce effect of investigator bias
	Admission of researcher's beliefs and assumptions
	Recognition of shortcomings in study's methods and their potential effects
	In-depth methodological description to allow integrity of research results to be scrutinized
	Use of diagrams to demonstrate audit trail

Source: Reprinted from Shenton (2004), p. 73, with permission from IOS Press.

Morse et al. (2002) recommended that establishing quality should be a formative process:

> We suggest that by focusing on strategies to establish trustworthiness (Guba and Lincoln's 1981 term for rigor) at the end of the study, rather than focusing on processes of verification during the study, the investigator runs the risk of missing serious threats to the reliability and validity until it is too late to correct them. (p. 14)

This consideration suggests determining legitimacy should be a process of verification used during the research as opposed to after analysis. The authors later referred to qualitative analysis as iterative rather than linear and the analysis process, if including mechanisms to ensure quality, as self-correcting (p. 17). Morse et al. (2002) concluded that "the lack of responsiveness of the investigator at all stages of the research process is the greatest hidden threat to validity" (p. 18).

Building Your Qualitative Research Skillset

The 10 competency areas for practitioners (ACPA/NASPA, 2015), as well as the standards for master's level preparation in the field (CAS, 2015) relate foundational outcomes for research. Specifically related to qualitative research, ACPA/NASPA's (2015) Intermediate Competencies relate the following:

> Apply the concepts and procedures of qualitative research, evaluation, and assessment including creating appropriate sampling designs and interview protocols with consultation, participating in analysis teams, contributing to audit trails, participating in peer debrief, and using other techniques to ensure trustworthiness of qualitative designs.

Closely reading texts (reviewing documents), watching people and places (observing), and asking questions and listening (interviewing) are skills practitioners use daily as part of their jobs that can facilitate qualitative research literacy. However, the difference between qualitative skills and skilled qualitative data collection and analysis is considerable. Learning can be aided under mentorship or through formal coursework. Several authors also can help aspiring researchers build expertise independently. These include Merriam and Tisdell (2015) for a more thorough introduction to qualitative design, Patton (2015) for a more comprehensive treatment of methods, and Saldana (2015) for additional details on data analysis and presentation.

References

Allen, T. O. (2016). (In)validation in the minority: The experiences of Latino students enrolled in an HBCU. *The Journal of Higher Education, 87*(4), 461–487.

American College Personnel Association & National Association of Student Personnel Administrators. (2015). *Professional competency areas for student affairs practitioners.* Washington, DC: Authors.

American Council on Education. (1937). The student personnel point of view. *American Council on Education Studies* (Series I, Vol. I, no. 3).

American Council on Education. (1949). The student personnel point of view. *American Council on Education Studies* (Series VI, Vol. XIII, no. 13).

Biddix, J. P., & Schwartz, R. (2012). Walter Dill Scott and the student personnel movement. *Journal of Student Affairs Research and Practice, 49*(3), 285–298.

Birnbaum, M. G. (2013). The fronts students use: Facebook and the standardization of self-presentations. *Journal of College Student Development, 54*(2), 155–171.

Bowen, G. A. (2008). Naturalistic inquiry and the saturation concept: A research note. *Qualitative Research, 8* (1), 137–152.

Boyatzis, R. E. (1998). *Transforming qualitative information: Thematic analysis and code development.* Thousand Oaks, CA: Sage.

Corbin, J., & Strauss, A. (2014). *Basics of qualitative research: Techniques and procedures for developing grounded theory* (4th ed.). Thousand Oaks, CA: Sage.

Council for the Advancement of Standards in Higher Education. (2015). *CAS professional standards for higher education* (9th ed.). Washington, DC: Author.

Coyne, I. T. (1997). Sampling in qualitative research. Purposeful and theoretical sampling: Merging or clear boundaries? *Journal of Advanced Nursing, 26*(3), 623–630.

Crabtree, B., & Miller, W. (1999). A template approach to text analysis: Developing and using codebooks. In B. Crabtree & W. Miller (Eds.), *Doing qualitative research* (pp. 163–177). Newbury Park, CA: Sage.

Creswell, J. W. (2007). *Qualitative inquiry and research design: Choosing among five traditions* (2nd ed.). Thousand Oaks, CA: Sage.

Denzin, N. K., & Lincoln, Y. S. (2011). *The Sage handbook of qualitative research* (4th ed.). Thousand Oaks, CA: Sage.

Denzin, N. K., & Lincoln, Y. S. (2017). *The Sage handbook of qualitative research* (5th ed.). Thousand Oaks, CA: Sage.

Emerson, R. M., Fretz, R. I., & Shaw, L. L. (2011). *Writing ethnographic fieldnotes.* Chicago, IL: University of Chicago Press.

Glaser, B., & Strauss, A. L. (1967). *The discovery of grounded theory: Strategies for qualitative research.* Chicago, IL: Aldine.

Guba, E. G., & Lincoln, Y. S. (1981). *Effective evaluation.* San Francisco, CA: Jossey-Bass.

Hornak, A. M., Ozaki, C. C., & Lunceford, C. (2016). Socialization for new and mid-level community college student affairs professionals. *Journal of Student Affairs Research and Practice, 53*(2), 118–130.

Jones, S. R., Torres, V., & Arminio, J. (2014). *Negotiating the complexities of qualitative research in higher education: Fundamental elements and issues* (2nd ed.). New York, NY: Routledge.

Levine, A., & Cureton, J. S. (1998). *When hope and fear collide: A portrait of today's college student.* San Francisco, CA: Jossey-Bass.

Lincoln, Y. S., & Guba, E. G. (1985). *Naturalistic inquiry.* Newbury Park, CA: Sage.

Manning, K. (1992). A rationale for using qualitative research in student affairs. *Journal of College Student Development, 33*(2), 132–136.

Marshall, S. M., Gardner, M. M., Hughes, C., & Lowery, U. (2016). Attrition from student affairs: Perspectives from those who exited the profession. *Journal of Student Affairs Research and Practice, 53*(2), 146–159.

Mason, M. (2010). Sample size and saturation in PhD studies using qualitative interviews. *Forum: Qualitative Social Research, 11*(3). Retrieved from http://www.qualitative-research.net/index.php/fqs/article/view/1428/3027

Maxwell, J. A. (2005). *Qualitative research design: An interactive approach* (2nd ed.). Thousand Oaks, CA: Sage.

Merriam, S. B. (2009). *Qualitative research: A guide to design and implementation.* San Francisco, CA: Jossey-Bass.

Merriam, S. B. & Tisdell, E. J. (2015). *Qualitative research: A guide to design and implementation* (4th ed.). San Francisco, CA: Jossey-Bass.

Miles, M. B., Huberman, A. M., & Saldana, J. (2015). *Qualitative data analysis: A methods sourcebook* (3rd ed.). Thousand Oaks, CA: Sage.

Morse, J. M., Barrett, M., Mayan, M., Olson, K., & Spiers, J. (2002). Verification strategies for establishing reliability and validity in qualitative research. *International Journal of Qualitative Methods, 1*(2), 13–22.

National Association of Student Personnel Administrators. (1987). *A perspective on student affairs: A statement issued on the 50th anniversary of the Student Personnel Point of View.* Washington, DC: Author.

Ortiz, A. M. (2016). The qualitative interview. In F. K. Stage & K. Manning (Eds.), *Research in the college context: Approaches and methods* (2nd ed., pp. 47–61). New York, NY: Brunner-Routledge.

Patton, M. Q. (2002). *Qualitative evaluation and research methods* (3rd ed.). Thousand Oaks, CA: Sage.

Patton, M. Q. (2011). *Essentials of utilization-focused evaluation.* Thousand Oaks, CA: Sage.

Patton, M. Q. (2015). *Qualitative research & evaluation methods: Integrating theory and practice* (4th ed.). Thousand Oaks, CA: Sage.

Rhoads, R. A. (2000). *Freedom's web: Student activism in an age of cultural diversity.* Baltimore, MD: Johns Hopkins University Press.

Saichaie, K., & Morphew, C. C. (2014). What college and university websites reveal about the purposes of higher education. *Journal of Higher Education, 85*(4), 499–530.

Sandelowski, M. (1995). Sample size in qualitative research. *Research in Nursing & Health, 18*(2), 179–183.

Saldana, J. (2015). *The coding manual for qualitative researchers* (3rd ed.). London, United Kingdom: Sage.

Saunders, K., & Cooper, R. M. (2009). Instrumentation. In J. H. Schuh & Associates (Eds.), *Assessment methods for student affairs* (pp. 107–140). San Francisco, CA: Jossey-Bass.

Shenton, A. K. (2004). Strategies for ensuring trustworthiness in qualitative research projects. *Education for Information 22,* 63–75.

Stage, F. K., & Manning, K. (Eds.). (2003). *Research in the college context: Approaches and methods.* New York, NY: Brunner-Routledge.

Stage, F. K., & Manning, K. (Eds.). (2016). *Research in the college context: Approaches and methods* (2nd ed.). New York, NY: Brunner-Routledge.

Strauss, A. S., & Corbin, J. (1998). *Basics of qualitative research: Techniques and procedures for developing grounded theory* (2nd ed.). Thousand Oaks, CA: Sage.

Webb, E. J., Campbell, D. T., Schwartz, R. D., & Sechrest, L. (2000). *Unobtrusive measures.* Thousand Oaks, CA: Sage.

CHAPTER SIX

REVIEWING DOCUMENTS

Learning Outcomes

By the end of this chapter, you should be able to:

- Understand the purpose and role of document review.
- Differentiate between the major types of document review.
- Read document review results in journal articles and reports.
- Evaluate document review results based on data collection, analysis, and reporting.
- Apply interpretations of document review methods to student affairs practice.

Document review involves examining existing information, inclusive of documents, records, or artifacts in text, visual, or mixed formats. In addition to analyzing words or images, researchers also are concerned with the presentation of materials, which can include authorship, context, medium, and format. Document review studies can be challenging to conduct because information about document authorship or context are not always available. As a result, determining intent, motivation, or other relevant circumstantial details require that the researcher use logic, deduction, and intuition to analyze and interpret the information.

Data used for document review are broadly referred to as documents. A *document* is a text or image data source. This general definition is consistent with common research terminology in qualitative methods (Merriam & Tisdell, 2015) as well as in the student affairs context (Love, 2003; Thompson, 2016). When it is necessary to differentiate the two, text-based documents, inclusive of nonprinted text such as emails or web-page copy, will be referred to as texts while visual images such as photographs or Web images will be referred to as images.

Document review data are generally used alongside other sources, such as interviews, to provide factual or procedural information, additional perspectives, or context and insight. Patton (2014) also noted that documents are valued by researchers because they provide paper trails that can be mined and followed to enhance knowledge and understanding. For Love (2003), existing documents lead to important contextual questions about a setting or event and its participants. This chapter begins with a general overview of document review then describes how to understand, read, evaluate, and apply results from document review-based studies.

Words Researchers Use—Distinguishing Documents

When researchers write about documents, they use several words synonymously. Following is a listing of the most commonly used words, along with some minor distinctions worth noting.

Artifact
Often used as a descriptor for an older document or record. An artifact can be a text or image, but most often is a physical object.

Document
Commonly used as an overarching term for document review data. A document can be a text or image. It can also be physical or digital.

Image
Generally used to mean photographs, but sometimes also films and other media. An image can be physical or digital.

Record
Typically only text-based data. Records can be physical or digital.

Understanding Document Review Research

Document review is often exploratory and investigative. Analysis can be superficial or extremely thorough depending on the goals of the study and role and types of data. While it is possible to review a document quickly to generate basic themes, a comprehensive analysis is much more complex and time-consuming. A detailed document review considers the text and/or images, medium, history, and context of

Table 6.1. Examples of Campus and Student Affairs–Specific Documents

	Institutional Records (Official)	General Records (Public)	Personal Documents (Private)
Campus	Budget and financial documents, policy manuals and handbooks, contracts, and annual reports	Meeting records, training materials, and strategic planning documents	Personal meeting notes, emails, or written reactions
Student Affairs	Student-group financial statements, constitutions, handbooks and bylaws, as well as office organizational charts, budget documents, contracts with vendors, individual, unit, and divisional annual reports and strategic plans	Meeting notes from student organizations or staff meetings and retreats, descriptions or instructions for activities related to student and employee training and/or orientation, annual reports or goals	Emails between specific individuals, personal notes from meetings, personal photographs or images of programs and events

Source: From Herdlein, Reifler, and Mrowka (2013). Reprinted by permission of Taylor & Francis Ltd.

creation, as well as intended and unintended use(s). Locating and reviewing documents is an analytical exercise involving logic, deduction, and intuition.

Researchers collect documents from a broad variety of physical and virtual sources. Beyond library or archive-based information, documents can be found in filing cabinets, in email records, stored on computers not accessible online, or in current or previously online materials such as websites, text, files, or posts. Table 6.1 is a listing of campus and student affairs-specific documents.

Metcalfe (2016) further distinguished campus documents as preexisting (found) and researcher prompted (generated). Found examples include campus maps, yearbooks, organizational charts, and photographs. Generated examples include videos taken by the researcher or the research participants, drawings by participants, or social media interactions initiated by the researcher.

Reviewing Documents

Researchers review documents to describe, explain, or relate information, or as supplemental data to reveal details or establish context. In addition, documents can be used to show how information developed and changed as well as how sources are directly or conceptually linked. Specific or personal records also can provide insight into thought processes, and can offer background information and context that may not be immediately visible. Student affairs researchers typically pair document review with other qualitative forms to establish context related to a research problem, refine data collection, or to supplement findings from additional methods. Document review is seldom used as a primary method, aside from historical research. Following are some ways researchers use document review in student affairs research.

Reasons for Understanding Document Review

- Discover or relate context.
- Refine data collection.
- Supplement or triangulate findings.
- Illuminate history.

Discover or Relate Context   Documents provide researchers with sources for understanding the setting, background, and details that influence other data and findings. Often, documents can reveal important contextual information. Such details can become the primary focus of an article, can help to explain results by providing background, or can be used to identify concepts that need further exploration. For example, Biddix, Somers, and Polman (2009) reviewed campus newspaper reports and editorials, flyers, announcements, press releases, and emails surrounding a living wage protest to create an event listing showing the sequence of events. This provided the context necessary for the researchers to examine civic learning that resulted from the revealed actions.

Refine Data Collection   Documents often are used as a first step in identifying or refining data collection. Researchers may know the phenomenon they want to study, but are unsure about the sources of data that can provide rich information. Barnhardt (2015) used methods from social movement studies to conduct a protest event analysis of national, local, and industry-specific newspaper articles tracing student anti-sweatshop mobilization. She considered variations in tactics, approaches, and motivations for collective actions as a means of identifying and comparing organizational contexts. Also, during their investigation of archival documents at Northwestern University, Biddix and Schwartz (2012) identified several new links to authors of the *Student Personnel Point of View* (American Council on Education, 1937) who had direct ties to Northwestern University's Personnel Department.

Supplement or Triangulate Findings   Used as a supplement, documents can confirm what researchers discover from a primary data collection method. Findings from interviews, for example, might be substantiated or verified (in other words, triangulated) by reviewing related documents. For example, to supplement interviews about women's gendered experiences working at a university, Broido, Brown, Stygles, and Bronkema (2015) examined employee handbooks, aspects of labor law, various campus reports, and curricula from programs designed to retain employees. The information revealed the policy context of the university environment including procedures and structures that inhibited women's advancement and development, adding legitimacy to the women's experiences.

Illuminate History   Historical studies have been relatively sparse in the published research in student affairs. Hevel (2016) recently located and synthesized more than 40 articles from various sources published over two decades related to the history of student affairs, finding that researchers explored positions and practice, professionalizing, and problems throughout the development of the field primarily using document review. Also, in *The Role of Student Affairs in Student Learning and Assessment*, Schuh and Gansemer-Toph (2010) reviewed influential documents in the field dating back to the *Student Personnel Point of View* (American Council on Education, 1937) to understand the role and development of assessment practice. This let the researchers explain and contextualize the emphasis on assessment by offering two broad conclusions (pp. 5–6): First, the work of student affairs (inclusive of their roles and contributions) has moved "from the periphery to the center of students' learning at college," and second, that assessment practice has moved from evaluating use and participation in programs to "measuring how programs and experiences contribute to students' learning."

Perspectives From the Field—Why Historical Research Matters to Student Affairs Research

Historical research provides perspective to contemporary problems and allows educators to learn from the past. In fact, the ability to learn from troubling actions of our predecessors may be history's most useful feature. Earlier generations of student affairs administrators held women students to stricter behavioral standards, organized conferences at racially segregated hotels, and expelled students for being gay. At the same time, some determined professionals promoted gender equality on campus, combatted racism in the field and in society, and quietly admitted students who were dismissed from another campus for their sexual orientation. Appreciating the ways in which the field perpetuated sexism, racism, and homophobia in the past—along with the efforts to subvert this discrimination—can redouble student affairs administrators' contemporary efforts to create equitable campuses today.

Michael S. Hevel—Associate Professor of Higher Education, University of Arkansas

Research Considerations

The basic approach to reviewing documents involves identifying a source, gaining access, and finding key information in the text(s) or image(s) relevant to the focus of the study. The extent of the review depends on the nature of the document, how it contributes to the research question, and the skill of the researcher. Following is an overview of research considerations including terminology, accessibility, availability, awareness, and standardizing the analysis. Understanding these considerations supports an ability to read and evaluate document review research.

Understanding the Terminology. Terminology can present some confusion when reading or working with documents. Many researchers refer to all forms of text and visual data broadly as documents and describe data analysis as document analysis. The range of data researchers can use as part of review methods can make this confusing. While text-based data basically fit this description, photographs and videos, as well any three-dimensional media or artifacts, complicate the classification. The existing literature in student affairs does not offer a consensus on these considerations.

Gaining Access to Data. The distinctions of official, public, or private relate to the accessibility of documents or the researcher's ability to access data. Various restrictions may limit access. For example, on most public campuses, institutional and general records are available to the public. This is also true of personal documents depending on how they are recorded, stored, and the information contained in them. Email messages sent using a university email account should be accessible to anyone who requests them unless the specific information is protected by state or federal law (e.g., FERPA, HIPAA). Private institutions may have different guidelines.

Determining Data Availability. Data availability is an important consideration when reviewing documents. For example, prior drafts of a document may no longer be available because they were deleted or the original record was edited. In the case of archives, a record may be damaged, missing, or otherwise incomplete. Electronic records can be beneficial when available, because they are seldom fully deleted. For example, many universities use backup or cloud-based storage for email and file sharing. Prior versions of files are often archived or retrievable. Information published online, such as websites, older files, and images, often can be found using a retrieval service. One issue with online information is stability of the record, as text and images can change faster than they are archived.

Knowing What Data Exists. Locating documents can be a highly deductive activity, requiring the researcher to speculate on what might be missing. Schuh, Biddix, Dean, and Kinzie (2016) noted, "Data typically do not exist without the influence of outside factors" (p. 202). The authors used the example of a restrictive campus policy on posting fliers listed in the student handbook. Without prior or insider knowledge pointing to specific questions, a researcher may not know the policy was derived directly from a series of offensive party fliers. There may or may not be meeting minutes where these fliers were referenced and prior versions of the handbook would only show a change, not the reason for it. Considering this, Love (2003) cautioned, "no document is a literal recording of an event" (p. 87).

Standardizing the Process. A document review guide is a standardized form researchers often use to investigate documents. Most document review guides begin with a set of standardized questions about the source, such as material, origin, author, or other visible details. Less evident questions involve the temporal, political, historical, or economic context (Merriam, 1998). Using a guide for data collection standardizes known and observable facts about the data, and provides consistency and continuity across different data formats, allowing for comparison (Saunders & Cooper, 2009). A guide also aids data analysis, and is especially beneficial when working with varied forms of data or when multiple researchers are involved in data collection. Guides can be highly structured or even semistructured, with common elements such as a checklist or open notes section.

Associated Designs

Most often, researchers use document review in case study designs to present a more holistic view of context and setting. In grounded theory, documents contribute to the development and verification of themes. In phenomenology, researchers use documents to explain factual conditions or to describe phenomena participants may or may not know existed. For example, Biddix (2010) used websites, blogs, news stories, and other documents to uncover unseen patterns of coordination and control affecting college women's work as activist leaders. Researchers using ethnographic methods incorporate documents as equivalent data sources to discover and reveal aspects of culture, as in Nathan's (2006) depiction of a first year on campus. A narrative design may be based primarily on a review of historical documents, or may incorporate elements of interview and documents to retell a story, as in Wolf-Wendel et al.'s (Wolf-Wendel, Twombly, Tuttle, Ward, & Gaston, 2004) first-person accounts of student affairs administrators from the Civil Rights Era.

Main Types of Review Methods

Student affairs researchers distinguish two main types of document review methods: document analysis for analyzing text and visual analysis for analyzing images and media. Some basic features apply to both. The data analysis process includes a literal examination of the content as well as consideration of its production and/or authorship, context, and other decisions affecting the data, such as its storage. It also incorporates investigation into the source's use(s). The process might be thought of as similar to in-depth interviewing; the researcher is asking the data questions to elicit meaning. Finally, effective data collection, especially within the same study, shares consistent questions and procedures. To accomplish this uniformity, researchers develop or use an existing document review guide. Following are descriptions of the main types of review methods including an overview of use and example types of data.

Document Analysis

Document analysis is the process of analyzing text-based data. When reviewing documents, researchers typically begin with a general reading of the text and then move to a form of thematic analysis. Bowen (2009) emphasized the importance of making a first pass at data in order to identify and separate relevant information into groups, categories, and examples (p. 32). Bowen (2009) described the process as iterative, combining elements of content analysis and thematic analysis. He specifically outlined the process as "skimming (superficial examination), reading (thorough examination), and interpretation" (p. 32). Although thematic analysis is completed separately for each document, researchers often are concerned with merging multiple data sources to reveal a more complete story through commonalities, divergence, and interconnections in the data (Love, 2003; Miles, Huberman, & Saldana, 2015).

Words Researchers Use—Document Versus Content Analysis

Some researchers use the terms document analysis and content analysis interchangeably, while others distinguish the two but use content analysis to also mean thematic analysis. Krippendorff (2004) stated, "Content analysis is a research technique for making replicable and valid inferences from texts (or other meaningful matter) to the contexts of their use" (p. 18).

For the purposes of clarity, this chapter follow's Bowen's (2009) definition, consistent with student affairs research conventions (e.g., Love, 2003; Schuh et al., 2016), to describe document analysis as including content analysis. Content analysis can be further divided into distinct techniques such as discourse analysis, analysis of narrative structures, and ethnography.

Visual Analysis

Visual analysis is the process of analyzing image-based data. When reviewing image-based documents, researchers typically distinguish between data and data generators. This distinction requires an understanding of how images are experienced by image viewers versus image creators. Schwartz (1989) also noted that while images show visible details of events, activities, and contexts, analysis can involve both what appears in the image and what meaning the image elicits for others. Metcalfe (2016) considered visual research methods as among the most underutilized techniques in higher education "given their potential to aid in the interpretation of the increasingly visual nature of academia and society at large" (p. 111). Considering both static (photographs) and dynamic (websites) data, she classified several forms of visual methods including content analysis, ethnography, archival practices, and photo elicitation. Two notable forms of visual methods used in student affairs research that she described were: (1) participatory visual methods (participants provide comments on images and videos) and (2) data visualization and mapping (researchers obtain or create charts and graphs for further analysis).

Variations of Review Methods

Two variations of review methods are used in student affairs research. Discourse analysis is an extension of content analysis, focusing on language. A further extension is critical discourse analysis, commonly used by researchers working with critical theory. Multimodal analysis is a relatively new approach to the combined study of text and visual media.

Discourse Analysis. *Discourse analysis* is the study of how language is used in text and other contexts. According to Gee (2014), it is the study of how to say and do things. People use language to communicate, cooperate, and build, as well as for doing harm. Gee (2014) listed several theoretical approaches and variations of research tools used for discourse analysis—some tied closely to the study of grammar and others concentrating more in ideas and issues expressed. Gulley (2016) used discourse analysis to examine discourse around how student affairs practitioners and academic affairs officers defined collaboration in a community college context. He was also concerned with how the terminology came into being and was perpetuated, noting, "I am interested in not only the forms that collaboration takes in the setting, as described by the participants, but how they conceptualize the actual concept of collaboration" (p. 500). When analyzing transcripts from interviews with participants, Gulley (2016) considered both the context and assumptions used by the speaker and listener, as well as intertextuality to understand the meaning generated when one person referred to something someone else said. This gave him a sense of how the language of collaboration contributed to and shaped campus practices.

Critical Discourse Analysis. *Critical discourse analysis* is an extension of discourse analysis that uses critical theory to study the use and meaning of documents. Fairclough (2010) described this method as having three properties: relational (the focus is not on individuals or entities, but social relations), dialectical (relations between objects that are different but not discrete), and transdisciplinary (incorporates different theories, disciplines, and frameworks) (pp. 3–4). Using a critical discourse framework (i.e., examining everyday language to raise awareness about issues), Saichaie and Morphew (2014) studied the language and images used on institutional websites from 12 colleges and universities across a number of characteristics. The researchers noted that while the content and images varied in subtle ways across the websites, there was a singular and relatively homogeneous focus on the promotion of higher education as a product:

> The messages de-emphasize IHEs' [institutions of higher educations'] public missions and purposes, as well as the goals that these colleges and universities have chosen for themselves. What appears is an idealized setting where students assemble to enjoy a collegiate experience chockfull of extracurricular activities and academic demands tailored to their interests and career preparation. (p. 523)

This led Saichaie and Morphew (2014) to ask rhetorically, "Why should we be surprised that students are leaving college knowing little more than they knew upon enrolling?" (p. 526).

Multimodal Analysis. *Multimodal analysis* is the study of both images and text in documents. Metcalfe (2016) recommended that researchers consider the interplay between both forms of media when examining data. Lynch (2015) related an example of how multimodal analysis works in an increasingly tech-reliant educational economy. In a study of online software for delivering courses in K–12 education, Lynch considered the text presented as well as how the tool (the online delivery system or interface) influenced the product. The researcher found that the interface shaped the content while being shaped by it. Applied to a student affairs context, a multimodal analysis of the review process for online admissions applications would consider both the product (applications) as well as the process of using them (online interface) and how the applications are shaped by interface.

Some questions might include: How are decisions facilitated by the use of the system? Is there automation? Are some applications submitted and routed while others are not due to formatting or other interface errors? Does everyone review in the same way? Machin and Mayr (2012) offered guidance for using both critical discourse and multimodal analysis in Chapter 2 of their textbook, which considered the use of visual media.

Reading Document Review Research

When writing about document review, researchers typically describe their thematic analysis or coding technique and showcase results in narrative format or data displays with excerpts from sources. Following are different ways document review data are presented in text, with examples from published studies, and general guidelines for reading document review research.

Narrative With Quotations

Gulley (2016) used discourse analysis of interview transcripts to study the concept of collaboration in the community college context. He organized findings by themes and elaborated using representative quotations from interview transcripts to show interconnections within the data. Gulley highlighted specific quotations from text to draw attention to underlying meanings:

> . . . these participants did not necessarily discuss collaboration as ongoing, long-term, and programmatic engagements but as communicating on particular issues in the short-term. Even the reverse of the above situation is true. For example, one chief academic affairs officer, Allison, told a story of having students enter her office in tears because their financial aid was short, and they needed tuition funds. This administrator recognized that the student had come to the wrong place to get assistance for this problem but felt obligated to assist him saying, "I call them up and say 'look 40 bucks—I got 20, you got 20?'—that's the kind of collaboration we have and I think that's the kind of relationship that we have built." Collaboration in this sense was about problem solving for a student and communicating with colleagues in the other division for that purpose. It was a one-time connection for a specific reason. (p. 501)

Synthesis Without Quotations

Certis (2014) reviewed policy documents, personal notes and correspondence, published works, academic records, and other materials from the Northwestern

University Archives to create a biographical sketch of Dr. Esther Lloyd-Jones. Jones's dissertation revealed insight into the work that shaped her perspective on the field. Certis showcased the results with a synthesis approach:

> Lloyd-Jones's dissertation conveys an overall theme of interest in individuals, which can be seen in sections of the work dealing with case studies and interviews with students (p. 263). . . . To organize such a wide variety of data on students, Lloyd-Jones (1929) provided detailed charts and graphs representing students by school: liberal arts, commerce, medicine, law, dentistry, journalism, speech, and music. Through graphs and charts, Lloyd-Jones was able to demonstrate that students with low grade point averages (GPAs) were more likely to drop out; however, she noted students who may have done well in high school did not necessarily do well in college. Lloyd-Jones showed administrators the need to be invested in admitted students as providing students with the skills to succeed is in their best interest. (p. 264)

Images

Saichaie and Morphew (2014) examined the language and images used on institutional websites from 12 colleges and universities across a number of characteristics. They showcased images as a way to bridge their review of the visual aspects of analysis with text, described as follows:

> Images were accompanied by descriptions ranging from the nebulous, such as "Inquiry and Discovery" on the Princeton site, to the very specific, such as "Students from Dance Marathon and KRUI share their experiences in a Life Design course" at Iowa. In most cases, the attached text connected the images to normative expectations about academic life in college, including the role of faculty and technology. (p. 510)

Themes Table

Herdlein, Riefler, and Mrowka (2013) studied desired skills and competencies in student affairs. Data, derived from articles published over 17 years focusing on student affairs competencies important for professional preparation and practice, were organized into summary themes:

> Table 4 identified student affairs skill sets, of which research, assessment, and evaluation were found to be the most frequently mentioned items in the literature. Other significant skills included communication, administration and management, supervision, leadership, and writing effectiveness. Sixteen studies also noted that a combination of skills is necessary for effective student affairs practice, while six articles did not specifically identify skills. (p. 261)

Table 4

Desired Characteristics of Student Affairs Professionals in Articles

Note: Percentages are based on number of articles analyzed (N = 22) and may exceed 100% given variables recorded in more than more category.

Skills (n = 157)	n	%
Research/Assessment/Evaluation	15	68
Communication	13	59
Administration and Management	13	59
Supervision	13	59
Leadership	13	59
Writing Effectiveness	11	50
Technology	10	45
Problem Solving	8	36
Personnel Management	8	36
Collaboration	7	32
Practicing Diversity	7	32
Conflict/Crisis Management	7	32
Advising Students	7	32
Promote Student Learning	6	27
Application — Theory to Practice	5	23
Implementing Assessment	5	23
Teaching and Training	4	18
Did not apply	6	27
Combination	16	73

Data Display

Biddix et al. (2009) used both text and visual materials to create an Event Listing Display as part of data analysis. The display provided a means of understanding how several forms of communication influenced the conduct and resolution of a campus protest. An excerpt from the article and the unpublished display follows:

> After constructing a reduced narrative based on this technique, the research team created an event listing display, which illustrated the sequence and nature of events. Miles and Huberman (1994) suggested using displays to analyze qualitative data when attempting to understand phenomena. For textual analysis, we used an open coding strategy proposed by Strauss and Corbin (1998) to construct a chronological listing of critical events. Coded categories included chronology (CHRON), critical events (CRIT), electronic tactics (EL), and real-life tactics (RL). We listed critical events and used arrows to indicate sequence. The refined display was shared with two key informants, a Student Worker Alliance (SWA) leader and a campus administrator for clarification and verification of critical events. (p. 137)

Developmental Experiences			Learning Outcomes (1-8)
Student Actions	Time Period	University Actions	
Internet-based research; Plan via email and cell phones with students at other campuses	Pre-Occupation 3/21 – 4/3		(7) Commit to global citizenry though involvement; (8) Recognize the importance of direct access and free information
Begin sit-in; Announce sit-in via email; Update website; Create Weblog; Create personal IM away messages for immediate updates; Create Facebook group; Create and distribute an e-newsletter; Email press releases	Early Occupation 4/4 – 4/10 Sit-in begins; Daily rallies begin		(1) Advance a community search for mutual agreement; (3) Examine and develop values; (4) Teach how to bring about change in society; (5) Develop a sense of community; (8) Recognize the importance of direct access and free information
			(6) Reconsider the role of individual vs. society
Send demands to administrators		Permit occupation; Permit use of University-owned Internet access, email, and Web space	(7) Preserve/legitimize expression (8) Recognize the importance of direct access and free information
Email administrators to warn of intent to hunger strike		(E1) RE: Address sit-in, preserve viewpoints; (E2) RE: Keep dialog open, students to leave	(1) Advance a community search for mutual agreement (2) Preserve/legitimize expression (3) Develop a sense of community
Begin hunger strike; Contact students at other campuses for health info, advice	Hunger Strike 4/11 – 4/16	(E3) RE: Reasonable response to demands	(7) Commitment to global citizenry though involvement
Mobilize 400 for rally		Judicial summons RE: out by 11:30 p.m.	
		Permit rally	(2) Preserve/legitimize expression
Students end hunger strikeaa		Discussions with SWA	(1)Advance a community search for mutual agreement
Email exchanges with university regarding demands	Final Days 4/17 – 4/22	(E4) RE: Outcome of negotiations, students altered originally agreed upon deal	(1) Advance a community search for mutual agreement; (8) Recognize the importance of direct access and free information
Email all undergraduates, RE: Misinterpretations		Discussions with SWA	
Students end sit-in; Email students to announce victory		(E5) RE: End of sit-in	(8) Recognize the importance of direct access and free information
Students respond to judicial summons in campus newspaper	Epilogue	Judicial sanctioning	(1) Advance a community search for mutual agreement; (3) Examine and develop values
Potential future student demonstrations		Draft; Request comment; Approve new policy	(1) Advance a community search for mutual agreement

Indicators: → Responses; (E) 1 of 5 Emails from the Chancellor to entire campus community (students, faculty, staff, etc.)

Guidelines for Reading Document Review

- Look for answers to questions.
- Follow the logic.
- Read the summaries.
- Consider the examples.

Look for Answers to Questions   Researchers develop, investigate, and answer research questions in a study. The results section should directly answer questions and/or provide evidence to support tentative answers in the subsequent discussion. When reading document review results, start by scanning the findings to get an overall sense (or macro view) of how (the evidence) and to what extent (how much data and/or detail in analysis) the researcher answered the questions with the data sources.

Follow the Logic   Researchers display results in a specific way to answer or to evidence their questions. Consider why they chose the method(s) they used to showcase findings. Why include quotations instead of synthesis? Why use a summary table of themes (or why not)? If the data included images, why were these specific images chosen (or not)? Seeking answers to these questions can reveal more about the available data and how the researcher used (or did not use) sources effectively.

Read the Summaries   The themes or categories researchers identified as part of the data analysis process represent summary findings. These are often reported in tables. When researchers do not include a listing of their themes, they incorporate summary or narrative text in the introduction to the results section. Locating and reading summary data reveals some of the decisions the researcher encountered when reducing data through analysis. Summaries should include explanations as well as examples (direct or referenced) to relate the data and findings to research questions.

Consider the Examples   If researchers included excerpts and/or examples in their results, read or review them carefully. In most cases, these are exemplars or outliers chosen to add legitimacy to results or to give readers a clearer picture of the data sources. If quotations or images are included, accompanying text should explain how the examples support the overall theme(s) of the results or if they were included to emphasize a key point, showcase an outlier, or serve as a representative example.

Evaluating Document Review Research

When evaluating document review research, it is important to consider how the text or visual material was produced, circulated, read, stored, and used. Atkinson and Coffey (2004) emphasized several important points that can be applied to text and visual analysis. They noted, "documents are 'social facts' in that they are produced, shared and used in socially organized ways. They are not, however, transparent representations of organizational routines, decision-making processes, or professional diagnoses. They construct particular kinds of representations using their own conventions" (p. 58). This suggests documents and images should not be viewed at face value, devoid of context, use, and meaning. As a research consumer, it is important to consider these multifaceted aspects. Prior (2003, p. 77) emphasized three related considerations when using documents as research materials that informed the following evaluative questions.

Questions for Evaluating Document Review

- Is the data analysis process clear?
- What circumstances influenced the materials?
- How are (or were) the materials used?

Is the Data Analysis Process Clear?   The most prevalent data analysis method for document review is thematic coding. A generalized approach involves reviewing initial sources, looking for "recurring regularities" (repeated concepts) in the data, checking for congruence, developing themes, evaluating themes, and connecting themes to objectives (Schuh et al., 2016). While replicating analysis is not possible with constructivist-based research, readers should be provided with enough detail to clearly understand the analysis process (for example, how codes and themes were identified). The information provided should enlighten the process, letting the reader "see" how the researcher moved from initial data sources through analysis and to presentation.

What Circumstances Influenced the Materials?   Documents and images are produced, used, and stored in context. Studying the background, setting, and/or environment in which data are produced can reveal important aspects beyond what is written or shown. Researchers should provide sufficient information to reveal these circumstances and include how they interpreted the meaning(s) of the material through this lens. For example, a context to consider could be the circumstances in which the document was produced. A demonstration policy revised during or directly after a campus protest may be worded differently than if it was written as part of a general revision to a student handbook. These are critical details a researcher should consider, reveal, and discuss.

How Are the Materials Used?   Documents typically are created for a specific purpose. For example, an email is meant to convey particular information between the sender and the audience. The information may be informational or directive, serious or humorous. Similarly, a photograph may have been taken to share a glimpse of an image with another person or the general public, to showcase positive results, or to emphasize needs. The use(s) of a document can reveal processes, decisions, and customs. Researchers should include any details that reveal a more complete understanding of their sources and how they incorporated those details into their analysis and interpretation.

Following are additional questions for evaluating documents review research based on different ways data may be presented.

Narrative Format With Quotations or Images
- Why did the researcher choose these specific quotations or images?
- Do the quotations or images clarify, support, or refute the research questions?
- Is the context for quotations or images clear, or could they be interpreted several ways?

Synthesis Without Quotations or Themes Table
- Why did the researcher choose not to use quotations?
- Does the synthesis or themes table reflect examination of all data?
- Are there enough data to support an overall synthesis or themes table?

Data Display
- Do the texts or images in the display clarify, support, or refute the research questions?
- Does the figure make conceptual and logical sense?
- Does the accompanying explanation include details about context of the data?

Applying Document Review Research

Document review research can be useful for helping understand how context affects programs and policies. It is also beneficial for understanding successes, challenges, or failures. Finally, it can be helpful for guiding policy development or revision.

Following are some opportunities for applying results from document review research studies to practice.

Opportunities for Applying Document Review

- Understand context to improve application.
- Reveal relatable successes and challenges.
- Guide policy development or revision.

Understand Context to Improve Application   Published materials that incorporate document review research generally include contextual information. Beyond simply details about the setting, a description about context may include organizational values, key players in decision making, individual or group norms and/or behaviors, historical overviews, or specifics about how the climate or setting influences actions, beliefs, and behaviors. These details help readers apply recommendations to specific situations, and reveal opportunities and/or potential difficulties that apply to similar circumstances. For example, in a study about Latino women majoring in STEM fields, Diaz-Espinoza (2015) analyzed recruitment materials used to attract potential students to STEM majors. The findings revealed ways images shown in print and online perpetuated a perception of male dominance in engineering. While the recruitment materials were specific to the case institution, the contextual details included about how the materials were used, intended, and experienced are relatable to other underrepresented fields and contexts. Understanding problematic aspects that the materials create for the culture of women in STEM can inform efforts to revise materials in other settings.

Reveal Relatable Successes and Challenges   Practitioners often seek supportive evidence when designing, implementing, or assessing a program or service. Document review research can aid these efforts by revealing relatable successes and challenges. For example, Peltier (2014) studied faculty and student affairs collaborative initiatives associated with experiential learning. A review of campus documents showed how experiential learning was described, emphasized, and implemented in institutional documents and records such as the vision statement, strategic plan, and educational philosophy. The researcher used these results to specify interview questions. Analysis of themes from document analysis and interviews suggested that a primary barrier to faculty and student affairs collaboration around experiential learning was the language surrounding the documentation of outcomes. Peltier also noted that faculty could not consistently articulate a definition of experiential learning or cocurricular programming and were unclear of institutional expectations. Further, Peltier observed that faculty members did not consider student affairs staff as potential collaborators. This miscommunication, both formally in documents and informally in role perceptions, is not unique in faculty/staff collaborations. Results suggested relatable ways to build collaboration and create shared language that can be applied to other issues and settings.

Guide Policy Development or Revision   Documents can be used to trace policy development. A prominent example is Stoner and Lowery's (2004) model student conduct code, which incorporated past legal proceedings and considerations about conduct approaches in student affairs. Although primarily a review of legal materials, the research showcased the origins and development of conduct policy. Another example is the Foundation for Individual Rights in Education's (FIRE) annual publication, *Spotlight on Speech Codes*, a listing of various institutional policies governing campus speech along with a grading system for whether or not the codes meet constitutional requirements. Research contributing to these reports traces regulations from campus codes.

Perspectives From the Field—Reviewing Documents for Practice

Reviewing documents for policy development is very important. Understanding the context and authorship behind the content of an existing policy or the context driving the need for the development of a policy can be extremely critical. In my role as a senior level administrator, I am often reviewing documents in order to inform recommendations or decisions policies to remove barriers to student success, enhance student involvement, and create division- or university-strategic plans.

So, for example, in order to understand barriers that inhibit student enrollment, it's important to review previous survey results in which students outline challenges they faced to re-enrollment. The open-ended survey responses provide valuable insight into understanding several issues that were easily addressed through process clarification or policy changes.

Additionally, in a strategic planning process, it is important the committee are provided results from listening sessions, university strategic plans, examples of print and social media communications, and information about each department in the division in order to help shape recommendations for strategic goals and tactical plans. This review of data can provide insight into areas of opportunity, success, and gaps which the divisional leader can use to outline strategic priorities for the next five years.

Melissa S. Shivers—Vice-President for Student Life, University of Iowa

Building Your Document Review Skillset

Working with documents engages logic, deduction, and intuition. It builds the ability to conceptualize, identify, and make associations. Writing skills are enriched through the process of fitting disparate information into meaningful and interpretable summaries. Further, collecting, preserving, and working with documents is relatable to effective organizational recordkeeping.

Additional texts for learning about document review include Silverman's (2014) edited volume, which contains three chapters on text analysis, one on visual analysis, and several others related to other types of documents. One of the richest and most approachable sources for learning how to use review data is Bowen's (2009) article "Document Analysis as a Qualitative Research Method," which provides an overview of documents as data sources and details research procedures. Specific to data analysis, Krippendorff (2013) published several frequently used and cited texts on content analysis, emphasizing a systematic approach to data reduction. For visual analysis, Rose (2016) outlined various forms of visual media, methods and approaches, and a theoretical approach for studying and understanding images. Student affairs authors also have provided some field-specific guidance for document review research. Stage and Manning's (2003, 2016) edited texts each include three chapters written by different authors on forms of document review data including visual, historical, legal, and policy-based documents.

Document review typically is not emphasized as a primary method in research courses. Basic qualitative design courses in educational research tend to focus on using all three forms, while advanced courses often detail specific designs, such as case study or ethnography, data analysis and coding, or advanced interviewing. Nonetheless, learning to locate, read, and evaluate documents enhances highly transferable practice skills in seeking information, asking important questions, and identifying relatable connections in text and image sources.

References

American Council on Education. (1937). The student personnel point of view. *American Council on Education Studies* (Series I, Vol. I, no. 3).

Atkinson, P. A., & Coffey, A. (2004). Analyzing documentary realities. In D. Silverman (Ed.), *Qualitative research: Theory, method and practice* (2nd ed., pp. 56–75). London, United Kingdom: Sage.

Barnhardt, C. L. (2015). Campus educational contexts and civic participation: Organizational links to community action. *The Journal of Higher Education, 86*(1), 38–70.

Biddix, J. P. (2010). Relational leadership and technology: A study of activist college women leaders. *NASPA Journal about Women in Higher Education, 3*(1), 25–47.

Biddix, J. P., & Schwartz, R. (2012). Walter Dill Scott and the student personnel movement. *Journal of Student Affairs Research and Practice, 49*(3), 285–298.

Biddix, J. P., Somers, P. A., & Polman, J. L. (2009). Protest reconsidered: Activism's role as civic engagement educator. *Innovative Higher Education, 34*(3), 133–147.

Bowen, G. A. (2009). Document analysis as a qualitative research method. *Qualitative Research Journal, 9*(2), 27–40.

Broido, E. M., Brown, K. R., Stygles, K. N., & Bronkema, R. H. (2015). Responding to gendered dynamics: Experiences of women working over 25 years at one university. *The Journal of Higher Education, 86*(4), 595–627.

Certis, H. (2014). The emergence of Esther Lloyd-Jones. *Journal of Student Affairs Research and Practice, 51*(3), 259–269.

Diaz-Espinoza, C. R. (2015). *You kind of have to prove it: Gender microaggressions within the lived experiences of women in engineering* (Unpublished doctoral dissertation). The University of Tennessee, Knoxville.

Fairclough, N. (2010). *Critical discourse analysis: The critical study of language* (2nd ed.). New York, NY: Routledge.

Gee, J. P. (2014). *How to do discourse analysis: A toolkit* (2nd ed.). New York, NY: Routledge.

Gulley, N. Y. (2016). A discourse analysis of collaboration between academic and student affairs in community colleges. *Community College Journal of Research and Practice, 40*(6), 496–507.

Herdlein, R., Riefler, L., & Mrowka, K. (2013). An integrative literature review of student affairs competencies: A meta-analysis. *Journal of Student Affairs Research and Practice, 50*(3), 250–269.

Hevel, M. S. (2016). Toward a history of student affairs: A synthesis of research, 1996–2015. *Journal of College Student Development, 57*(7), 844–862.

Krippendorff, K. (2004). *Content analysis: An introduction to its methodology.* Thousand Oaks, CA: Sage.

Krippendorff, K. (2013). *Content analysis: An introduction to its methodology* (3rd ed.). Thousand Oaks, CA: Sage.

Lloyd-Jones, E. (1929). *Student personnel work at northwestern university.* New York, NY: Harper & Brothers.

Love, P. (2003). Document analysis. In F. K. Stage & K. Manning (Eds.), *Research in the college context: Approaches and methods* (pp. 83–97). New York, NY: Brunner-Routledge.

Lynch, T. L. (2015). *The hidden role of software in educational research: Policy to practice.* New York, NY: Routledge.

Machin, D., & Mayr, A. (2012). *How to do critical discourse analysis: A multimodal introduction.* Thousand Oaks, CA: Sage.

Merriam, S. B. (1998). *Qualitative research and case study applications in education.* San Francisco, CA: Jossey-Bass.

Merriam, S. B., & Tisdell, E. J. (2015). *Qualitative research: A guide to design and implementation* (4th ed.). San Francisco, CA: Jossey-Bass.

Metcalfe, A. S. (2016). Visual methods in higher education. In F. K. Stage & K. Manning (Eds.), *Research in the college context: Approaches and methods* (2nd ed., pp. 111–127). New York, NY: Brunner-Routledge.

Miles, M. B., & Huberman, A. M. (1994). *Qualitative data analysis: An expanded sourcebook* (2nd ed.). Thousand Oaks, CA: Sage.

Miles, M. B., Huberman, A. M., & Saldana, J. (2015). *Qualitative data analysis: A methods sourcebook* (3rd ed.). Thousand Oaks, CA: Sage.

Nathan, R. (2006). *My freshman year: What a professor learned by becoming a student.* Ithaca, NY: Cornell University Press.

Patton, M. Q. (2014). *Qualitative research & evaluation methods: Integrating theory and practice* (4th ed.). Thousand Oaks, CA: Sage.

Peltier, M. (2014). *The impact of faculty perception of student affairs personnel on collaborative initiatives: A case study* (Unpublished doctoral dissertation). University of Nebraska–Lincoln.

Prior, L. (2003). *Using documents in social research.* Thousand Oaks, CA: Sage.

Rose, G. (2016). *Visual methodologies: An introduction to researching with visual materials* (4th ed.). Thousand Oaks, CA: Sage.

Saichaie, K., & Morphew, C. C. (2014). What college and university websites reveal about the purposes of higher education. *Journal of Higher Education, 85*(4), 499–530.

Saunders, K., & Cooper, R. M. (2009). Instrumentation. In J. H. Schuh & Associates (Eds.), *Assessment methods for student affairs* (pp. 107–140). San Francisco, CA: Jossey-Bass.

Schuh, J. H., Biddix, J. P., Dean, L. A., & Kinzie, J. (2016). *Assessment in student affairs: A contemporary look* (2nd ed.). San Francisco, CA: Jossey Bass.

Schuh, J. H., & Gansemer-Topf, A. M. (2010). *The role of student affairs in student learning assessment.* National Institute for Learning Outcomes Assessment, Occasional Paper #7. Champaign, IL: National Institute for Learning Outcomes Assessment. Retrieved from http://www.learningoutcomeassessment.org/documents/studentAffairsrole.pdf

Schwartz, D. (1989). Visual ethnography: Using photography in qualitative research. *Qualitative Sociology, 12*(2), 119–154.

Silverman, D. (Ed.). (2014). *Qualitative research: Theory, method and practice* (2nd ed.). London, United Kingdom: Sage.

Stage, F. K., & Manning, K. (Eds.). (2003). *Research in the college context: Approaches and methods.* New York, NY: Brunner-Routledge.

Stage, F. K., & Manning, K. (Eds.). (2016). *Research in the college context: Approaches and methods* (2nd ed.). New York, NY: Brunner-Routledge.

Stoner, E. N., II, & Lowery, J. W. (2004). Navigating past the "spirit of insubordination": A twenty-first century model student conduct code with a model hearing script. *Journal of College and University Law, 31*(1), 1–77.

Strauss, A. S., & Corbin, J. (1998). *Basics of qualitative research: Techniques and procedures for developing grounded theory* (2nd ed.). Thousand Oaks, CA: Sage.

Thompson, M. D. (2016). Document analysis, oral history, and historical methods. In F. K. Stage & K. Manning (Eds.), *Research in the college context: Approaches and methods* (2nd ed., pp. 128–140). New York, NY: Brunner-Routledge.

Wolf-Wendel, L., Twombly, S., Tuttle, K., Ward, K., & Gaston, J. (2004). *Reflecting back, looking forward: Civil rights and student affairs.* Washington, DC: National Association of Student Personnel Administrators.

CHAPTER SEVEN

OBSERVING PEOPLE AND PLACES

Learning Outcomes

By the end of this chapter, you should be able to:

- Understand the purpose and role of observation methods.
- Differentiate between the major types of observation techniques.
- Read observation data in journal articles and reports.
- Evaluate observation methods based on how data are collected, analyzed, and reported.
- Apply interpretations of observation methods to student affairs practice.

Observation involves selecting a person or group, or a time and location, and recording data about interactions, activities, or the environment. The focus can be on a single individual or a group, one location or multiple, in an everyday setting, or in the context of a specific event. Data collection can take place at a specific date and time or over several days and at different times. It can be concentrated and structured or open and emergent. A researcher may observe a natural setting or introduce a change to see what happens. Regardless of the approach, an observation typically is bounded (or restricted) by some criteria to keep the study focused. However, it is essential for the researcher to be open to what may occur (or emerge) during data collection.

Observation data are seldom published in single-method studies in student affairs. They often are used alongside other methods to lend context, additional insight, or to add rigor or legitimacy to a study. However, Russell and Kovacs (2003) noted that "a revival of these measures would enable college and university research to move beyond its dependence on reactive data" (p. 78). They further recommended that, "after you have scored the questionnaires, and transcribed the interviews, get out of the office and on to the campus and see what is really going on!" (p. 78). This chapter begins with a general overview of observation then describes how to understand, read, evaluate, and apply results from observation-based studies.

Understanding Observation Methods

Observation offers insight into people, places, and settings that may otherwise be difficult to learn using other forms of data collection. Observation research can be highly interactive, involving a researcher collecting data while also participating in the activity or setting. It also can be unobtrusive, involving data collection that is unknown to participants. The approach and setting can influence the nature, quantity, and depth of the data collected. An experienced observer (or even a novice after just one session) regards observation as more difficult than it seems. Researchers must decide what to record and ignore, develop an efficient system for taking notes, and resist distraction, monotony, and boredom. The complexity of data collection led Marshall and Rossman (1995) to note that observation requires a great deal of the researcher in managing their role while observing potentially large amounts of complex stimuli.

Observation settings often are physical places, but researchers also can collect data from virtual spaces. Similarly, observations typically occur in person and real time, but technology also allows for virtual observation (using a live camera for example) in real time or of recorded past settings. Traditionally, researchers collect observation data by taking field notes, but even this approach can vary from deep and detailed observation with copious notes (low-structured approach) to an initial observation that is used to create an observation form used for sustained data collection (high-structured approach). Finally, observations can vary based on time and location (or both), depending on the focus and goals of data collection.

Observing People and Places

Researchers use observation methods in a variety of ways to reveal and uncover insights about people, places, and events related to student affairs practice. Following is a listing of some of the more common uses for observation methods, including examples from research and practice.

Reasons for Observing People and Places

- Understand how people affect places.
- Learn how places affect people.
- Study the effect of changes to setting.
- Evaluate learning environments.
- Gain new insights for practice.
- Complement other methods.

Understand How People Affect Places   Individuals and groups use and repurpose environments to meet their needs. An example is a footpath between buildings on campus. A landscape architect may carefully plan traffic flow only to find that a dirt trail emerges once students begin to move between buildings. The use and function of a place can also change depending on the date and time. During business hours, a student activities office is staffed with professionals completing and filing event forms, advising students, or holding staff meetings. After hours, the same space may be used for student-group meetings and planning sessions. The furniture arrangements and the sounds and language change as the location shifts from a professional work environment to a student space. Understanding how people affect spaces can provide valuable insight into how to make spaces more efficient.

Learn How Places Affect People   Places can have positive or negative effects on people. Further, perceptions about a setting can alter its use. For example, a dimly lighted building, hallway, or parking garage may influence a student's willingness to visit those spaces after dark. Or, locating a conduct office next to a fraternity affairs office can send a passive message to students about administrative perceptions of fraternity involvement, which may create challenges for professionals hoping to build trust with members. Data focusing on how people perceive places can be challenging to collect, as sometimes even the participants may not be aware of how they are affected. Patton (2014) listed "experiencing empathy" as a strength of high-quality observations to suggest that researchers are able to experience settings similarly to the people they are studying by visiting those settings.

Study the Effect of Changes to Setting   Researchers sometimes change aspects of an environment to investigate potential effects. For example, practitioners at Indiana University–Purdue University Indianapolis (IUPUI) added chalkboard panels with questions to a little-used but highly trafficked campus space (Goldfinger, 2009). Observing student reactions to the panels, which included writing, reading, and initiating discussion about the content, revealed issues important to students, how they processed them, and the value of providing a space for engagement. Meade (2015) tested the effects of different posters with information about disinfecting gym equipment in campus recreation centers. Campus workers observed users' behaviors in rooms where different posters were displayed to determine which messaging was most effective in changing behavior.

Evaluate Learning Environments   A college campus is comprised of countless formal and informal learning environments. Formal learning spaces include classrooms and libraries, designated study areas, and laboratories. Informal learning spaces include residence halls and student unions, campus green spaces, dining facilities, and meeting rooms. Online spaces, facilitated by course management systems and social media, are also learning environments on campus. How college students learn and the ways practitioners and faculty work with them is influenced by these settings. The philosophical perspective on student affairs practice considers learning as a holistic activity that occurs regardless of place (American Council on Education, 1937). Understanding the role(s) of spaces (physical and online) in student learning is critical for creating, enhancing, and sustaining learning environments. Observational methods can provide insight into how students use, interact within, and create learning spaces (online and off) that enhance or inhibit learning.

Gain New Insights for Practice   Observation methods provide the unique ability to see the unseen or to perceive things that routinely escape awareness. Aspects of individuals' lives, such as choices, habits, and routines, may not be apparent to them. Observations by an outsider can offer new insights. For example, staff may not consciously realize why they typically sit in the same place in meetings or students may not recognize they avoid a certain route to get to their residence hall. A key to effective observation, according to Patton (2002), is being "open, discovery-oriented, and inductive." For example, in a study about roommate behaviors, Erlandson (2012) found nonverbal indicators were crucial to understanding roommate satisfaction. Using nonobtrusive observation methods, the researcher found that roommates who were highly concerned about sharing space were less relaxed and positive in their interactions with their roommates. This led to a recommendation for professional staff to be trained to watch for immediacy displays (such as tension and lack of positive affect toward one another) when discussing roommate conflict.

Complement Other Methods Observations often are used as supplemental data to provide context or lend validity to other methods. When used to support additional data collection, such as document review and interview data or descriptive statistics, observation can help researchers develop a deeper understanding about an issue. Findings may lead to recommendations for whom to select for interviews or which documents, images, or artifacts may be important but otherwise overlooked. For example, Literte (2010), in a study of the relationship between biracial college students and race-oriented student services, noted, "Observation provided another means to enhance my data collection. . . . Data attained from informal observation yielded contextual information to paint a fuller, more accurate picture of the campus sites and student populations" (p. 123).

Research Considerations

The basic design for observation research involves determining a source (person, place, event), negotiating access, gaining approval, and taking detailed notes. Variations relate to the depth of data collection and the availability of the observable phenomena. The extent of the observation also can be influenced by the richness of the sources and/or sites, the focus and perspective of the study, and the skill of the researcher. Each of these considerations can operate individually or in combination to affect the results of a study. Following is a list of decisions researchers consider when designing an observation study. Understanding these considerations supports an ability to read and evaluate observation research.

Identifying a Site. A primary consideration for observation is the accessibility of the site. Often, questions about access relate to whether a site is classified as public or private, due to various laws and regulations that have shaped and evolved with regard to campus spaces. It may be better to think about observable campus sites as accessible or not accessible, with the caveat that accessibility is a variable scale and individual contexts vary. For instance, a student union is often considered a public space, but certain areas may be designated as private depending on the use or time of day. In general, accessible sites on public campuses include outdoor and common areas in nonacademic or public buildings and public events. Less accessible sites on public campuses include instructional spaces in academic buildings, classrooms, and private events.

Negotiating Access. A researcher's role on campus influences access to data sites and sources. As with any type of data collection, a researcher with some affiliation to campus (such as being faculty or staff) will have easier access to data (individuals, documents, and sites) than a nonaffiliated researcher. The intent of the study also can influence accessibility of the site or setting. For example, in a study of gospel choir participants, Strayhorn (2011) used his familiarity first as an observer then as a participant-observer before, during, and after practice sessions to negotiate access to the site.

Gaining Approval. Observations can be completely nonobtrusive, meaning that a researcher would not directly interact with others and would be collecting data without anyone in the setting being aware. A study may be focused on routine behaviors in a public setting, and the researcher would not record information in a way that would identify any specific individual. In this case, institutional review board (IRB) approval for the research may seem unnecessary. However, this determination for approval should be left to an IRB, not to the researcher. Ethics reviews exist to help anticipate problems and how a researcher may handle them. What if, for example, the researcher witnessed a potentially harmful behavior? Rhoads (1995) faced this dilemma in a study of misogynistic behaviors in fraternities, ultimately deciding to advance a larger understanding of their culture.

Informing Participants. A major consideration for observation research is whether or not people being observed should be informed. In public or accessible settings, where there is no intent to identify individuals, this may not be necessary. Similarly, in classroom settings, the researcher may not want to alert individuals that they are conducting a study for concern that it may change their behaviors. A classic example of this is the "Hawthorne effect" (also referred to as the observer effect). In that study, researchers sought to improve worker productivity by manipulating aspects of the work environment. Researchers reexamining the data after the study suggested that the spike in productivity was due to the presence of the researchers (Sonnenfeld, 1985).

Collecting Data. Researchers typically either take open field notes or use an observation form when collecting data. The advantage of open field notes is their flexibility. This method provides the researcher with the unconstrained ability to record nearly anything in the setting. Unfortunately, observation can quickly become overwhelming without focus (Webb, Campbell, Schwartz, & Sechrest, 2000). Saunders and Cooper (2009) recommended developing a preset list of questions prior to beginning an observation. Chronology, key events, setting details, people, process, and issues should be recorded. The descriptions should be factual, accurate, and thorough without being cluttered by irrelevant minutia and trivia. A more structured approach is to use a predesigned observation form or checklist when in the field to record common behaviors or note the occurrence and frequency of specific behaviors and events. Emerson, Fretz, and Shaw (2011) recommended completing an initial observation to generate ideas and to understand the setting, then using these notes to develop a form. They cautioned that an observation should not simply turn into a counting activity, and that researchers should remain open to new data as they arise.

Associated Designs

Researchers often use observation methods to verify, supplement, or explore additional phenomena revealed from case study interviews. For example, Biddix (2017) was directed to specific study spaces by participants in his study about college study technology use and learning. Using grounded theory, researchers might develop or verify a conceptual model from observations, particularly about behavior and interactions. In phenomenology, researchers might focus on people, places, and events to clarify or illuminate the phenomenon of interest as it is experienced, in a naturalistic state. For example, in a study of hip-hop culture as related to sense of belonging on campus, Sule (2016) observed six campus events. The research led her to suggest that counterspaces (physical locations underrepresented students seek for self-affirmation and social support) can be transported to higher-education spaces; counterspaces on campus can embody diversity, and, as a cultural artifact, hip-hop can foster diversity outcomes.

Main Types and Variations of Observation Methods

Unlike other methods, there are no main or variation types of data collection for observation. Instead, observation is typically distinguished by common data collection approaches. Researchers select an approach by making choices about the sample selection, the role of the researcher, and the influence of the researcher. Table 7.1 is an overview of each data collection approach with associated options. A description of each follows with examples.

Table 7.1. Observation Data Collection Approaches and Options

	Data Collection Approaches		
	Sample Selection	Role of the Researcher	Influence of the Researcher
Data Collection Options	Time	Nonparticipant	Simple
	Location	Participant	Contrived
	Time-and-Location		
	Person		

Sample Selection. The focus of the study determines how researchers select a site. They generally use one of three procedures: time, location, or time-and-location sampling. A variation of this approach is person sampling, which focuses on an individual or group, regardless of the time or location.

- In *time sampling*, the researcher chooses a specific time at a location and observes the location one (or ideally more) days during that same time. In this case, the focus is on specific people, behaviors, or use of a space at that particular time. For example, the researcher might observe a single commuter student parking lot on campus at a specific time on multiple days to discover which days are busiest.
- In *location sampling*, the researcher chooses a specific location and observes the location one (or ideally more) days during different times. In this case, the focus is on specific people, behaviors, or use of a space beyond a specific time of day. For example, the researcher might observe a single commuter student parking lot on campus at multiple times to get a clearer sense of traffic patterns.
- In *time-and-location sampling*, the researcher chooses multiple locations and times and observes what takes place. For example, the researcher may want to know about commuter student parking across campus at various times to determine ways to reduce frustration for students seeking parking options.
- In *person sampling*, the researcher is concerned with how an individual or group behaves. Time and location may be considerations, but not the central focus. For example, the researcher might be interested in understanding a typical day on campus for a commuter student, so they may observe students over multiple times, locations, or days.

Role of the Researcher. The role of the observer may be nonparticipant, meaning they do not interact with the people, place, or event(s) they are observing, or participant-observer, meaning they interact with varying degrees of participation from fully participating to minor involvement (Patton, 2014). Related to non-participant observation is the conspicuousness of the researcher's role. A researcher may collect data overtly or covertly depending on whether or not participants know they are being observed.

- In *nonparticipant observation*, the researcher collects data in a location without direct interaction with people. The observer should not affect the site, setting, or individuals. For example, Matthews et al. (2009) rode the campus transit system as nonparticipant observers to understand how fraternity/sorority members enacted the values of their organizations in their dress and discussions. They described data collection in the following way: "Researchers began observations by noting natural occurrences to situate the environment. Also noted were details that might connote values, including student behaviors, conversation topics, and articles of clothing or other accoutrements" (p. 33).

- In *participant-observation*, the researcher intentionally becomes a noticeable part (or participant) in data collection. The observer typically interacts with others, although the level of interaction can vary. For example, some participant-observers are fully part of the research site while others maintain distance but may interact with participants by asking questions. Birnbaum (2013) collected data as a participant-observer to explore undergraduate students' self-presentations on social media. He described interacting directly with students' as they used Facebook, noting, "This immersion into SU student culture provided insights into the subjective logic and values on which the undergraduate community was built and the opportunity to feel, hear, and see the social experiences of my participants" (p. 159).

Influence of the Researcher. The researcher may choose to influence an observation in a simple or contrived way by creating conditions or stimuli in the setting that prompt observable changes.

- In a *simple observation*, the research has no control over the setting or participants. This is the more common and familiar approach. Using the prior example of transit system observations, Matthews et al. (2009) simply watched and listened to what occurred and recorded observations but did not change aspects of the environment.
- In a *contrived observation*, the researcher deliberately varies the setting in some way. Using the prior example of student self-presentation on Facebook, Birnbaum (2013) could have added comments to the students' profiles and observed the effects. Or, using a less directly interactive approach, he might have left information about Facebook profiles and security in the residents' campus mailboxes to see if it influenced what they posted.

Data Collection + Approach Examples

Rather than referring to a particular type of observation, researchers typically include information about the combination(s) of data collection approaches they used (sample selection, role of the researcher, influence of the researcher). For example, Matthews et al.'s (2009) study involved time-and-location sampling (researcher team members rode the same bus twice a week for 5 weeks), nonparticipant observation (researcher team members did not directly interact with fraternity/sorority members), and simple observation (researcher team members did not manipulate the setting). Conversely, in Birnbaum's (2013) study involving location sampling (collecting data from Facebook and in person), the researcher was a participant in data collection (also creating an account and posting on Facebook), and the observation remained simple as he did not intentionally stimulate changes such as facilitating online discussion.

Reading Observation Methods

When writing about observation methods, researchers typically describe the research procedures briefly in text and provide results as context in narrative format or incorporate findings with interview data. Tables or graphs generally are not used to display observation results. Unlike review or interview data, observation results seldom include quoted materials or images as examples. As a result, it can be difficult to determine which part(s) of the analyses or results directly correspond with the observations. In most cases, observation results either serve as the primary analysis of data, add legitimacy to a study as a secondary source or triangulation strategy, or provide context to a study to help situate or describe results. Following are three generalized ways observation methods appear in text along with steps for reading results.

Observation as Primary Analysis

When observation is the only method or a primary form of data collection, researchers either report results as reconstructed from field notes (an aggregate format), or they may provide descriptions (thick description or brief and illustrative). This arrangement is intended to help readers create a mental picture of the setting or what occurred. For example, in their study of espoused values among fraternity/sorority members riding a campus transit system, Matthews et al. (2009) described the theme of homogeneity in the following way:

> Nearly all riders were White, a higher concentration than the overall student body, which had a minority student enrollment of 10.65 percent in fall 2007. Virtually everyone wore expensive, name-brand clothing in similar styles and brands. Nearly all carried technological devices including cell phones and mp3 players, and students articulated the need to have up-to-date or "cool" cell phones. Most female students wore makeup, expensive jewelry, and had their hair styled. (p. 35)

Birnbaum's (2013) experiences collecting data from Facebook lent insights into students' online behaviors and the culture it exhibited. For example, one frequent observation he noted was when women changed their relationship status from single to in a relationship. He recalled:

I attributed this behavior to possible psychosocial or cognitive-structural stages related to identity and sexuality. When I asked my RAs about these observations, they suggested a more practical and dramaturgically consistent explanation: female students were simply signaling to unknown males that they were not interested in uninvited communications. (p. 159)

Words Researchers Use—Qualitative Terms

Holistic
Considering multiple aspects of a phenomenon. In a research context, a holistic approach uses multiple forms of data or data collection methods to describe or tell a more complete story.

Immersion
The researcher becomes embedded and invested in the setting. Immersion in research may include being involved or engaged in the activity or practice under study.

Thick Description
A detailed explanation that describes and/or enlightens the focus of the research (people, places, and/or events) in a way that the setting and context is meaningful to a nonobserver (the audience). This is also referred to as rich, thick description.

Observation as Supplemental Analysis

Researchers discuss their use of observation data as a means of generating questions for interviews, or to provide context for data analysis. Several examples illustrate this approach. McCoy and Winkle-Wagner (2015), in a multisite case study on the role of summer institutions in preparing students of color for doctoral programs, conducted observations of students both in class and in informal settings, such as during meals and walks across campus, to build an understanding of the settings and experiences. This gave the researchers greater insight into questions to ask during interviews, but also provided them with an opportunity to understand how their participants engaged with the campus, faculty, and their peers.

Ward, Thomas, and Disch (2014), in a study about mentoring relationships among undergraduate students, described using observation methods as a means of building themes for data analysis.

As part of her study of hip-hop culture, Sule (2016) observed six campus events: a poetry slam, two rap performances, two dance battles, and a hip-hop symposium.

Attending the events was important for her to see first-hand who attended, how participants interacted in the settings, and how culture was fostered and enacted. These observations served to "reveal the potential for hip-hop to engender the very form of interactional diversity championed by colleges" (p. 192).

Observation as Context or Description

Often, researchers aggregate results from observations with other forms of qualitative data collection to present a fuller picture of a setting. For example, Literte (2010) noted that using informal observation, along with archival data collection, "provided me with salient supplemental and contextual data, which allowed me to better depict the institutional environment within which student services and students themselves are acting" (p. 123).

Diaz-Espinoza (2015) offered examples in her dissertation focused on women's experiences in STEM. Walking around the same building as the women allowed her to experience some of the apprehensions they associated with the dimly lit hallways, as well as the negative feelings they described in seeing all-male images on fliers and posters. In her description of the first-floor atrium, she noted:

> Each glass image, bolted to the wall, contained a photo and description of the work done by the named engineer. The first woman appeared to be awarded this title in 2003. While this display of award recipients emphasized the work of several individuals and had visible ethnic diversity with several of them being African-American men, there was only one woman along the entire wall. I watched women walking by looking at these images often as they were waiting to enter the lecture hall that has an entrance near these images. (p. 45)

Guidelines for Reading Observation Research

- Understand the function.
- Recognize the approach.
- Determine the point of view.

Understand the Function Observation data can serve several functions in a study. Researchers should explain the function(s) when describing data collection, analysis, and reporting. When observation serves as a primary method, researchers typically describe the four relevant components of methodology. However, when observation is used as a secondary method (for context or to inform a primary method such as refining interviews), researchers seldom provide details about its role or how the data were analyzed or incorporated.

Recognize the Approach   The lack of main or variation types of observation methods requires unraveling the methodology to understand how the observation functions in a study. Sometimes, but seldom explicitly, researchers state their approach to sample selection, role, and influence. Understanding these facets of an observation study is critical to understanding how the method and purpose aligned with research techniques to yield results.

Determine the Point of View   When researchers write about observation, they relate what they see from either their point of view or from the perspective of others. This is an important distinction that skilled researchers work hard to capture and present. When taking the view of participants, researchers sometimes will include quotations but most often they present results in a more generalized manner. This is a purposeful distinction that should reflect the overall purpose of the study.

Evaluating Observation Research

Rigorous observations can yield powerful insights as a primary or supplemental method, revealing aspects about a phenomenon that are otherwise difficult or not possible to learn. Conversely, poorly done observations (for example, working with a vague or absent focus, failing to take good notes, spending little time in the field, misinterpreting or overinterpreting what is observed) can result in faulty assumptions that confuse instead of enhance study results. Attentive researchers help minimize these concerns by describing the purpose and function of the observation, providing a systematic description of data collection and analysis, and recognizing limitations and personal influences (subjectivity). Following are considerations for evaluating observation research.

Questions for Evaluating Observation Research

- Did the researchers adequately describe the setting and context of the observation?
- Is the point of view of the observation apparent?
- What strategies did the researcher use to enhance credibility and believability?
- Could the study be replicated with the information provided?

Did the Researchers Adequately Describe the Setting and Context of the Observation?   A description of the setting should include details about the place, time, and frequency of the data collection. This setting is important for understanding situational influences. Readers should be able to determine why a particular place, time, and context were selected. The answer should not be convenience. Ideally, the researcher(s) chose the setting and context because it was optimal for answering the research question or addressing a focus in the study. Even if the choices were based on a typical day, the criteria for determining what is typical should be included. If there are special contextual circumstances, these should also be described.

Is the Point of View of the Observation Apparent?   Observation can be conducted from the point of view of the researcher or the individual(s) being observed. It is important that the researcher indicate the point of view, either directly or in a way that can be inferred, as perspective can significantly influence the results. This consideration is particularly important when the focus of the study is on people. In a blended approach, rich, thick descriptions might be accompanied by quotations from the participant(s) interviewed from their point of view and as they interpret and/or experience a setting or event. The way the setting is described, either by the researcher or participant(s) or both, can affect the reader's interpretation of the findings and should be clear in the results.

What Strategies Did the Researcher Use to Enhance Credibility and Believability? Conceptions of believability are vital in qualitative research, especially given the longstanding criticism of subjectivity. To enhance credibility across audiences, researchers should include details about the accuracy of the data collection. For example, if data collection involved multiple researchers observing the same phenomenon, the methods section should include information about how they ensured congruence. If data collection involved multiple locations or times, researchers should discuss consistency (or lack thereof) between sessions to strengthen reliability. Finally, whether observing people, places, or events, the exact same circumstances rarely occur with multiple observations. Often, researchers will report similarities but fail to report any differences or anomalies which should raise questions about authenticity.

Could the Study Be Replicated With the Information Provided?   It is not always possible or feasible, within the space constraints of a published study, to provide enough details that another researcher could replicate a study. However, sufficient information should be included to provide a clear understanding of the data collection and analysis processes. This includes techniques used for taking field notes, contextual information about the time and setting, and a description of the details documented. Patton (2002) noted, "the quality of observational reports is judged by the extent to which that observation permits the reader to enter into and understand the situation described" (p. 262). The critical question is, given the details provided, could another researcher conduct the study and reach similar conclusions?

Applying Observation Research

Practitioners gain significant insight both directly from observation-focused studies and indirectly from contextual information presented from observation-supplemented results. Following are some suggestions for how to apply results from observation studies to student affairs practice.

Opportunities for Applying Observation Research

- Learn about people to understand experiences.
- Learn about places to enhance environments.
- Learn about events to improve effectiveness.

Learn About People to Understand Experiences Observation data can reveal how people are affected by places, how people affect places, how people behave in specific places, and what might be changed to influence behaviors. These insights can be applied to practice by considering how changing demographics on college campuses benefit from or may be constrained by physical and online aspects of campus spaces. For example, Diaz-Espinoza (2015) considered how the physical aspects of an engineering building related to women's perceptions of their success. In addition to walking the same halls, she attended classes, visited faculty offices, and observed study spaces from the perspective of a female STEM major as a way to understand participants' experiences. In considering the large classrooms with immovable desks and constrained study spaces, she observed:

> The physical space within the engineering building appeared neither outwardly welcoming nor discouraging to women but there were elements that made me question how much students in general were welcomed in the space to study or build community. There was very little space for students to sit outside of a classroom and the study desks with lined panels did not encourage collaboration. (p. 52)

Birnbaum's (2013) study about self-presentation on Facebook revealed how students presented themselves (through pictures and personal information), which the researcher labeled as taking on one of six identities: the partier, the socialite, the risk-taker, the comic, the institutional citizen, and the eccentric. Observational methods suggested how student behavior was influenced by digital space, which allowed them to load numerous images quickly, post public statements, hold private conversations, and reveal details about relationship status. Brimbaum (2013) noted, "The advent of affordable digital technologies make it possible for nearly everyone to document and display their daily activities and social interactions, thus blurring the boundaries between public and private spaces" (p. 168).

Perspectives From the Field—How Does Observation Research Inform Practice?

Observations are first-hand data collected by a researcher. Observing participants and their environments can be a powerful experience and comes with significant responsibility. Ranging from complete observer to active participant, researchers choose how they want to interact with their participants and the level to which they become a part of their own study. Learning how to consciously observe environmental factors takes a great deal of practice but adds a richness that goes beyond the second-hand recollection of an interview.

When studying women in engineering, I observed the same hallways and classrooms they walked daily. It gave me insight into how unwelcoming these spaces were for them as they navigated majors historically underrepresented by women. I saw desks with dividers between them, dark hallways in all directions, and almost no furniture that allowed multiple students to sit together. Directly observing participants or their environment allows researchers to present a richer context in which the reader can orient findings. In this case, it was important to me that readers could picture the hallways and classrooms these women in engineering experienced.

Observation data also helps a researcher think differently about questions he or she asks participants. While I did not ask about the engineering building directly when conducting my interviews, because I had seen the space, I did ask participants to describe where they spent most of their time as an engineering student and with whom they interacted on a daily basis. Beyond my dissertation study, these observations equipped me with data-driven ideas for the dean about ways we might improve the physical space within the building to better facilitate academic collaboration and community among engineering students. I also worked to help connect women in engineering with one another outside of the classroom by creating programs centered on community building and sharing their experiences.

Crystal Diaz-Espinoza—Director of Enrollment and Alumni Services, Diana R. Garland School of Social Work, Baylor University

Learn About Places to Enhance Environments   Results from observation studies focused on places can reveal how a location is used (intended versus actual), how adaptable it may be to its use, what may enhance or inhibit use, and what might be changed to influence use. These insights can be applied to practice by considering how changes in the environment, minor or major, could enhance student learning experiences. Using observation methods to learn about and to optimize campus environments is prevalent in studies about academic libraries (Oliveira, 2016) and student unions (Rief, 2014). Understanding how students use campus spaces has benefits for renovation as well as strategic planning.

Goldfinger's (2009) research on Democracy Plaza revealed how aspects of an environment could be used to promote learning. The plaza, constructed under a breezeway at the center of the campus, evolved into an area promoting free speech when chalkboards were added to facilitate discussion for civic-oriented events. Any member of the campus community could add to the discussion at any time by posing or answering "provocative and constructive" questions. In addition to details about the origin and construction of the plaza, Goldfinger (2009) provided examples of the discussions. Recalling ACPA's call to align campus spaces to student learning, the researcher concluded Democracy Plaza was a good example of the innovative use of public space "where people go to read, write, hear, and talk about issues of public concern. . . . There is no reason why Democracy Plaza's success cannot be repeated at other campuses as long as proper attention is given to location, maintenance, and programming" (p. 76).

In her study of roommate boundaries in residential life, Erlandson (2012) used data collected from observations to evaluate measures of nonverbal immediacy, or behaviors that send messages about approachability and positive affect towards others. Specifically, the researcher wanted to understand how nonverbal immediacy and territoriality (real or perceived boundaries in the same room) affected roommate satisfaction. The study was conducted in an office configured to resemble a typical living room. Roommates (51 pairs) were given a prompt and 10 minutes to discuss an event that required them to negotiate an issue such as quiet times or chores. The researcher videotaped their interactions and coded the nonverbal interactions using a predetermined scale. Combined with a survey of territoriality (boundary defining), results showed that students who were more concerned with having personal space were less satisfied with their roommates. Erlandson (2012) noted, "Perhaps a sense of private space is more important to satisfaction than the personalization of that space. In other words, roommates may care more about having a desk for their exclusive use than they care about the kinds of posters or personalized pictures that are displayed in or on that space" (p. 57).

Learn About Events to Improve Effectiveness   Numerous activities take place on a college campus daily, ranging from large sporting events, concerts, and talks to small gatherings of students raising awareness about a campus issue. While there are some apparent facts about events (such as start time and duration, number of people in attendance, features of the setting), people experience them in different ways. Observing people's reactions offers details about who participates in terms of student demographics, how they engage, who is missing, how topics or events affect individuals (directly and indirectly), and pragmatic insight on space and time management. These insights can be applied to practice by considering how the space, time, content, and context of an event can shape outcomes.

Understanding how people and places interact in an event can influence planning, policy, and practice for its development and management. This understanding also can add insight about how these factors might interact to produce both positive and negative outcomes. Unfortunately, research focused on campus events is largely absent in student affairs publications. Insights gained from observations of orientation, campus activities, and commencement could considerably advance a practical understanding of their effectiveness.

Building Your Review Skillset

Observation can yield considerable insight about the people, places, and events central to student affairs practice. It can be used to build knowledge directly from context and provide awareness about behaviors that otherwise might not be visible. Observation skills can enhance practitioner abilities in watching and listening, as well as in precise record keeping and note taking. These skills also build logic and puzzle-solving abilities by emphasizing questioning (both of people and places). Finally, observation-informed studies can direct assessment and planning efforts by enhancing what is known about the effects of people, places, and events in learning environments.

Training to be a skilled observer requires two broad skillsets: the ability to observe and the ability to record. Patton (2014, p. 331) expanded these skills as learning to pay attention, writing descriptively, acquiring expertise in recording field notes, knowing how to separate detail from trivia, triangulating observations, and acknowledging the strengths and limitations of one's perspective. Research courses in student affairs seldom emphasize observation as a primary field method. Learners seeking formal training should consider coursework in anthropology, communication, psychology, or sociology, which have deeper traditions of incorporating observation into primary research. Self-directed learners could pair Patton's (2014) chapter on observation methods with Emerson et al.'s (2011) guide to writing field notes.

References

American Council on Education. (1937). The student personnel point of view. *American Council on Education Studies* (Series I, Vol. I, no. 3).

Biddix, J. P. (2017). *The convergence of mobile technology, social media, and online and collaborative practices* (Unpublished manuscript). Department of Educational Leadership and Policy Studies, The University of Tennessee, Knoxville.

Birnbaum, M. G. (2013). The fronts students use: Facebook and the standardization of self-presentations. *Journal of College Student Development, 54*(2), 155–171.

Diaz-Espinoza, C. R. (2015). *You kind of have to prove it: Gender microaggressions within the lived experiences of women in engineering* (Unpublished doctoral dissertation). The University of Tennessee, Knoxville.

Emerson, R. M., Fretz, R. I., & Shaw, L. L. (2011). *Writing ethnographic fieldnotes.* Chicago, IL: University of Chicago Press.

Erlandson, K. (2012). Stay out of my space: Territoriality and nonverbal immediacy as predictors of roommate satisfaction. *The Journal of College and University Housing, 38*(2), 46–61.

Goldfinger, J. (2009). Democratic plaza: A campus space for civic engagement. *Innovative Higher Education, 34*(2), 69–77.

Literte, P. E. (2010). Revising race: How biracial students are changing and challenging student services. *Journal of College Student Development, 51*(2), 115–134.

Marshall, C., & Rossman, G. B. (1995). *Designing qualitative research.* Thousand Oaks, CA: Sage.

Matthews, H., Featherstone, L., Bluder, L., Gerling, A. J., Loge, S., & Messenger, R. B. (2009). Living your letters: Assessing congruence between espoused and enacted values of one fraternity/sorority community. *Oracle: The Research Journal of the Association of Fraternity Advisors, 4*(1), 29–41.

McCoy, D. L., & Winkle-Wagner, R. (2015). Bridging the divide: Developing a scholarly habitus for aspiring graduate students through summer bridge programs participation. *Journal of College Student Development, 56*(5), 423–439.

Meade, T. (2015). Disinfect the Rec: Creating and implementing a disinfection campaign at gyms using the theory of planned behavior. *Recreational Sports Journal, 39,* 157–169.

Oliveira, S. M. (2016). Space preference at James White Library: What students really want. *The Journal of Academic Librarianship, 42,* 355–367.

Patton, M. Q. (2002). *Qualitative evaluation and research methods* (3rd ed.). Thousand Oaks, CA: Sage.

Patton, M. Q. (2014). *Qualitative research & evaluation methods: Integrating theory and practice* (4th ed.). Thousand Oaks, CA: Sage.

Reif, Z. (2014). *Building community through physical space: A visual ethnography of college union utilization by community college transfer students* (Unpublished doctoral dissertation). Texas Tech University, Lubbock.

Rhoads, R. A. (1995). Whales tales, dog piles, and beer goggles: An ethnographic case study of fraternity life. *Anthropology and Education Quarterly, 26*(3), 306–323.

Russell, R. V., & Kovacs, A. (2003). Unobtrusive measures. In F. K. Stage & K. Manning (Eds.), *Research in the college context: Approaches and methods* (pp. 63–80). New York, NY: Brunner-Routledge.

Saunders, K., & Cooper, R. M. (2009). Instrumentation. In J. H. Schuh & Associates (Eds.), *Assessment methods for student affairs* (pp. 107–140). San Francisco, CA: Jossey-Bass.

Sonnenfeld, J. A. (1985). Shedding light on the Hawthorne studies. *Journal of Organizational Behavior, 6*(2), 111–130.

Strayhorn, T. L. (2011). Singing in a foreign land: An exploratory study of gospel choir participation among African American undergraduates at a predominantly White institution. *Journal of College Student Development, 52*(2), 137–153.

Sule, V. T. (2016). Hip-hop is the healer: Sense of belonging and diversity among hip-hop collegians. *Journal of College Student Development, 57*(2), 181–196.

Ward, E. G., Thomas, E. T., & Disch, W. B. (2014). Mentor service themes emergent in a holistic, undergraduate peer-mentoring experience. *Journal of College Student Development, 55*(6), 563–579.

Webb, E. J., Campbell, D. T., Schwartz, R. D., & Sechrest, L. (2000). *Unobtrusive measures.* Thousand Oaks, CA: Sage.

CHAPTER EIGHT

INTERVIEWING INDIVIDUALS AND GROUPS

Learning Outcomes

By the end of this chapter, you should be able to:

- Understand the purpose and role of interview methods.
- Differentiate between the major types of interview techniques.
- Read interview data in journal articles and reports.
- Evaluate interview methods based on how data are collected, analyzed, and reported.
- Apply interpretations of interview methods to student affairs practice.

Interviewing involves identifying key informants, determining questions to ask, recording responses, and (often) seeking others who can confirm, contradict, or otherwise provide additional perspectives on a topic. Interviews typically are highly interactive research methods, requiring the researcher to cooperate directly with the individuals or groups (Maxwell, 2013). Gerard (1959) referred to an interview as "a conversation with a purpose" and emphasized both getting and giving information as part of the "art of listening" (p. 126). Unlike other methods, interviews add considerable flexibility to data collection by allowing the instrument (often the researcher) the ability to adjust questions as needed during an interview. Through interaction, the interviewer and participant cocreate meaning (Corbin & Strauss, 2014). This major advantage is also its greatest criticism. Both aspects will be discussed in this chapter.

Interviewing is the most prevalent form of qualitative data collection in the college context (Ortiz, 2016). Researchers utilize two basic types of interview methods: individual and focus groups. These can be further differentiated by the structure of the questions or by theoretical, philosophical, or disciplinary perspectives. *Individual interviews* typically are scheduled and can involve highly structured questionnaires or a loose guide with questions serving as prompts, and can take place multiple times depending on the nature and depth of the research. *Focus groups* typically involve small groups that are tightly focused on a specific topic or group perspective, and can take place once or multiple times. Individual interviews generally involve asking questions, and focus groups generally involve facilitating conversations. This chapter begins with a general overview of interviews then describes how to understand, read, evaluate, and apply results from interview-based studies.

Understanding Interview Research

In the beginning of his chapter on qualitative interviewing, M. Q. Patton (2002) noted "The very popularity of interviewing may be its undoing as an inquiry method . . . so much interviewing is being done so badly that its credibility may be undermined" (p. 340). Qualitative interviewing is not a journalistic or simply question-and-answer activity, focused on gathering facts from participants and communicating responses. Skilled interviewers are highly effective researchers. Knowing who and what to ask, when to dwell on a topic, push a point, or change directions, and how to capture perspectives requires considerable expertise. Effectively used, interviewing is a shared conversation intended to capture an experience from someone's perspective. Qualitative researchers describe interviews as "collaborative accomplishments" rather than simply "a pipeline for transporting knowledge" (Holstein & Gubrium, 2004, p. 141).

Describing the general purpose of interviewing, Seidman (2006) emphasized the need to understand the "lived experience of other people and the meaning they make of that experience" (p. 9). This is very different from simply getting answers to questions. Researchers using interview methods seek to gain insight beyond facts and general observations. Some researchers focus on one or a few participants to build understanding. Others seek multiple perspectives to gain a more generalized perspective, while still preserving a constructivist focus on individuality. Ortiz (2016) clarified interviewing as "immersion in data" (p. 47). Depending on the goals of a study, capturing and working to understand perspectives helps researchers uncover ways to sustain, enhance, or change experiences. While it may seem more advantageous to gather the most possible perspectives about a research topic or problem through survey methods, carefully collected interview data can highlight individual perspectives often lost in aggregated responses.

Interviewing Individuals and Groups

Interview methods allow researchers to uncover personal realities or group perspectives that make up understandings, acknowledging that experiences are embedded in environments, such as organizations or structures and social interactions within those environments. The *Student Personnel Point of View* values the needs and experiences of the individual student as a means of facilitating success (American Council on Education, 1937). Interviewing individuals and groups offers an opportunity to understand those experiences. Published interview research in student affairs ranges from theoretical perspectives focusing on constructing and revealing meaning to more pragmatic considerations that reveal successes, challenges, and opportunities. Following is a list of ways researchers use interviews in student affairs research.

Reasons for Understanding Interviewing

- Learn about programs and services.
- Understand common and conflicting experiences.
- Add overlooked, missing, or marginalized perspectives
- Explore personal or sensitive issues.
- Reveal known or unknown processes.
- Examine complex issues.

Learn About Programs and Services   Researchers conduct interviews about programs and services to learn about associated successes, challenges, and outcomes. Understanding individual and group perspectives can have broader implications for enhancing the design or redesign of learning experiences. For example, Bradbury and Mather (2009) conducted interviews to understand the integration experiences of first-generation Appalachian college students. The researchers found that the students spent less time with roommates and had a difficult time interacting with diverse individuals. This finding raised questions about the practice of pairing roommates with different backgrounds to facilitate peer interaction and build community. Almeida (2016) used sense-making theory (how one makes sense of information based on prior knowledge and aspects of the social context) to explore the experiences of Latino students at low-income high schools with a college readiness program. Part of the researcher's argument for the significance of the study was to "help those who design and implement a program like the EAP to do so in ways that best serve the students who can arguably benefit most—low-income and Latino students" (pp. 330–331).

Understand Common and Conflicting Experiences   A fundamental acknowledgment of qualitative research is that each individual experiences the world in a personal, unique way. Interviews can enlighten how people's backgrounds, prior experiences, and viewpoints create different interpretations of experiences. For example, Tillapaugh and Haber-Curran (2016) found that the experiences of male leaders of campus organizations were influenced by the socialization they experienced growing up, their institutional environment, and the influence of peers within their organizations. Similarly, Silver and Jakeman (2014) interviewed student affairs master's students who considered leaving the field early to pursue other careers. Although all students began their graduate program with the intent of pursuing a student affairs career, the researchers uncovered ways these intentions were initially formed and how they changed for some students during their program of study.

Add Overlooked, Missing, or Marginalized Perspectives A considerable amount of research in student affairs, particularly in the past 30 years, has been focused on student development based on college experiences (L. D. Patton, Renn, Guido, & Quaye, 2016). As acknowledgment of the broad diversity of individuals in college expanded, researchers worked to capture and enlighten their experiences and perspectives. Literte (2010) interviewed students and administrators at two universities to clarify misunderstandings about race-based student services (e.g., Office of Black Services). Literte's work challenged the effectiveness of support services for a broader group of marginalized students and advocated for a reconsideration of work with biracial students, in particular. Vaccaro (2015) added the unique voices of student veterans to research on socialization and campus programming to highlight how within-group differences affect student experiences. Specifically, findings revealed a common misperception that veterans (as a group) experience higher education similarly.

Explore Personal or Sensitive Issues Promoting student and staff success involves understanding influences that inhibit or limit potential. Researchers have explored aspects of identity, previous experiences, and ongoing concerns beyond academic issues that impact success. Individuals often conceal or guard their issues and concerns, making it difficult to learn what affects them. Skilled interviewers work to build rapport with participants that can lead to these revelations. Some researchers recommend taking a personal interest and working from an advocacy perspective to help by offering counsel or referral. Others take a more distant approach at gathering experiences, prompting interviewees to work through sensitive issues to reveal potential solutions that can help others. Jaggers and Iverson (2012) used focus group interviews to explore the experiences of Black undergraduate men living in residential halls at a predominantly White institution (PWI). The students relived experiences of roommate conflict, including interracial tensions, negative racial stereotypes, unevenly applied disciplinary actions, and lack of support.

Reveal Known or Unknown Processes   Interviews can focus on how things are done, which can reveal processes known or unknown to participants. For individuals, processes might be developmental, such as acculturation or socialization. Theorists construct models based on interviews with individuals and groups whose experiences and perspectives reveal (or create, depending on perspective) developmental frames, phases, or stages (L. D. Patton et al., 2016). An example is King and Baxter Magolda's (2005) description of intercultural maturity, a developmental process the researchers hypothesized as a model based on interviews with students. Interviews might also be used to render or reveal organizational processes. In a study focused on leadership development among women in activist organizations, Biddix (2010) uncovered an engagement model showing how female leaders used technology to get involved, stay involved, and get others involved.

Examine Complex Issues   The changing nature of higher education and student demographics means that the boundaries of student affairs work continue to be shaped, expanded, and refined (Zhang & Associates, 2011). An example is the term engagement, which is considered a product of student affair work for its link to graduation and retention (Kuh, 2009). While there have been efforts to standardize the term through operationalization, the field continues to struggle to identify a common definition. Wolf-Wendel, Ward, and Kinzie (2009) considered this problem using interviews with experts and scholars to explore the concepts of involvement, engagement, and integration. The researchers noted that the terminology is confusing because "all three [terms] focus on student development and success, each concept contributing a unique and nuanced piece of understanding to the puzzle" (p. 426). Reybold, Halx, and Jimenez (2008) interviewed student affairs professionals to understand their conception and application of professional ethics. The researchers identified different dimensions of ethics, concluding that the "intentional and purposeful practice of modeling professional decision making (at all levels, but especially by senior student affairs staff members) in the context of daily interaction and conversation will provide the reminders needed to encourage ethicality in higher education" (p. 123).

Research Considerations

The basic process for interviewing involves writing questions, identifying individuals or groups who have a valuable perspective, asking questions, recording and then transcribing responses, analyzing data, and presenting the results. Research considerations relate to specifying and identifying informants, choosing a questionnaire format, and collecting perspective and meaning. Following is an overview of these considerations for conducting interview research.

Specifying and Identifying Informants. An interview can be an in-depth exploration of a very specific topic, or it may be a general overview of an issue. In either case, the researcher may need one or many participants to explore the topic fully. For example, a narrative study focusing on the experiences of one person as she navigated the complexities of a job change in student affairs may only include one person with questions focused only on the event, context, and related influences, such as Jones's (2016) study of Dr. Ruth Simmons's journey to the presidency as the first African American women at Brown University. A study more broadly focused on career mobility in student affairs may require more perspectives to portray a broader look at the topic, as Biddix et al.'s (2012) look at women's career paths and choices leading to the senior student affairs officer (SSAO) in a community college.

Researchers identifying sources have a variety of sampling options, ranging from convenience (generally not recommended) to random selection. Because interviews are generally focused on exploring or understanding a specific phenomenon, most methods for identifying participants are either based on specific criteria (criterion sample) or selected based on recommendations (snowball sample). To identify a criterion sample, researchers specify a shared phenomenon, experience, or event and find participants who meet the criteria. To identify a snowball sample, researchers identify information-rich sources based on recommendations from informants. The process continues (in other words, snowballs) until data collection is complete.

Developing a Questionnaire. Researchers often develop questions or topic prompts before interviewing participants. The types of questions can vary based on the focus of the interview. For example, an interviewer may ask about background/demographics, experiences and behaviors, opinions and values, feelings, knowledge or factual information, or sensory experiences (Schuh, Biddix, Dean, & Kinzie, 2016). Questionnaires also differ by format; specifically, the degree of standardization and structure of the questions. Berg (2004) described questionnaires as a continuum ranging from formal (or directed) to informal (or nondirected). Most student affairs researchers refer to three basic formats of interview questionnaires: structured, semistructured, and unstructured. Each format might be used to interview individuals or groups. Table 8.1 summarizes the key features of each approach.

A standardized questionnaire is highly structured and might be described as facilitating a formal interview. It is contrasted by an unstructured questionnaire that tends to take a more casual or conversational approach. The terms formal and casual do not suggest how an interviewer behaves during the interview, but how the questions are phrased and ordered. A semistructured questionnaire, prominently used in student affairs research, is a blend of both approaches. Specific questions are listed and the approach can be more or less formal or structured. A semistructured questionnaire provides the flexibility to alter interviews or pursue specific topics, as needed based on the direction, flow, and content of the interview.

Table 8.1. Interview Questionnaire Continuum

Structured	Semistructured	Unstructured
Highly standardized	Moderately standardized	Loosely standardized
All questions must be asked	Questions are listed but not all required	May only have one question or topic
Question order is followed exactly	Question order can be modified	No specific question order
Emphasizes standardization	Emphasizes flexibility	Emphasizes exploration

Words Researchers Use—Instrument/Guide/Protocol/ Questionnaire

Synonyms for questionnaire include instrument, guide, or protocol. Although there are some theoretical differences in the terms, they are most often used synonymously in student affairs research based on researcher preference. For purposes of clarity, instrument should be thought of as a category for data collection formats, so that a survey is also a type of research instrument, as is an observation form. Following this logic, guides or questionnaires are types of instruments used to collect interview data. A difference is that a guide typically is used when researchers develop topics and ask questions based on these as opposed to a questionnaire where most questions are composed beforehand. While a protocol is sometimes used to describe a questionnaire, it might be more precisely thought of as the steps and format of an interview.

Gathering Perspective and Making Meaning. Ortiz (2016) described interviewing as "[revealing] the varying perspectives participants have regarding the research problem in order to obtain a deep understanding of the interaction between the participant, setting, and topic under study" (p 47). Conceptualized by M. Q. Patton (2002), "We interview to find out what is in and on someone else's mind, to gather their stories" (p. 341). The concept of perspective is fundamental to this goal. Put simply, perspective is how someone views or sees the world. What someone sees can be affected by their background and identity, prior events they experienced, what they have been exposed to (or not) related to the topic, or any other influence. Another common word for this is lens, which invokes the image of each person having their own glasses to see the world. The need to view a problem through someone's perspective illustrates the complexity of interviewing. Simply asking questions does not allow a researcher to arrive at perspective. Keeping with the image, the skilled researcher attempts to see through the participant's lens to understand the participant's perspective.

The concept of meaning can have multiple connotations depending on how researchers use it. From a constructivist standpoint, meaning has to do with how individuals view and make sense of their world. Each person experiences an individual reality by interpreting and making meaning of personal experiences. From a data collection standpoint, researchers ask questions to solicit the meaning during an interview. From a data analysis standpoint, researchers attempt to make meaning of realities by describing and depicting them from the perspective the interviewee provided. From a data interpretation standing, the researcher interprets participants' meanings as coexisting with their own perspectives, which creates a shared meaning. In summary, the meaning-making process is developed with:

1. The interview participant.
2. The researcher.
3. How the researcher interprets and presents the information.

Perspectives From the Field—Using Interviews for Research

Interviews are most likely the most commonly used method for collecting detailed information from participants. They are useful in that they provide us both content and process. We learn insight into what the participant shared, but interviews also allow us to see how participants respond, providing additional insights. Interviews are both a methodological and research tool, in that they influence research design and form the foundation of the methods employed (i.e., grounded theory, phenomenological, narrative, etc.). We are able to use the insights of interview research in our qualitative and quantitative designs to understand numerous student populations.

Whether the researcher utilizes unstructured, semistructured, or structured interviews and regardless of the delivery of these interviews (face to face, email, phone, focus groups, etc.), interview research provide us with a deeper understanding of social phenomena and experiences of our students. Much of our work in student affairs and higher education is about serving marginalized groups and those who have had their voices silenced, those impacted and underserved by institutional systems. As such, effective interviewing allows for giving voice from our participants as they share their experiences. In short, they help us get the story behind the student's experience. As these student narratives emerge, the narratives help us refine our theories and assumptions about student groups and populations.

Tony W. Cawthon—Alumni Professor of Educational and Organizational Leadership Development, Clemson University

Associated Designs

Most often, researchers use interviews as primary data sources in qualitative studies. Following is a listing of the major qualitative research designs in student affairs with examples of how interviews were incorporated.

Basic—Silver and Jakemen (2014) used basic interpretive qualitative interviews to understand master's students' perceptions of student affairs and their future careers.

Case Study—Garcia and Okhidoi (2015) considered culturally relevant practices intended to meet diverse students' needs at Hispanic Serving Institutions (HSIs).

Ethnography—Nathan (2005) interviewed students about their first-year experience while becoming a freshman student.

Grounded Theory—Ward, Thomas, and Disch (2014) studied mentoring practices to create a theoretical framework for understanding student experiences.

Narrative—Mintz (2011) used narrative-based interviews to enlighten transgendered student experiences on campus.

Phenomenology—Harrison (2014) used phenomenological interviewing to explore ways student affair professionals learned advocacy skills within and beyond graduate study.

Main Types of Interviews

Student affairs researchers typically distinguish two main types of interview methods: individual interviews and focus groups. Researchers sometimes use both in a single study to obtain different perspectives. Kneiss, Havice, and Cawthon (2015) used both types to inform their study of second-year transitions for African American students. Following is their rationale:

> Focus groups served as the primary means of collecting data, and secondary sources of data, such as key informant interviews, observations at events, and artifacts, were also utilized (Yin, 2009). Compared to individual interviews, focus groups allowed participants to discuss their experiences at a PWI more freely among a group of peers (Krueger & Casey, 2000). Additionally, since the primary researcher's race is White, focus groups allowed for more candid discussion among a group of same-race peers. (p. 149)

A brief overview of individual interviews and focus groups follows. Next is a description of four variations used in student affairs research: basic, exploratory, narrative, and phenomenological.

Individual Interviews. An *individual interview* is a direct approach to qualitative data collection using open-ended questions or prompts to gain perspectives from individuals. Individual interview studies may include one person or several. Either the individual or the phenomenon of interest can be the focus of the study. An interview study, for example, might include only one individual who represents a unique case, such as a dean of students. Individual interviews with this participant (the focus of the study) might explore her career pathway. A study with multiple individual interviews could also focus on the position of the dean of students, but include multiple individuals to explore similar or conflicting aspects of the pathway to the position (the focus of the study).

Focus Groups. A *focus group* is a direct approach to qualitative data collection using open-ended questions or prompts to gain perspectives from a group that shares one or more characteristics. A researcher intentionally selects participants based on specific criteria, which allows them to gain insight from group interactions about a topic. A focus group is not simply an interview with a group of people. According to Savin-Baden and Major (2012), a focus group involves a limited number of individuals who, "through conversation with each other, provide information about a specific topic, issue or subject" (p. 375). Because of the emphasis on encouraging and promoting interaction, a focus group can reveal group dynamics and social processes.

Perspectives From the Field—How Are Focus Groups Beneficial in Student Affairs Research?

Focus groups are incredibly effective ways of soliciting, producing, and making sense of data as part of research, as well as assessment projects. One of the real benefits of conducting focus groups is the ability to check for shared understandings of lived experiences, along with the places that no consensus for meaning exists. The opportunity to discuss these (mis)alignments for further meaning is invaluable. This data collection method can also be part of the analytic technique, as is the case when used within the framework of collective memory work. I recently completed a research study on the experiences of White faculty at historically Black colleges and universities and employed collective memory work as a participatory action research methodology to understand the root and collective phenomenon of being a White faculty member in the setting. Hosting a focus group allowed for participants to contribute their unique perspectives on the stories shared by others. The push and pull and desire to find meaning across participants could only really happen in a nurturing focus group setting.

Needham Yancey Gulley—Assistant Professor of Higher Education, Student Affairs, Western Carolina University

Variations of Interviews

Variations of interviews are based on different perspectives. Merriam (2009) identified six types of interviews based on philosophical orientation and two based on disciplinary perspective. M. Q. Patton (2014) classified 12 types of interviews, differentiating each by the purpose or focus of a specific inquiry, as well as theoretical, philosophical, and methodological approaches to data collection and analysis. Following are four common approaches used in student affairs research.

Basic Interview. A *basic interview* is an in-depth individual or focus group interview that does not follow a specific perspective. A basic interview is characterized as an in-depth focus aimed at eliciting perspective and meaning. In most cases when researchers use interview methods (and do not indicate a guiding perspective), they are likely following a basic interview approach. Similar to Merriam's (2009) description of basic qualitative research, M. Q. Patton (2014) referred to this interviewing format as pragmatic, describing the approach as asking "straightforward questions about real-world issues aimed at getting straightforward answers that can yield practical and useful insights" (p. 436). The emphasis remains on "[building] a rich understanding of a person, setting, or situation through the perspective of those experiencing it" (Schuh et al., 2016, p. 149).

Exploratory Interview. An *exploratory interview* is a focus group interview that broadly explores an issue or topic to develop a more specific research question or agenda. Typically, a group is asked open-ended questions as a way to develop a focus on a specific topic or issue. The findings can be used within the same study to refine subsequent data collection (for example, a mixed methods approach) or as recommendations for continued research. For example, Kinzie (2010) led focus groups with academic deans, provosts, presidents, and directors of institutional research from a variety of 2- and 4-year institutions to learn about the role and prioritization of learning outcomes in assessment efforts.

Narrative Interview. A *narrative interview* is an in-depth interview with an individual aimed at understanding an experience as narrated by the person who experienced it. This type of interview is typically conducted in multiple sessions to relate the story of a single individual (referred to as a life-history) or to identify themes from several individuals that converge across stories describing a common experience. For example, Broido, Brown, Stygles, and Bronkema (2015) interviewed women working in administrative and faculty positions at a single institution to learn about their experiences with gendered dynamics over a 25-year career. Although the researchers did not specify their approach as narrative, their method description is aligned with its basic tenets:

We conducted individual semistructured, face-to-face interviews lasting 30–180 minutes. Interview questions focused on work history; gender-related changes in institutional policies, culture, or climate over time; experiences of sexism or sexual harassment; and the relationship between work and family life. (p. 604)

Phenomenological Interview. A *phenomenological interview* focuses on capturing perspectives from lived-through moments, experiences, and remembered stories with the goal of describing a phenomenon. While there are different approaches to using phenomenological interviews, Seidman (2006) described a common technique of combining life history with focused, in-depth interviews. The three-step process involves an initial interview to establish the context of a participant's experience (focused life history), a second to allow them to reconstruct the detail of the experience within its context (the details of the experience), and a third to encourage the participant to reflect on the meaning of the experience (reflection on the meaning). For example, McCoy (2014) asked undergraduate students to share their stories about the experiences of being first-generation students of color enrolled at an "extreme" predominantly White institution (PWI).

Words Researchers Use—Writing About Interviews

Researchers write about interviews in various ways. Following are three common terms to know.

Emic Approach
The researcher is describing an experience or aspect in a way a person from a culture understands it, using an insider's own words.

Etic Approach
The researcher is describing an experience or aspect in broad terms, from their perspective using terms that might be applied across different settings.

Essence
The researcher is describing the core or underlying aspect of an experience.

Reading Interview Research

Presenting results from interviews can be challenging, as researchers attempt to balance preserving the individual perspectives of participants with the need to produce a concise account of the study findings for their audience. It is common for a researcher to struggle with reducing the amount or density of direct quotations out of concern for not giving voice to their participants. As with most qualitative research, results are typically presented as themes derived from coding data. Researchers typically write about interview research by describing themes and then integrating direct quotations with their own synthesis of the findings. Following are three common approaches (with examples) of how interview results are presented in text. Afterward are general guidelines for reading interview research.

Direct Quotations

Petchauer (2010) described his approach to using frequent, direct quotations from participants to ensure the voice and tone of their comments conveyed their cultural lens (hip-hop practices):

> In the following sections, I share detailed portraits of Barry and JB to illustrate some contextualized ways that hip-hop existed in these students' lives and the more salient themes of hip-hop sampling and the importance of hip-hop spaces and practices. I share these two portraits specifically because they illustrate these themes most clearly and because of how they are interwoven with students' lives on campus. (p. 364)

Synthesis

Biddix (2010) chose to limit the use of direct quotations to present a common or pervasive perspective of how activist women leaders used technology in student organizations:

> Because this inquiry focused on understanding everyday experiences at a macrolevel, the voices of individual informants were aggregated following [institutional ethnography] convention (DeVault & McCoy, 2002). Giving voice to individual experiences can shift the focus of analysis away from the institution (Devault & McCoy); therefore, results contain very limited quotations. From this portrait, the social processes that connect and influence the experiences of [the participants] become more visible. (p. 34)

Direct Quotations and Synthesis

Kniess, Havice, and Cawthon (2015) included direct quotations with synthesis to present themes:

> . . . Thea described her commitment to the mentoring program, which also had a living-learning community in residence life: "I can't let these people down. Lord, you know me, I can't just give up on these people." Brian, who was also involved in the mentoring program, indicated that his reasons for coming back were "solely, primarily 100% the people that I met . . . the people that I had met and

became my circle . . . I wouldn't find anywhere else." Finding a supportive peer group was a commonality among all nine participants' decisions to return for the second year, which indicates how important social support is in determining persistence for African American students (Gloria et al., 1999). (p. 52)

Guidelines for Reading Interview Research

- Identify the focus of the study.
- Recognize the use of theory.
- Look for the prevalence of themes.

Identify the Focus of the Study   Researchers conduct interview studies with several purposes in mind. A study may be intended to provide details about programs and services, enlighten individual or group experiences, add perspectives or missing voices, explore sensitive issues, or reconstruct events. A single study may also incorporate multiple purposes. Reviewing the problem statement and use of theory and research questions can help determine the focus. While reading results, consider how those aspects of the methodology align with what the researcher reported about the interviews as well as how they presented the findings (individual narratives with direct quotations, generalized themes with some examples, descriptions with no quotations, or a blended approach).

Recognize the Use of Theory   Researchers using interviews often incorporate theory into their methodology. Although there are many variations, two basic approaches to using theory can be described. First, researchers may use a specific theory to guide participant selection, development of questions, and/or data analysis. Sometimes when using this approach for data analysis, researchers begin with tenets of the theory and look for examples in interview transcripts (*a priori* coding). Second, researchers may use several theories to develop their own conceptual framework to guide participant selection and question development. While they also may let the key aspects of theory guide coding, they often use a grounded theory approach to let results emerge from the data (*a posteriori* coding). Regardless of how researchers use theory in interview research, recognizing its role is essential in understanding intended outcomes and potential applications of the study.

Look for the Prevalence of Themes   Researchers using interviews often indicate the prevalence of findings, either by listing word or concept counts and percentages or simply by denoting major and minor themes. More prevalent themes should not necessarily be viewed as more or less important than others, as deviants can lead to a greater understanding of a problem. Just as too few commonalities in data may seem problematic, too much cohesion also could seem questionable. Providing prevalence data helps the reader make sense of the findings within the context of the study. Kniess et al. (2015) described the prevalence of themes in the following excerpt:

> Throughout data collection, nine out of the 11 participants indicated that they seriously thought of not returning for a second year. Three of them indicated that finances were a factor in deciding whether or not to return, two indicated grades as a factor, and one noted that it was a combination of money and grades. The remaining three participants indicated that family and campus culture were factors in their hesitation to return. (p. 52)

One important caveat to keep in mind is that some researchers reject the notion of adding prevalence data, considering the use of frequency information counter to constructivist approach.

Evaluating Interview Research

While several practices are commonly used for ensuring quality in interview research, there are no standard formulas and few agreed-upon procedures for validating or replicating interview data collection or analysis. Some researchers even regard the search for validation as counter to constructivism's focus on individual context and meaning. However, this does not mean readers should not question methods or results. Decisions about the research process should be supported by clearly documented procedures. Two concepts are important to consider when evaluating interview result authenticity and trustworthiness. Following is a description of each.

Issues With Data Collection: Authenticity

Authenticity relates to the genuineness of interview data and is concerned with data collection. Seidman (2006) summarized several key questions about authenticity readers might have when reviewing interview findings:

- How do we know that what the participant is telling us is true?
- And if it is true for this participant, is it true for anyone else?
- And if another person were doing the interview, would we get a different meaning?

- Or if we were to do the interview at a different time of year, would the participant reconstruct his or her experience differently?
- Or if we had picked different participants to interview, would we get an entirely dissimilar and perhaps contradictory sense of the issue at hand? (p. 23)

According to M. Q. Patton (2002), "The quality of the information obtained during an interview is largely dependent on the interviewer" (p. 341). A constricted focus on a specific concept, preconceived notions about results, or even time restrictions can result in leading questions that lend themselves to evident responses. Further, a researcher's opinion about a question can be detected by a participant through the wording of the question, physical prompts such as facial expression, or verbal cues such as voice intonation. Interviewers often acknowledge potential concerns directly when writing about methodology and mention the steps they used to minimize (or capitalize on) them.

Words Researchers Use—Journaling, Bracketing, Positionality

Researchers using interviews often keep a journal of their thoughts throughout the research process (journaling). As they begin to form personal opinions, they jot these down and consider them later, during data analysis. These notes allow researchers to bracket, or set aside, their thoughts, notions, and considerations that might adversely affect the study. While researchers seldom include specific information about their journaling or bracketing procedures during data collection or analysis, many will include a statement that outlines their perspectives on the study topic (positionality). Bourke (2014) offered some considerations related to positionality, describing his processes for bracketing, or accounting for, his perspective:

> At one point during the [research] process, I began writing about limitations in the context of my positionality as a White man studying issues of race and in collecting data from students of color. But now reflecting on the research process in the context of positionality, I realize that my positionality is not a limitation. My positionality meets the positionality of participants, and they do not rest in juxtaposition to each other. The research in which I engage is shaped by who I am, and as long as I remain reflective throughout the process, I will be shaped by it, and by those with whom I interact. (p. 7)

Issues With Data Analysis: Trustworthiness

Trustworthiness relates to confidence in interview data and is concerned with data analysis.

Trustworthiness for interview research has two aspects with associated concepts: internal as verified by participants (credibility) and external as verified by the reader (dependability, confirmability, transferability). Following is an overview of each associated concept.

> *Credibility* is providing assurance that participants can verify the quality of the results. Researchers typically establish credibility by including procedures for member-checking, or giving participants an opportunity to review findings.

> *Transferability* is conceptually related to the concept of generalizability, or whether the results from the sample data can be reflected in the population; however, qualitative researchers make no explicit claims at generalizability, and instead focus on whether some of the findings might be similar in related contexts.

> *Dependability* considers whether a study could be replicated, given the procedures described (participant selection, instrumentation, data analysis). Researchers typically include a detailed account of the study procedures to enhance dependability.

> *Confirmability* is generally thought of as a data analysis concern. Researchers include clear details about data analysis procedures, such as how transcripts became codes and codes became themes, that could allow another researcher to follow the steps and arrive at similar results.

Following is an excerpt showing how Kneiss et al. (2015) described enhancing trustworthiness in their study:

> Trustworthiness in the data was achieved through triangulation, which included review of transcripts by the participants, other analysts, and data collected from different sources (Patton, 2002). First, participants were asked to review the themes derived from the transcriptions, known as member-checking (Creswell, 2009). Second, the clusters of meaning from the transcribed data were discussed and verified with a scholar educated in qualitative research methods and analysis. Third, a peer debriefer served as an independent reviewer for the research data to ensure that the researcher-created meanings were accurate (Creswell, 2009). Finally, key informant interviews, observations at campus events, and a review of key artifacts further served to triangulate the data from the focus groups and interviews (Patton, 2002). (p. 151)

Questions for Evaluating Interview Research

- Did the researcher provide sufficient details about the interview process (authenticity)?
- Are the details about data analysis detailed enough to be convincing (trustworthiness)?

Did the Researcher Provide Sufficient Details About the Interview Process (Authenticity)?   Authenticity is concerned with the research process, which includes participant selection and data collection. A critical reader should first consider the participant selection process to determine if the data sources match the focus of the study. Next, data collection should be questioned with regard to the content, depth, and frequency of interview sessions. A key consideration is the believability of the content, given the participants and instrument. If the full questionnaire is not provided (for example, if the interview was semi- or unstructured), the description of the instrument should suggest an alignment between what was asked and what was learned. Researchers also should provide some detail about the session(s), indicating the length of the interviews. Multiple sessions with participants are beneficial for promoting authenticity, as they allow for correction or elaboration (Seidman, 2006).

Are the Details About Data Analysis Detailed Enough to Be Convincing (Trustworthiness)?   Trustworthiness relates to data analysis and concerns believability in the results of the study. Establishing credibility generally is accomplished by asking participants to review results, then providing information about consistency or revisions. The researcher is not asking a participant, "Is this what you said?" but rather, "Does this reflect what you said?" Further, readers should be able to clearly understand how researchers generated results, or themes, from the data. A detailed description of the data analysis procedure should be included to reveal how the researcher arrived at the conclusions. This enhances both dependability and confirmability of the study. Merriam (2002) suggested that credibility issues can be offset by using multiple researchers when conducting data analysis. Researchers often describe this as peer review. Finally, transferability asks whether the results might be transferred to a similar context. A critical reader might ask, how likely is it that these findings would be similar in a different context. For example, given the participants and setting, are these findings comparable at another institution?

Applying Interview Research

Interview findings uniquely add individual and group perspectives to research. Understanding how and/or why students, faculty, and staff experience the college environment provides invaluable insight for how to create inclusive and effective policies, practices, and programming. Interviews can reveal ways to enhance services, create or revise practices, and promote student development. Following are some suggestions for how to apply interview results to student affairs practice.

Opportunities for Applying Interview Research

- Learn ways to develop or enhance programs and services.
- Understand experiences to improve practices.
- Relate student development theory to practice.

Learn Ways to Develop or Enhance Programs and Services Learning about student and staff experiences can reveal successes, challenges, and opportunities associated with programs and services. While interview studies often are focused on a single campus or context, key findings are often relatable. For example, Smith's (2015) year-long study of living–learning communities (LLCs) at a regional institution in the southeast revealed the critical roles student affairs/faculty partnerships played in the success and sustainability in LLCs. The interviews uncovered aspects of the program administration that at first enhanced, then limited the continued development of a successful LLC. Incorporating these findings, Smith (2015) offered recommendations transferable to LLC administration beyond the study campus.

Interviews also can help practitioners who are developing a new program or service anticipate challenges with implementation. They may also be beneficial for understanding best practices that inform program enhancement or revision. Finally, interviews add perspectives about how individuals and groups experience programs and services that may not be discovered with close-ended (survey) questions. Such findings can suggest underlying issues that affect the viability and longevity of programs and services. Considered beyond their context, interviews can offer a richer understanding of a program or service through the perspective of those experiencing it.

Perspectives From the Field—Using Interview Research to Inform Student Affairs Practice

Interview research, and qualitative research in general, is an important practitioner tool that complements survey data. The quantitative results that come from survey tools can give a useful sense of the overall sampling population—the general direction of their collective responses. Interview research has the opportunity to add much texture to quantitative outcomes. It enables the telling of stories and the provision of examples that illuminate the thoughts of the subjects that quantitative data is limited in its ability to do. The interview setting creates the chance to understand the subjects in a more nuanced and deeper manner and when paired with quantitative outcomes provides a richer and more complete picture of not only the entire population but also of individuals who comprise the focus of the research. This research dynamic strengthens the practitioner's ability to deliver services in a highly effective manner.

Michael Segawa—Vice president of student affairs and dean of students, University of Puget Sound

Understand Experiences to Improve Practices   Large-scale quantitative studies can reveal attitudes, values, and beliefs held by a population or group. Interviews tend to focus more on detailed experiences and perspectives missing from generalizable studies. Specifically, rigorously conducted, well-reported, in-depth interviews can expose new or unfamiliar phenomena that affect student experiences. For example, while interviewing students of color about their experiences transitioning in to doctoral programs, McCoy and Winkle-Wagner (2015) learned that fostering confidence, cultivating a passion for scholarship, and identifying as an emerging scholar were fundamental to recruiting and retaining underrepresented students in doctoral programs. Also important was facilitating ways for students to develop a new identity while maintaining their prior backgrounds and identities.

Practices in student affairs might range from procedural (registering events on campus) to personalized (counseling students in crisis). Experiences are how students, staff, and other stakeholders encounter and make meaning of those practices. By focusing more directly on experiences with practices, interviews can reveal ways to sustain or improve them. For example, Hornak, Ozaki, and Lunceford (2016) conducted semistructured focus group interviews across seven 2-year institutions to understand how student affairs professionals were socialized into their roles. Results revealed the importance of education and on-the-job experiences in their socialization and development. The researchers provided recommendations that could be broadly applied to help professionals find success though institutional and professional experiences.

Relate Student Development Theory to Practice   Results from interview studies used to develop or refine theory can be informative sources for practitioners designing or revising policies, programs, and learning environments. The broad dimensions of student development theory suggest how students grow though identity formation, life issues, intellectual improvement, moral reasoning, and self-authorship (L. D. Patton et al., 2016). Results from interview-based studies incorporating theory into program development and administration can reveal ways theory can be operationalized for practice.

For example, Huerta and Fishman (2014) used mattering and marginality (key concepts from Schlossberg's transition theory) as lenses to explore the transition experiences and success of ten first-generation, low-income urban Latino males. Guided by theory, the researchers asked questions about college and financial aid plans, college perceptions, peer relations, and ethnic identity. The findings led to implications and program recommendations focused on better supporting and understanding Latino male students. One specific recommendation from the findings was the development of a male support program that includes professional mentoring.

Building Your Interview Skillset

Effective interviewing is a research skill that directly translates to good student affairs practice. Many aspects of fieldwork relate to identifying and understanding problems while searching for solutions. Marshall and Rossman (1995) specified that interviewers must have excellent listening skills and be skillful at personal interaction, framing questions, and gentle probing for elaboration. Swanbrow Becker and Drum (2015) recommended interviewing as an essential skill for helping students. Although they specifically were referring to promoting well-being and intervening with students in distress, their considerations can be applied broadly to practice:

> At the heart of the counseling process is a set of counseling interview skills crucial to guiding the self-discovery process and developing a clear understanding of students' sources of distress as well as their available resources to cope with their circumstances. (p. 205)

> Positive intervention starts with developing a thorough awareness of the students' understanding of their problems, their attempts to solve them, their internal and interpersonal resources, and their goals. (p. 206)

Coursework in educational research often emphasizes interviewing as a primary research skill. A few programs offer classes specifically on interviewing, although counseling courses, even if the content is not directly related to college students or personnel, can provide a basis in effective interview skills. Finally, there are several approachable introductory textbooks focused on interview research, including works by Merriam (1998; Merriam & Tisdell, 2015) and Seidman (2013). Researchers seeking a specific design perspective, are referred to Yin (2013) for case study, Corbin and Strauss (2014) for grounded theory, or Van Maanen (2014) for phenomenology.

References

Almeida, D. J. (2016). Low-income Latino students and California's early assessment program: The role of sensemaking in the use of college readiness information. *Journal of Hispanic Higher Education, 15*(4) 310–339.

American Council on Education. (1937). The student personnel point of view. *American Council on Education Studies* (Series I, Vol. I, no. 3).

Berg, B. L. (2004). *Qualitative research methods.* Boston, MA: Allyn & Bacon.

Biddix, J. P. (2010). Relational leadership and technology: A study of activist college women leaders. *NASPA Journal about Women in Higher Education, 3*(1), 25–47.

Biddix, J. P., Giddens, B. M., Darsey, J., Fricks, J. B., Tucker, B. A., & Robertson, J. W. (2012). Pathways leading to the SSAO for women at community colleges. *Community College Journal of Research & Practice, 36*(9), 713–732.

Bourke, B. (2014). Positionality: Reflecting on the research process. *The Qualitative Report, 19*(33), 1–9.

Bradbury, B. L., & Mather, P. C. (2009). The integration of first-year, first-generation college students from Ohio Appalachia. *NASPA Journal, 46*(2), 258–281.

Broido, E. M., Brown, K. R., Stygles, K. N., & Bronkema, R. H. (2015). Responding to gendered dynamics: Experiences of women working over 25 years at one university. *The Journal of Higher Education, 86*(4), 595–627.

Corbin, J., & Strauss, A. (2014). *Basics of qualitative research: Techniques and procedures for developing grounded theory* (4th ed.). Thousand Oaks, CA: Sage.

Creswell, J. W. (2009). *Qualitative inquiry and research design: Choosing among the five approaches* (3rd ed.). Thousand Oaks, CA: Sage.

DeVault, M. J., & McCoy, L. (2002). Institutional ethnography: Using interviews to investigate ruling relations. In J. Gubrium & J. A. Holstein (Eds.), *Handbook of interview research* (pp. 752–776). Thousand Oaks, CA: Sage.

Garcia, G. A., & Okhidoi, O. (2015). Culturally relevant practices that "serve" students at a Hispanic serving institution. *Innovative Higher Education, 40*(4), 345–357.

Gerard, S. A. (1959). The interview: A conversation with a purpose. *Hospital Progress, 40*(7), 126–130.

Gloria, A. M., Robinson Kurpius, S. E., Hamilton, K. D., & Wilson, M. S. (1999). African American students' persistence at a predominantly White university: Influences of social support, university comfort, and self-beliefs. *Journal of College Student Development, 40*(3), 257–268.

Harrison, L. M. (2014). How student affairs professionals learn to advocate: A phenomenological study. *Journal of College and Character, 15*(3), 165–177.

Holstein, J. A., & Gubrium, J. F. (2004). The active interview. In D. Silverman (Ed.), *Qualitative research: Theory, method and practice* (2nd ed., pp. 140–161). London, United Kingdom: Sage.

Hornak, A. M., Ozaki, C. C., & Lunceford, C. (2016). Socialization for new and mid-level community college student affairs professionals. *Journal of Student Affairs Research and Practice, 53*(2), 118–130.

Huerta, A. H., & Fishman, S. M. (2014). Marginality and mattering: Urban Latino male undergraduates in higher education. *Journal of the First-Year Experience & Students in Transition, 26*(1), 85–100.

Jaggers, D., & Iverson, S. V. (2012). "Are you as hard as 50 Cent?" Negotiating race and masculinity in the residence halls. *Journal of College & University Student Housing, 39*(1), 186–199.

Jones, P. Y. (2016). *HerStory: Dr. Ruth Simmons' journey to the presidency* (Unpublished doctoral dissertation). The University of Tennessee, Knoxville.

King, P. M., & Baxter Magolda, M. B. (2005). A developmental model of intercultural maturity. *Journal of College Student Development, 46*(6), 571–592.

Kinzie, J. (2010). *Perspectives from campus leaders on the current state of student learning outcomes assessment.* NILOA Focus Group Summary 2009–2010. Urbana, IL: National Institute for Learning Outcomes Assessment.

Kniess, D. R., Havice, P. A., & Cawthon, T. W. (2015). Creating networks that facilitate successful transition to the second-year for African American students at a PWI: Implications for residence life. *Journal of College and University Student Housing, 42*(1), 144–159.

Krueger, R. A., & Casey, M. A. (2000). *Focus groups: A practical guide for applied research* (3rd ed.). Thousand Oaks, CA: Sage.

Kuh, G. D. (2009). What student affairs professionals need to know about student engagement. *Journal of College Student Development, 50*(6), 683–706.

Literte, P. E. (2010). Revising race: How biracial students are changing and challenging student services. *Journal of College Student Development, 51*(2), 115–134.

Marshall, C., & Rossman, G. B. (1995). *Designing qualitative research.* Thousand Oaks, CA: Sage.

Maxwell, J. A. (2013). *Qualitative research design: An interactive approach* (3rd ed.). Thousand Oaks, CA: Sage.

McCoy, D. (2014). A phenomenological approach to understanding first-generation college students of color transitions to one "extreme" predominantly white institution. *College Student Affairs Journal, 32* (1), 155–169.

McCoy, D. L., & Winkle-Wagner, R. (2015). Bridging the divide: Developing a scholarly habitus for aspiring graduate students through summer bridge programs participation. *Journal of College Student Development, 56*(5), 423–439.

Merriam, S. B. (1998). *Qualitative research and case study applications in education.* San Francisco, CA: Jossey-Bass.

Merriam, S. B. (2002). *Introduction to qualitative research.* In S. B. Merriam & Associates (Eds.), *Qualitative research in practice* (pp. 3–17). San Francisco, CA: Jossey-Bass.

Merriam, S. B. (2009). Qualitative research: A guide to design and implementation. San Francisco, CA: Jossey-Bass.

Merriam, S. B., & Tisdell, E. J. (2015). *Qualitative research: A guide to design and implementation* (4th ed.). San Francisco, CA: Jossey-Bass.

Mintz, L. M. (2011). *Gender variance on campus: A critical analysis of transgender voices* (Unpublished doctoral dissertation). University of California, San Diego.

Nathan, R. (2005). *My freshman year: What a professor learned by becoming a student.* Ithaca, NY: Cornell University Press.

Ortiz, A. M. (2016). The qualitative interview. In F. K. Stage & K. Manning (Eds.), *Research in the college context: Approaches and methods* (2nd ed., pp. 47–61). New York, NY: Brunner-Routledge.

Patton, L. D., Renn, K. A., Guido, F. M., & Quaye, S. J. (2016). *Student development in college: Theory, research, and practice* (3rd ed.). San Francisco, CA: Jossey Bass.

Patton, M. Q. (2002). *Qualitative evaluation and research methods* (3rd ed.). Thousand Oaks, CA: Sage.

Patton, M. Q. (2014). *Qualitative research & evaluation methods: Integrating theory and practice* (4th ed.). Thousand Oaks, CA: Sage.

Petchauer, E. (2010). Sampling practices and social spaces: Exploring a hip-hop approach to higher education. *Journal of College Student Development, 51*(4), 359–372.

Reybold, L. E., Halx, M. D., & Jimenez, A. L. (2008). Professional integrity in higher education: A study of administrative staff ethics in student affairs. *Journal of College Student Development, 49*(2), 110–124.

Savin-Baden, M., & Major, C. H. (2012). *Qualitative research: The essential guide to theory and practice.* New York, NY: Routledge.

Schuh, J. H., Biddix, J. P., Dean, L. A., & Kinzie, J. (2016). *Assessment in student affairs: A contemporary look* (2nd ed.). San Francisco, CA: Jossey-Bass.

Seidman, I. (2006). *Interviewing as qualitative research: A guide for researchers in education and the social sciences* (3rd ed.). New York, NY: Teachers College Press.

Seidman, I. (2013). *Interviewing as qualitative research: A guide for researchers in education and the social sciences* (4th ed.). New York, NY: Teachers College Press.

Silver, B. R., & Jakeman, R. C. (2014). Understanding intent to leave the field: A study of student affairs master's students' career plans. *Journal of Student Affairs Research and Practice, 51*(2), 170–182.

Smith, D. L. (2015). *Unintended consequences of collegiate living-learning community programs at a public university* (Unpublished doctoral dissertation). The University of Tennessee, Knoxville.

Swanbrow Becker, M. A., & Drum, D. J. (2015). Essential counseling knowledge and skills to prepare student affairs staff to promote emotional wellbeing and to intervene with students in distress. *Journal of College and Character, 16*(4), 201–208.

Tillapaugh, D., & Haber-Curran, P. (2016). Research college men's perceptions of their leadership practice: Unpacking power and influence. *Journal of Leadership Education, 15*(3), 131–150.

Vaccaro, A. (2015). "It's not one size fits all": Diversity among student veterans. *Journal of Student Affairs Research and Practice, 52*(4), 347–358.

Van Maanen, J. (2014). *Phenomenology of practice: Meaning-giving methods in phenomenological research and writing.* New York, NY: Routledge.

Ward, E. G., Thomas, E. T., & Disch, W. B. (2014). Mentor service themes emergent in a holistic, undergraduate peer-mentoring experience. *Journal of College Student Development, 55*(6), 563–579.

Wolf-Wendel, L., Ward, K., & Kinzie, J. (2009). A tangled web of terms: The overlap and unique contribution of involvement, engagement, and integration to understanding college student success. *Journal of College Student Development, 50*(4), 407–428.

Yin, R. (2009). *Case study research: Design and methods* (4th ed.). Thousand Oaks, CA: Sage.

Yin, R. (2013). *Case study research: Design and methods* (5th ed.). Thousand Oaks, CA: Sage.

Zhang, N., & Associates. (2011). *Rentz's student affairs practice in higher education* (4th ed.). Springfield, IL: Charles C. Thomas.

CHAPTER NINE

Learning Quantitative Research

Learning Outcomes

By the end of this chapter, you should be able to:

- Understand the purpose and role of statistics in research.
- Differentiate between the major types of statistics.
- Know answers to basic questions about statistics in research.
- Apply basic statistical terminology.
- Relate statistical research to student affairs practice.

Many students and novice research consumers are intimidated by quantitative research. Having to identify, use, and interpret quantitative data can be daunting and confusing for novice consumers. Some learners are simply overwhelmed by the thought of statistics, based on poor prior experiences, lack of exposure, or a general aversion to math. Unfortunately, few graduate statistics courses help to ease these apprehensions. The need to cover numerous topics in a limited time frame often results in a general scan of foundational concepts, favoring breadth over depth. Often missing or underemphasized is a genuine consideration of the essential terminology and material needed to understand quantitative research and statistics.

The purpose of the chapter is to serve as an introduction and reference guide for understanding, reading, evaluating, and applying quantitative research. It was written with a single question in mind:

What essential concepts do student affairs practitioners and researchers need to know to understand quantitative methods?

The question is answered with an overview and a series of questions and answers, derived from common challenges and difficulties for new and returning learners to quantitative research. The format is intended to establish pre-requisite knowledge, based on an assumption that learners either have never taken a statistics course or need a review. Readers with prior knowledge of statistics also will find the chapter valuable, as the concepts are explained from a student affairs perspective with applicable examples from published research and reports.

The chapter begins with a general overview of quantitative methods. This is followed by a specific review of uses in student affairs research and practice. Next is an introduction to essential concepts, followed by common questions (and answers) about statistics. The chapter closes with suggestions for developing foundational skills.

Understanding Quantitative Research

Quantitative research seeks to identify and explain reality as it exists. Quantitative research is characterized by the use of numerical data. As a result, the term quantitative is often synonymous with statistics. Quantitative research is generally associated with a postpositivist perspective. *Postpositivism* is a philosophical perspective that views truth as a discoverable reality. It seeks to determine causes that influence outcomes through reductionist methods and objectivity.

Overview of Quantitative Research

Perspective: Postpositivism

- Determinism: Causes probably determine outcomes; the goal is to identify and assess causes that influence outcomes.
- Reductionism: The intent is to reduce ideas into small, testable ideas to examine phenomena, such as variables used for hypothesis testing.
- Objectivity: An objective reality exists out there. There are laws that govern the world that need to be tested or verified and refined to build our understanding of the world.
- (Sometimes) Theory verification: Researchers start with a theory, then follow a path of discovery including identification and development of a research question and/or hypothesis, selection of a population, establishment of sampling strategies, specification of research strategies, and standardized methods of analysis.

Type: Qualitative Methods

- Emphasis on understanding and explaining: Seeks to understand, explain, and predict trends and behaviors of groups and processes.
- Empirical measurement: Data are collected and analyzed using standardized approaches such as hypothesis testing.
- Goals are to identify trends or to generalize: Findings are intended to reduce large amounts of data to identify trends, or to make inferences or estimations about data.

Design: Nonexperimental, Quasi-Experimental

- Nonexperimental design: A default quantitative design involving distributing a survey to a sample or population.
- Quasi-experimental design: Typically a pre/post survey involving a treatment (such as participation in a program or organization, or the passage of time) and comparison.

Methods: Descriptive, Difference, Relationship, Prediction

- Descriptive: Summary of or trends in data.
- Difference: Comparisons between groups and inferences about populations.
- Relationship: Correlations between two or more characteristics.
- Prediction: Estimating changes in outcomes based on predictors.

Quantitative Methods in Student Affairs Research

Student affairs work was largely codified and legitimized with quantitative methods (Biddix & Schwartz, 2012). Nearly a century ago, pioneering student personnel workers at Northwestern University used surveys, descriptive statistics, and associational models to standardize admissions procedures, track academic and social progress, and help place students in jobs before graduation (Certis, 2014). Staff in the office, including eventual *Student Personnel Point of View* (SPPOV) lead author Esther Lloyd-Jones, conducted rigorous studies on college students using quantitative measures to enhance student success and improve student services.

The use of quantitative methods in student affairs research gained further prominence with the work of Alexander Astin at the American Council of Education (ACE) in the 1960s and 1970s. In 1966, Astin developed a large-scale longitudinal survey program to determine and evaluate involvement and environmental trends among college on students (Higher Education Research Institute, 2017). In 1977, he published an influential book detailing findings, *Four Critical Years: Effects of College on Beliefs, Attitudes, and Knowledge.* Astin subsequently expanded his conceptions of student involvement (Astin, 1984), revisited the effects of college on outcomes (Astin, 1993), and contributed to the literature on the value of service (Astin & Sax, 1998). Much of the conceptual theory and foundational work in student affairs is built from Astin's work, which along with Kuh's significant contributions to student success research (Kuh, 1999, 2009; Kuh, Kinzie, Schuh, Whitt, & Associates, 2005/2010) added important empirical support to the legitimacy of student affairs work.

A substantial amount of contemporary research in student affairs focuses on demonstrating outcomes such as intellectual gains, retention, and graduation rates using prediction statistics (Mayhew et al., 2016). Published articles, research reports, and other empirical sources provide practitioners with evidence to justify new programs and services, legitimize current practices, and forecast future needs. Table 9.1 shows several functions of quantitative methods useful for student affairs practice.

Table 9.1. Functions of Quantitative Research in Student Affairs

Function	Application and Explanation
Informs decisions.	Summarized statistics can be used to inform decisions at all levels and functional areas in student affairs.
Allows for generalizations and prediction.	Statistical results collected from a random sample can be generalized to other populations. Inferential results can be used to inform policy and practice.
Provides efficient methods for summarizing and interpreting information.	Data can be reported in confusing and unnecessarily complicated ways; however, statistics promote and standardize effective ways to communicate results.
Ensures information is presented and interpreted accurately and informatively. Standardizes practices and procedures for the research community.	With some exceptions, statistics are generally reported consistently, regardless of the topic. Although topics and outcomes can vary, statistical data collection and analysis are mostly standardized across disciplines.
Evidences the need for new programs and legitimizes the value of existing programs.	Quantitative research can be used efficiently to determine needs, advocate for additional resources, and demonstrate accountability.

Perspectives From the Field—Why Practitioners Need Quantitative Research Skills

Student affairs professionals may find learning quantitative research an intimidating notion. So why do it? Instead of viewing these skills as a chore, student affairs professionals can view them as tools that will help accomplish their goals for student learning and success.

Our field needs professionals who can do student affairs fast and slow (Sriram, 2017).

When discussing the importance of quantitative research skills for student affairs professionals, I often draw from Nobel Laureate Daniel Kahneman's (2011) work, *Thinking, Fast and Slow*. Kahneman discusses two types of thinking. Thinking fast is the use of our intuition. This mode of thinking identifies patterns and draws conclusions quickly. The problem is that our intuition can be wrong, and therefore it needs a partner. This partner is our logic and reason, what Kahneman calls thinking slow. The best thinkers and doers are those who can think both fast and slow.

A great way to do student affairs slow is through the use of quantitative research and statistics. Quantitative research provides a check against our biases and allows us to measure aspects of student learning, development, and success that are important to student affairs work.

Rishi Sriram—Associate Professor of Higher Education and Student Affairs, Associate Chair for Department of Educational Leadership, Baylor University

Table 9.2. Key Questions and Associated Essential Concepts

Key Question	Essential Concepts
What are the main quantitative methods?	Descriptive, difference, relationship, prediction
Where do quantitative data come from?	Survey, existing database
What is a statistic?	Population, parameter, sample, statistic
How do researchers classify statistics?	Descriptive, inferential
What is a variable?	Independent, dependent, covariate, extraneous
How and why do researchers classify variables?	Levels of measurement, parametric, nonparametric
How do researchers choose statistical tests?	Decision tree

Essential Concepts in Quantitative Methods

Anxiety and apprehension about statistics often result from a lack of understanding foundational concepts. Table 9.2 is a summary list of key questions along with associated concepts that comprise the primary features of quantitative research encountered when reading or evaluating research. Each question and associated concept is examined in subsequent sections.

What Are the Main Quantitative Methods?

There are four main categories of quantitative methods: descriptive, difference, relationship, and prediction. Following is a broad description of each.

1. Descriptive methods consist of trends and characteristics in data. Calculating descriptive statistics condenses individual units of information into interpretable, manageable, and useful summaries that can be efficiently displayed in graphics or text.
2. Difference methods make comparisons between two or more samples. Testing differences between groups allows researchers to make evidenced guesses about a population, to differentiate groups, and to track changes over time.
3. Relationship methods examine correlations between two or more variables. Assessing relationships can be used to show how one variable affects another, to verify or support a theory, to evaluate potential predictor variables, and to assess validity and reliability.

4. Prediction methods consider how individual measures such as characteristics, attitudes, values, and beliefs produce change. Making predictions lets researchers estimate the influence of one or more measures on an outcome.

Schuh, Biddix, Dean, and Kinzie (2016) suggested that these methods could be used as keywords for researchers to directly incorporate as research questions:

- What are the *descriptive* characteristics of college graduates?
- What *differences* exist between college graduates in terms of job skills?
- What is the *relationship* between major and job skills among college graduates?
- What characteristics of college students *predict* acquisition of specific job skills?

Where Do Quantitative Data Come From?

Student affairs researchers collect quantitative data by distributing surveys or using information from existing datasets. Surveys generally require direct interaction with individuals—either in person or mediated by technology. Existing databases can involve direct or indirect interaction, such as downloading a dataset or working with a data manager such as an admissions officer or institutional researcher. Following is a more detailed overview of each concept.

Survey. A *survey* is a data collection tool, or instrument, that researchers use to collect numerical data. Generally, a researcher uses a survey to collect a sample of data from a larger population. When collected from a random sample, the data can be used to make informed guesses, or inferences, about the population. Table 9.3 shows some characteristics about surveys, differentiated by which formats are more or less often preferred. It is important to note that preferences are audience-dependent. For example, a journal reviewer might favor an existing survey while a researcher might argue that a survey they create is more directly applicable to the research question.

Table 9.3. Survey Characteristics

More Often Preferred	versus	Less Often Preferred
Existing		Researcher-created
Administered in person		Technology-mediated
Longitudinal design		Cross-sectional design
Direct measures		Indirect measures
Highly focused content		Loosely focused content
Simple format		Complex format

An (accessible) existing survey offers the advantage of being available and already evaluated. Depending on how often it has been used, it also can offer the ability to benchmark, or compare results to other studies. However, accessing an existing survey often requires permission and sometimes also a cost.

A researcher-created survey offers the advantage of specifying questions that mirror the focus of the study. However, adequately pilot-testing and validating a new survey prior to use can be a lengthy process.

Surveys can be administered in-person by paper or online or with a mobile device or computer. The primary advantage of in-person administration is the potential for a higher return rate. However, if random sampling is a goal, directly surveying can be more challenging and potentially time-consuming. Another potential disadvantage is the need to input results from paper-based surveys.

Technology-mediated surveys generally involve sending an email with an online version of the survey in text or linked to a website. An advantage of indirect surveying is the potential to reach a larger and more diverse sample quickly. A limitation is a lower response rate from electronic-based surveys.

A survey may be longitudinal, or intended to examine something over time, or cross-sectional, intended to capture data at a particular moment. Longitudinal surveys are often referred to as pre/post because they tend to follow the same individuals over two or more administrations. A cross-sectional survey can be administrated and completed quickly and efficiently whereas a longitudinal survey is managed through multiple administrations, creating other challenges such as tracking participants.

Survey questions can be direct measures or indirect measures. Direct measures generally ask respondents to demonstrate what they know. Indirect measures focus on attitudes and perceptions, asking respondents to indicate how they feel about something. Demonstrating the value of programs and services using direct learning measures is a major emphasis in assessment and accreditation (Tucker, 2014). For example, rather than asking students if they learned about leadership approaches after a training (indirect), a more direct measure would be to ask them to identify definitions for each approach.

A survey can have highly focused content—meaning that the questions align closely with a central topic. This is contrasted with loosely focused content, which is intended to gather broad information on several unrelated topics. A highly focused content survey can be shorter and allow the researcher to obtain a larger sample of participants willing to complete it. A loosely focused content survey may be longer, but can give the researcher more information about associated behaviors to identify linked intervention strategies.

A simple format or complex format survey refers to the consistency or variability in questions and responses. Simple formats can be quicker to administer and score; however, the repetition of too many questions asked in the same way can affect reliability. A complex format helps address this problem, but too much variation can create confusion for respondents. Further, complex questions can be difficult to score and analyze—especially when the response types differ.

Existing Datasets. An *existing dataset* is an organized collection of numerical data. A benefit of using an existing dataset is efficiency, since the data is already collected in a database format. Often, existing datasets are also complete and formatted, reducing the preparation time needed prior to data analysis. Existing datasets share the same characteristics as surveys, since they generally are derived from survey data. Datasets can also be generated from institutional records such as admission and enrollment profiles and merged for large-scale or longitudinal analysis. There are two major types of datasets, internal and external. Following are some examples.

Internal datasets include records collected, stored, and maintained for institutional decision making and research. Example sources of student data include admissions, financial aid, registrar, academic, housing, and alumni records. Some student affairs units, such as service learning and community service and sorority and fraternity affairs maintain records on student involvement and participation. Other sources of existing data may not be publicized or apparent, such as databases containing assessments or survey results from individual programs and services. Finally, institutional research offices generally maintain institution-specific datasets from large-scale survey participation.

External datasets include large-scale surveys administered by external agencies. Examples are the cross-sectional and longitudinal designs used in the CIRP and National Survey of Student Engagement (NSSE) national surveys. An advantage to using existing external data is that it is already collected and stored for analysis. A disadvantage can be access, which can involve considerable cost. Another advantage is that existing datasets generally are based on surveys that have been extensively pilot-tested, validating measurement of broad concepts from attitudes, values, and beliefs on academic and social engagement.

What Is a Statistic?

The terms quantitative and statistic are often used interchangeably. Although closely related, the two are not synonymous. Quantitative refers to data that can be counted (or quantified). While quantitative data are mostly numeric, some start as categorical. For example, gender is a qualitative descriptor; when counted, it becomes a quantitative variable. When researchers summarize data into numerical formats, either with raw counts, averages, or percentages, they are quantifying data. Data must be quantified in a numerical format to be considered a statistic. Four essential concepts are necessary to distinguish: population, parameter, sample, and statistic.

Quantitative measures generally are associated with a population. A *population* is all members in a specific group. Researchers identify and define populations based on the goals of a study. For example, a population might be specified as all undergraduate college students in the United States or it might be more narrowly defined to all college freshmen taking first-year studies (FYS) courses. A *parameter* is a value that exists in a population. Sometimes researchers know the parameter value and other times the information is not accessible. For example, if the average age of all freshmen taking FYS courses is known, the researcher can report the parameter for that population.

If the researcher wanted to know how many freshmen taking FYS courses participated in intramural sports their first semester, things get more complicated. The parameter (all freshmen taking FYS courses who participated in intramural sports their first semester) is likely not accessible unless existing data tracks extra-curricular participation by student characteristics. Since it is also unlikely that each freshman can be surveyed, the researcher asks individual students who are members of the population. A *sample* is a group selected from a population. A *statistic* is the value calculated from a sample. Another word for statistic is parameter estimate, which suggests the researcher is estimating the true value (parameter) based on a sample.

How Do Researchers Classify Statistics?

There are two major designations of statistics, descriptive and inferential. *Descriptive statistics* describe data and include measures used to summarize population and/or sample information. They are sometimes referred to as trend statistics. Inferential statistics make inferences or estimated guesses about population data using a sample. When all of the data of interest are available, researchers use descriptive statistics to answer questions. In most cases, however, access to all data is not possible. *Inferential statistics* give researchers the ability to infer values in a population based on a statistic calculated from a sample. Figure 9.1 shows how the four essential concepts and two major designations interact with associated quantitative methods.

FIGURE 9.1. ESSENTIAL CONCEPTS AND MAJOR DESIGNATIONS IN STATISTICS

Essential Concepts		
Population All members of a group.	→	**Sample** A set of members selected from a population.
Parameter A collected value representing an entire population.	→	**Statistic, Parameter Estimate** A calculated value that may or may not represent the population
↓		↓

Major Designations		
Descriptive Statistics Associated Methods: Description, Relationship		**Inferential Statistics** Associated Methods: Difference, Relationship, Prediction

What Is a Variable?

After collecting data, researchers choose or develop variables to analyze. A *variable* is a measured or manipulated quantity or trait. Variables broadly are classified into two types, independent and dependent.

An *independent variable* is a measured or manipulated quantity or trait that is believed to affect an outcome. When individuals or their records are data sources, independent variables can be demographic characteristics, responses to survey questions, or cognitive or psychological measures. When objects or records are data sources, independent variables can be collected or derived characteristics or measures. For statistics concerned with group differences and prediction, the independent variable is considered the presumed cause of the change in an outcome. Independent variables also are sometimes referred to as inputs or predictors.

Words Researchers Use—Covariates and Extraneous Variables

There are several types of independent variables, each differentiated by the functions they serve for analysis. Two prominent independent variable types are important to understand, covariates and extraneous variables.

A covariate is a variable used to account (or control) for a known, existing effect. For example, in a study of college student drug use, Palmer, McMahon, Moreggi, Rounsaville, and Ball (2012) wanted to know whether men used marijuana more often than women. The researchers hypothesized that alcohol use was related to marijuana use among men so they controlled for (statistically removed the effect of) drinking frequency (a covariate). This enabled them to focus only on differences in marijuana use.

An extraneous variable is a measure not accounted for in a study that influences the result. For example, Palmer et al. (2012) did not account for (measure) how peer culture might affect drug use. Peer culture is considered to be extraneous (unmeasured) effect on the outcome. There are always extraneous variables in measurement.

A *dependent variable* is an outcome affected by one or more independent variables. Dependent variables can be directly collected as a question or measure on a survey or acquired from an existing dataset. They also can be derived by summing or statistically combining several questions into one measure (called a factor). Dependent variables can be measured in many ways, from numerical outcomes such as an engagement score to discrete categories such as retention (yes/no). For statistics concerned with group differences and prediction, the dependent variable is considered the presumed outcome or effect influenced by an independent variable. Dependent variables are sometimes referred to as outcomes or effects.

How and Why Do Researchers Classify Variables?

Researchers specify independent and dependent variables when identifying a research question and choosing data sources. *Scales of measurement* is a classification system used to differentiate variables. Scales of measurement include nominal, ordinal, interval, and scale:

- *Nominal variables* are typically qualitative and thought of as names or characteristics such as sorority membership (yes/no).

- *Ordinal variables* are ordered lists of categories, such as class standing (freshman, sophomore, junior, senior).
- *Interval variables* are ordered ratings such as Likert scales (strongly disagree, disagree, agree, strongly agree).
- *Scale variables* are continuous numbers such as service hours (0–infinite).

Variables also have a distribution, or shape, classified as nonparametric or parametric:

- *Nonparametric* measures are nonnumeric variables (typically nominal or ordinal) that do not follow a normal distribution.
- *Parametric* measures are numeric variables (interval or scale) that follow a normal distribution.

Normal distribution means that when plotted on a bell curve, most values will group around a central mean and narrow off equally at the two ends, looking like a small hill. Nonparametric measures do not group around a central mean. In most cases with nonparametric measures, calculating the mean would not be appropriate.

To illustrate the difference, consider sorority membership, a categorical, non-parametric measure. A survey question would ask whether a student is a member of a sorority (yes) or not a member (no). Calculating a mean value for responses to this question is not accurate, since a student is either a member or is not. For this variable, percentage would be a better summary statistic (60% members, 40% nonmembers). Recognizing scales of measurement is a useful skill for reading and evaluating quantitative research. Distinguishing scales of measurement is an essential skill when conducting quantitative research and analysis. Differentiating variables helps researchers select the appropriate statistical test.

Words Researcher Use—Likert Scale and Likert-Like Scale

The most commonly used responses for survey questions are ratings often referred to as Likert scales. The Likert scale was developed by psychologist Rensis Likert (1903–1981) as a way to measure attitudes by asking respondents the extent that they agree or disagree to a series of statements that when summed, would give a single score. Likert believed this this scale engaged cognitive and affective components of attitudes. Since then, Likert has become synonymous with a question that has a qualitative rating, or fixed choice response measuring attitudes, beliefs. Typically, a Likert scale assumes a linear intensity, with a lower intensity at one end of the scale (for example: strongly disagree), and a higher at the other (strongly agree).

Uebersax (2006) clarified the difference between a Likert scale and Likert scoring. A Likert scale is a series of several items that when summed or calculated, provide a score for a particular factor or construct. NSSE Engagement indicators are examples of Likert scales. Following is an example of the Student–Faculty Interaction construct (2016), made up of four questions.

During the current school year, how often have you: (Very often, often, sometimes, never)
Talked about career plans with a faculty member.
Worked with a faculty member on activities other than coursework.
Discussed course topics, ideas, or concepts with a faculty member outside of class.
Discussed your academic performance with a faculty member.

In contrast, a Likert-scored or Likert-like question would either not be a series of questions intended to provide a single score or be intended to measure intensity of response.

Tucker (2014) challenged student affairs professionals to stop using Likert-like items to measure student outcomes. Her argument was attitudes and perceptions are indirect indicators of learning. She noted, "Asking students to 'agree' that they learned something specific from a program is not measuring student learning; rather, it's measuring what students *think* they know" (p. 30). When professionals want to know what students learned, they should ask direct measures that demonstrate co-curricular learning, such as asking students to define or apply a concept. Following are examples of typical Likert-like items used in a student affairs context:

The Diversity Training Program increased my understanding of privilege.
Strongly Disagree, Disagree, Moderately Agree, Strongly Agree
Rate the level of importance to you from 1 (Not at all important) to 7 (Extremely important)
Finding a job that lets me make a positive contribution to society 1 2 3 4 5 6 7

FIGURE 9.2. SELECTING A STATISTICAL TEST

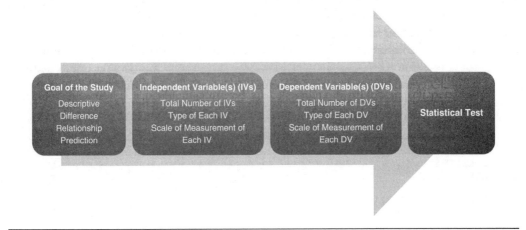

How Do Researchers Choose Statistical Tests?

Quantitative researchers choose which statistical tests to use based on alignment between the goals of the study, details about the independent variables, and details about the dependent variables. They often use a type of flow chart called a decision tree to help make these determinations. Figure 9.2 is a diagram illustrating this sequence. A more detailed version of this diagram would list choices underneath each listing for independent variables and dependent variables with lines or arrows leading to specific statistical tests.

Building Your Quantitative Research Skillset

The 10 competency areas for practitioners (ACPA/NASPA, 2015), as well as the standards for master's level preparation in the field (CAS, 2015) relate foundational outcomes for research. These broadly include selecting appropriate methods, facilitating data collection, and communicating results. ACPA/NASPA's (2015) Intermediate Competencies specify the following:

> Participate in the design and analysis of quantitative AER studies including understanding statistical reporting that may include complex statistical methods such as multivariate techniques, and articulating the differences in practical and statistical significance, validity, and reliability.

Practitioners seeking to cultivate quantitative skills that apply broadly across methodologies should seek to develop and enhance skills in statistical data collection (survey selection and design as well as sampling procedures), statistical data reporting (standardized as well as for specific audiences), and database creation and management (setting up an initial dataset as well as maintaining it during data collection and beyond). Several authors also can help aspiring researchers build expertise independently. These include Schuh et al. (2016) for specific recommendations on facilitating data collection and management (Chapter 3) and developing and selecting instruments (Chapter 6). Pryczak (2014) offers an introductory and approachable guide to basic descriptive and inferential statistical testing. Field (2013) is recommended for a more comprehensive consideration of advanced statistical analysis using advanced software.

References

American College Personnel Association & National Association of Student Personnel Administrators. (2015). *Professional competency areas for student affairs practitioners.* Washington, DC: Authors.

Astin, A. W. (1977). *Four critical years.* San Francisco, CA: Jossey-Bass.

Astin, A. W. (1984). Student involvement: A developmental theory for higher education. *Journal of College Student Personnel,* 25, 297–308.

Astin, A. W. (1993). *What matters in college? Four critical years revisited.* San Francisco, CA: Jossey-Bass.

Astin, A. W., & Sax, L. J. (1998). How undergraduates are affected by service participation. *Journal of College Student Development, 39*(3), 251–263.

Biddix, J. P., & Schwartz, R. (2012). Walter Dill Scott and the student personnel movement. *Journal of Student Affairs Research and Practice, 49*(3), 285–298.

Certis, H. (2014). The emergence of Esther Lloyd-Jones. *Journal of Student Affairs Research and Practice, 51*(3), 259–269.

Council for the Advancement of Standards in Higher Education. (2015). *CAS professional standards for higher education* (9th ed.). Washington, DC: Author.

Field, A. (2013). *Discovering statistics using IBM SPSS statistics* (4th ed.). Thousand Oaks, CA: Sage.

Higher Education Research Institute. (2017). *CIRP freshman survey.* Retrieved from https://heri.ucla.edu/cirp-freshman-survey/

Kahneman, D. (2011). *Thinking, fast and slow.* New York, NY: Farrar, Strauss and Giroux.

Kuh, G. D. (1999). How are we doing? Tracking the quality of the undergraduate experience, 1960s to the present. *The Review of Higher Education, 22*(2), 99–119.

Kuh, G. D. (2009). Understanding campus environments. In G. S. McClellan & J. Stringer (Eds.), *The handbook of student affairs administration* (3rd ed., pp. 59–80). San Francisco, CA: Jossey-Bass.

Kuh, G. D., Kinzie, J., Schuh, J. H., Whitt, E. J., & Associates. (2005/2010). *Student success in college: Creating conditions that matter.* San Francisco, CA: Jossey-Bass.

Mayhew, M. J., Rockenbach, A. N., Bowman, N. A., Seifert, T. A. D., Wolniak, G. C., Pascarella, E. T., & Terenzini, P. T. (2016). *How college affects students: 21st century evidence that higher education works* (Vol. 3). San Francisco, CA: Jossey-Bass.

National Study of Student Engagement. (2016). *NSSE 2016 engagement indicators.* Retrieved from http://nsse.indiana.edu/2016_Institutional_Report/pdf/NSSE16%20Engagement%20Indictors%20(NSSEville%20State).pdf

Palmer, R. S., McMahon, T. J., Moreggi, D. I., Rounsaville, B. J., & Ball, S. A. (2012). College student drug use: Patterns, concerns, consequences, and interest in intervention. *Journal of College Student Development, 53*(1), 124–132.

Pryczak, F. (2014). *Making sense of statistics: A conceptual overview* (6th ed.). New York, NY: Routledge.

Schuh, J. H., Biddix, J. P., Dean, L. A., & Kinzie, J. (2016). *Assessment in student affairs: A contemporary look* (2nd ed.). San Francisco, CA: Jossey-Bass.

Sriram, R. (2017). *Student affairs by the numbers.* Sterling, VA: Stylus.

Tucker, J. M. (2014). Assessment matters: Stop asking students to "strongly agree": Let's directly measure cocurricular learning. *About Campus, 19*(4), 29–32.

Uebersax, J. S. (2006). *Likert scales: Dispelling the confusion.* Retrieved from http://www.john-uebersax.com/stat/likert.htm

CHAPTER TEN

DESCRIBING TRENDS

Learning Outcomes

By the end of this chapter, you should be able to:

- Understand the purpose and role of descriptive statistics.
- Differentiate between the major types of descriptive statistics.
- Read descriptive statistics in journal articles and reports.
- Evaluate descriptive statistics based on how data are collected, analyzed, and reported.
- Apply interpretations of descriptive statistics to student affairs practice.

Descriptive statistics condense numerical information into interpretable, manageable, and useful summary data. They exchange the context and uniqueness of single data points for the ability to examine trends and tendencies. This concession is a key feature of positivism, which emphasizes data reduction and efficiency to promote a broader understanding of data.

Descriptive statistics are appealing to student affairs decision makers. Knowing common characteristics, preferences, and/or tendencies can suggest or reveal the effects of policy and programmatic decisions. Descriptive data also are appealing to research consumers. They can show summary information about data points of importance or concern as well as trends in attitudes, behaviors, and values of groups in similar contexts. In both cases, descriptive statistics can be valuable when making resource decisions or requests.

There are many ways to summarize data. Familiar measures include percentage, average, and range. Although these and other summary statistics are calculated using standardized formulas, researchers can choose how to report them. This is essential to realize when reading and evaluating statistics. Researchers can accurately report statistical results while highlighting beneficial findings. For example, reporting that 25% students do not participate in extracurricular activities is statistically the same as reporting that 75% do participate. However, emphasizing the smaller percentage might be more helpful when arguing to expand extracurricular programming.

This chapter focuses on three main classifications of descriptive statistics: frequency, central tendency, and variability. Reading descriptive measures reported in text, tables, or figures is not difficult. Evaluating descriptive statistics can be misleading, depending on how values are emphasized or reported. This chapter begins with a general overview of descriptive statistics then describes how to understand, read, evaluate, and apply results.

Understanding Descriptive Statistics

Descriptive statistics are the mostly widely used measures in research and practice. They are valued because they are widely interpretable and easy to calculate and to report. Descriptive statistics are commonly used to show trends, opinions/perceptions, needs, utilization of services, and attitudes and beliefs of people or groups. In published research, descriptive statistics are nearly always included although they rarely serve as the primary results. In most cases, they are used to complement more sophisticated techniques by adding essential and contextual details.

Descriptive statistics are associated with most research designs, inclusive of qualitative, quantitative, and mixed methods. Qualitative researchers may include descriptive statistics to summarize participant demographics, word counts from transcripts, time and date information from observations, or quantity data from documents. All types of quantitative and mixed methods designs generally include descriptive results, which might be used as the primary analysis, to show the progression of a more complex analysis, or to enhance validity and reliability by demonstrating how the sample aligns with the population.

Describing Trends

Researchers use descriptive statistics to condense or summarize data, provide context and promote transferability of results, and to add credibility or legitimacy to research designs. Following are explanations of each function.

Reasons for Understanding Descriptive Statistics

- Condense or summarize data.
- Provide context and promote transferability.
- Add credibility and legitimacy.

Condense or Summarize Data   Descriptive statistics are used to reduce, or condense, data into manageable and interpretable units. Understanding the average response to a question, most frequent preference, or percentage of individuals who share a demographic trait provides quick and understandable answers. Data can be summarized in many ways, depending on the goals of a study and type(s) of data. For example, in their case study of counseling-center planning and assessment, Reynolds and Chris (2008) included results from 37 Likert-scale survey questions ranging from 1 (Strongly Agree) to 5 (Strongly Disagree). The researchers reported mean and standard deviation scores for each item in a table, and also included a ranking system. Condensing data in this way let them efficiently show all 94 responses to the question. Results from some large-scale survey reports are only intended to provide descriptive information. For example, the 2015 NIRSA Salary Survey (NIRSA—Leaders in Collegiate Recreation, 2015) compared collegiate recreation staff salaries by position, university size, department size, average staff size, enrollment, operating budget, and other factors.

Provide Context and Promote Transferability   While studies may be composed entirely of descriptive statistics, in scholarly research they are often used to provide and/or promote transferability of results. For example, if the purpose of a study is to determine the relationship between extracurricular involvement and likelihood of graduation, the researcher would report demographic information about the sample (i.e., students) and site (i.e., institution) to give the readers some understanding of how the study might relate to their contexts. Results from large-scale surveys often include demographic information about the findings to suggest applicability and relevance in broader contexts. For example, in *The American Freshman: Fifty-Year Trends, 1966–2015*, Eagan et al. (2016) provide detailed tables and graphs showing how incoming freshmen have changed over time in terms of demographics, precollege experiences, academic preparation, goals and aspirations, and college expectations.

Perspectives From the Field—Using Descriptive Data to Inform Practice

In the work of prevention and health promotion, the ability to utilize descriptive statistics is critical to creating buy-in. Within a campus population, you have a wide range of stakeholders—administrators, faculty, staff, and students. Developing support for significant behavior or environmental change requires an understanding of what "is." In the work dedicated to prevention on university campuses, you must begin by understanding the phenomenon. Take, for example, incoming first-year student alcohol use. If you were to rely solely on students' own personal evaluation of other students' alcohol use you would likely find their perceptions informed by their own biases or use. Similarly, a faculty member may have a guess about student alcohol use, based on personal experience. By providing descriptive statistics, practitioners can help to create a shared understanding of the facts, grounded in data rather than speculation and personal opinion. Let's consider this issue in a practical application. In new student orientation you ask, "How much do you think your peers in this room drink?" In an online poll students respond and typically overestimate the drinking by their peers. Then you ask the question "How much do you drink?" Within any given cohort, 48–51% of students will report that they do not routinely drink. Inevitably, the room erupts, "Someone is lying!" You ask the question, "How many of you think they are lying?" Immediately you have a visual of your phenomenon—about 50% of the room has their hands raised. You can correct a bias in the moment *and* you can use the data to further support future prosocial decision making. Over time, you can begin to see whether there is a trend in first-year students' response to this exercise and to your survey results. Although this exercise may seem simplistic, it can become a valuable starting place for student engagement and future data collection. Then, you can begin to investigate whether your internal data look similar to the data that other institutions are sharing and how much human and fiscal resources should be dedicated to the issue?

Ashley Blamey—Title IX coordinator, The University of Tennessee

Add Credibility and Legitimacy   Quantitative researchers use specific measures to demonstrate the validity and reliability of their research; however, many audiences base their initial reactions to a study simply on how many people participated. For example, if a researcher conducted a survey but had few responses, or used existing data to describe a sample that was different from the population, readers may be concerned about the legitimacy of the study. A study highlighting differences in career paths based on race or gender characteristics that does not include African American female administrators loses some credibility when the field includes members of this demographic. Descriptive data are also used with qualitative and mixed methods research. Researchers may report summary statistics about interviews or word counts from observation notes or existing records. For example, Biddix (2010) was asked to report details about interview transcripts in a study of technology use in campus activism. He noted,

> Transcribed data for each interview ranged from 1,452 to 6,250 words per interview ($m = 3,153$, $sd = 1,147$). Most interviews took place over several sessions, ranging from 1 to more than 2 hours in length per session. (p. 683)

Method Considerations

The four primary criteria for inferential statistics (random sampling, sample size, independence, and normality) do not apply for descriptive statistics. Requirements for descriptive statistics are specified by the format of the data. For example, mean and standard deviation should not be calculated for nominal variables such as gender, class standing, or political affiliation. Similarly, percentages should not be used for scale data, such as a GPA or engagement score. There is flexibility with some types of data. For example, Likert scores might be reported as percentage responses or shown as averages (or both) depending on the goals of the analysis.

Categories of Descriptive Statistics

There are three basic categories of statistics: frequency, central tendency, and variability. Each is displayed in Table 10.1 with a brief description and listing of common types. All three categories and their associated types are prevalently used and reported in student affairs research.

Frequency is a summarized count of values. Researchers report all data as a single number (total count) or divide data into categories and then summarize the data (percentages, class intervals, or cross tabulations). A percentage is a grouping of numerical data used to summarize total count data, sometimes referred to as a proportion. When researchers group data and then summarize the data in each grouping, they create class intervals. A *class interval* is a grouping of numerical data

Table 10.1. Basic Categories of Descriptive Statistics

Category	Description	Types
Frequency	Summary of Values	Class Interval Percentage Cross Tabulation
Central Tendency	Most Common or Average Value	Mean Median Mode
Variability	Spread of Data	Range Standard Deviation

into categories based on a range. Class refers to a category and interval refers to a grouping range. The range (or size) of the interval is determined by the researchers depending on how they want to display the data. Researchers also may be interested in how data are distributed into categories. A *cross tabulation*, or crosstab, is a grouping of numerical data into categories by combining two or more variables. Cross refers to the point where the data merge and tabulation is the merged value. For example, a researcher may want to determine how many individuals in three different groups are males (crossing group by sex). Cross-tabulated data are often displayed in tables, where the cross tabulation appears at the intersections of columns and rows.

Central tendency is the most common or average value. Mean is the arithmetic average. It is most appropriately used to summarize numerical data. Median is the number falling in the 50th percentile, or the midpoint of data. Half of the values are higher than this number, half are lower. It is best used when there are outliers or extreme values in the data and is often used with income data. Mode is the most frequently occurring value. It is preferable to use with categorical data or when there is little variation in values, such as with small Likert scales (< 5 values).

Interpreting Standard Deviation

Another way to think of standard deviation is as an average score, representing the mean difference between each value and the mean for the total data. It is reported as *SD, sd, s^2*, or simply in parentheses following mean, for example, 2.2 (.5). In most cases, researchers want a smaller standard deviation because it means there is less spread, or variability, in the data.

The first word, standard, indicates that the statistic is based on a normalized value. This standardization allows for consistent interpretation. A principle to remember is the 68–95–99 rule, which is expanded as:

1 standard deviation above or below the mean contains 68% of the values.[*]

2 standard deviations above or below the mean contains 95% of the values.

3 standard deviations above or below the mean contains 99% of the values.

The second word, deviation, indicates that the statistic is based on a varying value. This deviation reveals how distant the values are from the average. In other words, it is the average of the deviations.

To read standard deviation (*SD*), simply subtract 1 *SD* away from and add 1 *SD* to the mean. A shorthand reminder for this is +1/−1. Following are examples with notes on interpretation.

_____

[*] Note that the majority of values (68%) falls within one standard deviation of the mean.

Example 1

In a study of career paths in student affairs, Biddix (2011) reported that it took men an average of 21 years to become senior student affairs officers (SSAOs). In text, the statistical notation is $M = 20.8$, $SD = 7.1$. This finding suggests that while the average number of years it took to become an SSAO was 20.8, there was considerable variability, 7.1 years. Adding and subtracting one standard deviation (+/− 7.1) from the mean (20.8), reveals that the majority of men (68%) took between 13.7 and 27.9 years to reach the SSAO. Looking only at the mean would cause a reader to mistakenly assume that 21 years was the common length of time it took to become SSAO at a master's-level institution.

Example 2

Another example from the same article (Biddix, 2011) shows a more problematic example. The column data in Table 10.2 shows each functional area stop future SSAOs took. Mean and standard deviation are reported as M and SD at the bottom of the table. For men at early/mid-career, the M number of years in that position was 4.6, with an SD of 3.4. This indicates that the majority of men stayed in the second role between 1.2 and 8.0 years, which is less helpful for an aspiring SSAO when deciding how long he should stay at this career stage.

Table 10.2. Career Areas Leading to the SSAO

	Early		Early/Mid		Mid		Mid/Late		Late		Last[a]	
	M	W	M	W	M	W	M	W	M	W	M	W
n	34	19	59	29	64	30	69	33	71	35	71	35
Dean of Students	X	X	X		X[b]	X	X[b]	X[b]	X[b]	X[b]	X[b]	X[b]
Residential Life	X[b]	X[b]	X[b]	X[b]	X	X[b]	X	X	X			
Student Activities			X	X								
Business			X		X							
K–12 Teaching	X											
Years in Area												
M	4.2	5.2	4.6	4.0	3.3	3.2	3.1	3.2	3.5	2.5	2.6	2.9
SD	3.5	3.8	3.4	2.5	2.3	2.0	1.9	2.3	3.8	1.5	2.7	2.5

[a]Area preceding the SSAO.
[b]Most frequent career area selected.
Source: Biddix (2011), Table 5, p. 451. Reprinted by permission of NASPA—National Association of Student Personnel Administrators/Student Affairs Administrators in Higher Education.
Note. X indicates career area selected.

Variability is the spread of data. It is also referred to as dispersion and is among the most informative statistics in quantitative research. The larger the variability, the larger the spread in data; the smaller the variability, the smaller the spread in data. Range shows the highest and lowest values in a dataset. *Standard deviation* is the average variability (or deviation) of a set of numbers. In other words, range reveals how far apart the data are in total; standard deviation reveals how far apart the responses are on average. Variability statistics are among the most often overlooked and underreported descriptive statistics in student affairs research.

Reading Descriptive Statistics

Researchers list descriptive statistics in text, tables, and graphs. The reporting format can depend on the type of data, researcher preferences, or publication guidelines. When reported in text or tables, researchers may use letters or symbols as abbreviations for the total data or participants, mean, and standard deviation. Generally, when letters are used, lowercase indicates sample while uppercase is used for population. Statistical notation is generally shown in italics. Mean and standard deviation have both letter and symbol abbreviations that are acceptable to use, although letters seem to be more commonly reported in student affairs research. Table 10.3 is a reference table for common abbreviations.

This section is divided into common formats, showcasing results in text, tables, and graphs. Excerpts from articles and reports showing descriptive statistics along with general notes on interpretation follow.

Table 10.3. Common Mean and Standard Deviation Abbreviations

	Sample	Population
Total Data or Participants	*n*	*N*
Mean	*m* $\bar{x}$ (x bar)	*M* μ (mu)
Standard Deviation	*sd* s	*SD* σ (sigma)

Descriptive Statistics in Text

Researchers provide descriptive statistics in the methods or results sections to summarize details about the study population and sample. When studies involve multiple demographic characteristics, survey questions, or other measures, a large number of descriptive statistics can be difficult to read when reported in text format. This is especially true with frequency statistics. More commonly appearing in text are overall population trends, sample numbers, central tendency, and variability. Following are examples of how descriptive statistics appear in text from a study on academic advising and first-year students.

Population and Sample

In Fall 2009, approximately 10,500 undergraduates were enrolled at the university with gender and racial compositions as follows: 58% female and 42% male; 60% Caucasian, 25% African American, and 15% other. First-generation students comprised approximately 30% of the incoming 2009 freshman class.

Reports generated by a university information-technology staff member included data for all first-time, full-time, first-generation students ($N = 437$) who matriculated in Fall 2009.

The final sample consisted of 363 records. (Swecker, Fifolt, & Searby, 2013, p. 48)

Mean and Standard Deviation

The mean number of advising meetings was 3.4 (SD = 2.02). (Swecker, Fifolt, & Searby, 2013, p. 48)

Review the statistics reported in the text examples. Following are interpretation notes:

- Population and sample include total counts and percentages by demographic category. The example includes all undergraduates enrolled and percentages for gender, race, and first generation status.
- Also included is a total count for the population of interest (all first-time, full-time, first-generation students [$N = 437$] who matriculated in Fall 2009) and the final sample (363).
- Mean is interpreted as the average response, but not as the most common because it can be significantly affected by outliers. The average number of advising meetings was 3.4.
- Standard deviation shows the spread of the data. There was a lot of variability in the example. Most students met with advisors between 1.38 and 5.42 times (3.4 − 2.02 and 3.4 + 2.02).

Descriptive Statistics in Tables

Researchers often include a table to display demographic results or other independent variables. They may also include a full listing of questions from a survey along with frequency, central tendency, and variability measures. The format for the values (raw numbers, class intervals, percentages) is sometimes influenced by researcher preferences but most often is dictated by the number and type of variable. Following are examples of how descriptive statistics appear in a table from a study of student affairs master's students' career plans.

Frequency, Mean, Standard Deviation, Percentage, Cross Tabulation. Examine the statistics reported in Table 10.4. Following are some notes for interpretation:

- Frequency data are the numbers listed under n (for example, in Group 1, Male = 3, Female = 7).
- Mean (M) and standard deviation (SD) are listed in the first row and only for ages between the two groups (for example, in Group 1, M age = 27.0 and SD = 4.6). The other variables do not have these central tendency measures because they are not scale level (numerical).
- Percentages are listed for each of the nominal variables (for example, in Group 2, 78% of the sample was middle class).
- Cross tabulations are listed under the column headings as Groups 1 and 2, to show comparisons between the two samples. Totaling a column or row provides counts for the full sample.

Table 10.4. Participant Demographics

	Group 1 (Plans to remain in the field)		Group 2 (Plans to leave the field)	
	M	*SD*	*M*	*SD*
Age				
Years	27.0	4.6	25.9	2.5
	n	%	*n*	%
Gender				
Male	3	43	4	57
Female	7	55	6	46
Race				
African American	3	100	0	0
Asian American	1	33	2	67
Latino/a	1	50	1	50
White	6	50	6	50
Class				
Lower/Lower-Mid.	4	80	1	20
Middle	2	22	7	78
Upper/Upper-Mid.	4	80	1	20
Employment Status				
Part-time	5	45	6	55
Full-time	5	56	4	44

Source: From Silver and Jakeman (2014), p. 174. Reprinted by permission of NASPA—National Association of Student Personnel Administrators/Student Affairs Administrators in Higher Education.

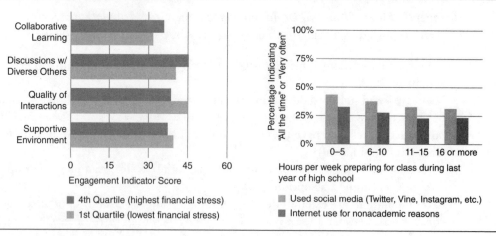

FIGURE 10.1A. SELECTED ENGAGEMENT INDICATORS

FIGURE 10.1B. USE OF SOCIAL MEDIA AND INTERNET

Source: Reprinted with permission by the National Survey of Student Engagement.

Descriptive Statistics in Graphs

Researchers use different types of graphs for displaying descriptive statistics. Variations of bar charts and line graphs are most common. Following are examples from two research reports. The bar charts are from the *NSSE 2015 Report: Engagement Insights: Survey Findings on the Quality of Undergraduate Education* (National Survey of Student Engagement, 2015). The line graph is from *The American Freshman: National Norms Fall 2015* (Eagan et al., 2015).

Horizontal, Vertical, and Stacked Bar Charts. Figure 10.1A shows a horizontal bar chart showing combined percentages for four engagement indicators among first-year students, related to their financial stress levels.

Figure 10.1B shows a vertical bar chart showing combined Very Often and All of the Time percentages for hours per week spent preparing for class by nonacademic social media and Internet use.

Figure 10.2 shows a stacked horizontal bar chart. Stacked refers to all responses being included on each line, totaling to 100%. In the example, all Likert-like responses are shown by multiple categories for how the faculty believe their institution supports people by different identity categories.

FIGURE 10.2. EXTENT TO WHICH FACULTY BELIEVE THEIR INSTITUTION SUPPORTS PEOPLE BY DIFFERENT IDENTITY CATEGORIES

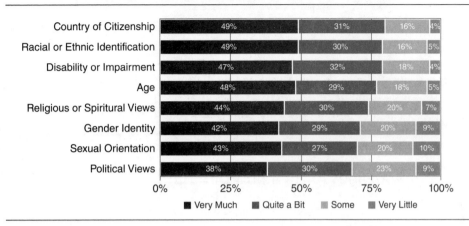

Source: Reprinted with permission by the National Survey of Student Engagement.

Line Graph. Figure 10.3 shows responses for seven different questions related to how students value different civic engagement activities. The data are aggregated to include a percentage of respondents indicating Very Important and Essential for each question by year from 2011 to 2015. The data is also cross tabulated to merge response and year. Each question is displayed with a different type of line to help the reader quickly differentiate responses.

FIGURE 10.3. THE IMPORTANCE OF CIVIC ENGAGEMENT

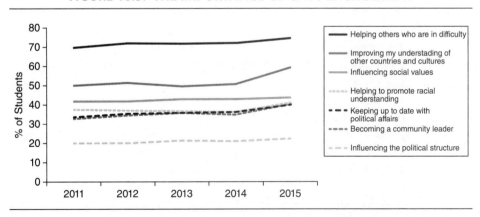

Source: From Eagan et al. (2016). Reprinted by permission of the Higher Education Research Institute.

Examine the statistics in each graph example. Following are general notes for interpretation.

- Consider how data are distributed in bar charts. Understanding distribution can reveal details about the raw data. Values can be gathered around a central number, skewed to higher or lower numbers, or evenly spread.
- Locate the scale (or range) of data in graphics. Sometimes researchers adjust the scale to highlight similarity or variation.
- Look for whether or not lines intersect in line graphs, which can reveal similarities, differences, and relationships in the data.

Guidelines for Reading Descriptive Statistics

- Locate or determine the population and sample.
- Disaggregate the data.
- Interpret mean with standard deviation.

Locate or Determine the Population and Sample   The population and sample generally are listed at the beginning of a methods section. In a published article, the data also might appear in the abstract. These two values add context and legitimacy to the study by letting the reader determine the representativeness of the sample. It is seldom possible to obtain a completely representative sample of a population, including all variables of interest. As a result, samples always involve decisions that lead to compromises. Researchers typically target specific characteristics and then explain why others either were unrepresented, unobtainable, or unnecessary. When reading descriptive statistics, look for information about the population along with rationale for any differences in the sample.

Disaggregate the Data   Researchers make intentional decisions when summarizing findings. Often as part of the data reduction process, researchers aggregate (or reduce and/or combine) data either to promote interpretability, highlight a specific pattern, or to conceal a deficiency. When reading aggregated data, it is important to consider the original raw data. This does not have to be a precise exercise. It can simply be an estimate based on the percentages or class intervals. Understanding the origin of combined data leads to a clearer comprehension of the sample and population.

Interpret Mean With Standard Deviation   Mean is an imprecise measure that is often misinterpreted. At best, it represents roughly the middle of a set of data, but in many cases, even this is inaccurate because of outliers. Researchers hesitate to use the word average, because it suggests the value is an approximation of a normal or most common response. Unfortunately, many readers view mean as an actual average. Variability statistics, in particular standard deviation, help to improve this misinterpretation. Standard deviation is literally a uniform measure of the spread in a dataset, the average of all deviations from the mean. Mean and standard deviation are intrinsically linked to help offset problems in misinterpreting average, normal, or common among a set of values. The prior examples for how to interpret standard deviation illustrate issues with only interpreting mean.

Evaluating Descriptive Statistics

Descriptive statistics are the most recognizable research results to most readers. Interpreting summary statistics is relatively intuitive. Unfortunately, this familiarity also causes readers to overlook important aspects when evaluating research, resulting in potential misinterpretations. This is especially problematic with basic reports or when descriptive statistics are the precursor to a sophisticated main analysis in a published study. Standardized formulas cannot be altered and still produce accurate results. While a researcher summarizing data cannot change the result of a calculation, they can choose which aspects to highlight. For example, 90% agreement on a statement is statistically the same as saying 10% disagreement, but there are situations when highlighting one over the other is more advantageous. Following are some considerations for evaluating descriptive results, focusing on questions to ask when reviewing specific statistics.

Questions for Evaluating Descriptive Statistics

- Are the statistics appropriate for the data?
- When was the study conducted?
- What is not reported?
- How did the researchers aggregate data?
- What is the scale of the table or chart?

Are the Statistics Appropriate for the Data?   When reviewing descriptive statistics, a first procedural consideration is whether or not the data fit the measure. This requires some consideration about the scales of measurement, or format of the data. For example, if several of the descriptive variables are nominal (such as race/ethnicity and year in school), while others are scale (such as entering ACT score or first-semester GPA), the accompanying statistics should include percentage (for nominal variables) and mean (for scale variables). Researchers sometimes mistakenly report mean and (even standard deviation) values for all variables.

When Was the Study Conducted?   The context of a study, inclusive of timing, location, and unaccounted factors, can affect results. A survey about political attitudes among college students is likely to produce different findings when administered on a majority liberal campus versus a majority conservative campus. Giving the same survey to either group of students during an election year is also likely to produce different results. As another example, asking first-year student affairs practitioners about job satisfaction and graduation preparation is likely to yield different results just after orientation than after winter break or spring graduation. The functional area of the sample is likely to affect this rating also, as a high concentration of housing professionals is likely to respond differently to contextual factors than professionals primarily involved in academic advising or programming. Unfortunately, researchers seldom include sufficient details to evaluate specific campus factors that can influence results. One indicator that unaccounted factors may have influenced results is surprising findings, such as unexpectedly variable statistics.

What Is Not Reported?   Although calculations making up descriptive statistics are for the most part standardized, researchers have some flexibility in how they choose to present data. Choices may be intentional or dictated. For example, if the focus of an article is on reporting retention rate, showing it as 80% as opposed to providing the actual number may simply be the preferred format for displaying the data. The calculations forming the values likely are valid. The critical reader should question both what has been reported and what might have been deemphasized.

How Did the Researchers Aggregate Data?   Researchers summarize, or aggregate results in tables for efficiency or to use higher-level statistics. There are no standardized guidelines for how to aggregate or combine data (such as, which class intervals to choose). For example, researchers sometimes combine categories using class intervals if responses to questions are too low or unevenly distributed for further analysis. Aggregating or combining response is not problematic if there is a good rationale to do so. However, the reader should have enough information to infer what was merged. In most cases, this means including the total number of responses to a question with total size of the sample.

Highlighting and Underemphasizing Results

Researchers can report data in a way that, while still true, can emphasize a particular point of view while leaving controversial or disconfirming results underemphasized or unstated. Following are several fabricated examples based on published studies and reports.

Example 1

A social norms approach to marketing suggests that actions are influenced by what individuals perceive as the norm, or common behavior. In the case of alcohol use, if a student believes binge drinking is the norm among her peers, she is more likely to also binge drink. For example, a researcher surveyed 1,000 female students, asking if they consumed more than four drinks in a 2-hour period at least once in the past 2 weeks. Summarized results might show that 620/1,000 of women fit the category of binge drinker. Instead of saying that 62% of women binge drink, or 38% do not, a social norms approach would emphasize the less drastic numerical statistic, highlighting that, "About 2 out of 5 college women do not binge drink."

Example 2

Compare the two columns of demographic data in the following table. Both the actual counts and the percentage values are accurate. However, if the researcher wanted to suggest more diversity in a sample to the audience, they might only show the percentages in the table.

Race/Ethnicity Identification ($n = 30$)

Race/Ethnicity	Actual Count	Percentage
African American	4	13.3%
Asian Pacific Islander	3	10.0%
Caucasian	14	46.67%
Latino/a	4	13.3%
No response	5	16.7%

Example 3

To highlight advantageous or detrimental responses, a researcher might combine the upper or lower ends of a Likert-like scale. Below, the researcher could combine the highest two categories to say that 60% of students agree that campus dining options are acceptable. Alternatively, the researcher might say that 40% are not satisfied with campus dining.

Satisfaction With Campus Dining Options
(Level of Agreement)

Response	Percentage
Strongly disagree	10%
Disagree	15%
Neither agree or disagree	15%
Agree	45%
Strongly agree	15%

What Is the Scale of the Table or Chart?   When displaying results in a table or chart, researchers choose the scale, or units of measure. Similar to choosing which statistics to highlight, researchers can decide the size of intervals to display. Depending on the values shown, manipulating scales to be smaller or larger can give the appearance of confirming or unexpected results. Other ways to manipulate graphed data include:

- Making the vertical or horizontal scales too large or small.
- Skipping numbers or not starting at zero.
- Mislabeling table of chart.
- Not including data.

Following is a fabricated example incorporating some these issues. Additional examples can be found in *Misleading Graphs: Real Life Examples* (Statistics How To, 2017).

Since 2015, service-learning staff have tracked participation of student volunteers at a local elementary school. The staff created several graphics to show results. Figure 10.4 shows the total average number of hours per week students volunteered over a 3-year period. In the graph on the left, the scale is changed to 2 and does not

FIGURE 10.4. HOURS PER WEEK SPENT VOLUNTEERING BY YEAR (COMPARISON GRAPHS)

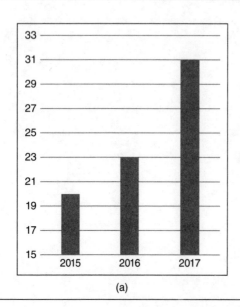

(a)

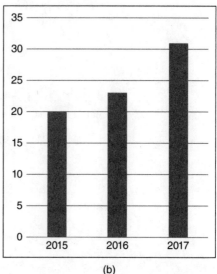

(b)

FIGURE 10.5. HOURS PER WEEK SPENT VOLUNTEERING BY CLASS STANDING (COMPARISON GRAPHS)

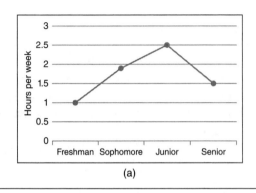

(a)

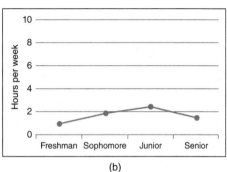

(b)

begin at 0. The graph on the right shows a scale of 5 and begins at 0. The staff could highlight either result to show how average hours changed, either at a steep rate (left), or more consistently (right). The graphs also do not include titles, the total sample size, the number of respondents per year, or variability.

Figure 10.5 shows the average hours per week students volunteered by class standing. Even though the mean for all years is about the same (1–2.5 hours), the shift in the scale from .5 (left) to 2 (right) changes the perception of how many volunteer hours the students contributed as well as the differences by class. The graphs also do not include titles, the total sample size, the number of respondents per class, or variability.

Table 10.5 shows the percentage of student visits per week by major. It is not possible to tell how many total students were included or how many students were from each group. According to the table, Communication majors visited the least; however, if there were more communication majors than all others, 5% could be a

Table 10.5. Visits per Week by Major

Major	Visits per Week
Business	14%
Communications	5%
Education	48%
Science	33%

high number. Conversely, it appears that Education students visited the most at 48%, but that percentage may be comprised of only a few students.

Applying Descriptive Statistics

Descriptive statistics can be useful for interpreting data, examining trends, and making comparisons related to participation, trends, needs, utilization, and outcomes. Their prevalence in research is associated with the ease of data collection, analysis, and reporting. They are also widely used because they are interpretable by most student affairs audiences and stakeholders. Following are some suggestions for how to apply descriptive statistics results to practice.

Opportunities for Applying Descriptive Statistics

- Using summarized data to support decisions.
- Reviewing and evaluating trends.
- Making comparisons and benchmarking.

Using Summarized Data to Support Decisions   The ability to interpret and evaluate summarized data effectively is essential for a decision maker. Descriptive statistics in published reports can show what is successful in other settings as well as suggest areas for potential growth. Descriptive information also can be used to support or legitimize resource decisions about services or programs. Descriptive statistics provide quick and broadly interpretable numerical values suggesting how the typical student, most students, or students on average might be characterized as well as how they experience campus services and programming. When this data is not available locally, findings from studies in similar contexts (institutional settings, student demographics, or programs) can be useful for supporting decisions. Institutional reports from large-scale surveys also can provide decision makers with a national pulse useful in considering the potential impact of initiating, revising, or expanding academic and extracurricular services related to student engagement, development, and learning.

Reviewing and Evaluating Trends   Trend comparison supports resource requests and funding allocation. Trend data can be generated from existing data on campus or they can be created by locating, recording, and modeling comparisons appearing in published research and reports. Being able to interpret, evaluate, and display existing or projected summary outcomes for programs and services in various reporting formats is invaluable for supporting funding proposals. The ability to show trend comparisons, particularly when multiple measures are taken of the same program over time, is also an applicable use of existing descriptive statistics. Further, understanding and being able to apply (and explain) variance statistics such as standard deviation can help distinguish differences or similarities in group trends even when the means are nearly identical.

Making Comparisons and Benchmarking   *Benchmarking* involves locating and evaluating existing data to make comparisons. Benchmarking also can include generating data locally for comparison to external trends. For the purposes of applying descriptive statistics, a practitioner might identify a comparison metric and one or more similar groups. Often, benchmarking includes peer groups that are considered similar as well as peer groups that might be considered aspirational. Peer groups usually are identified based on similarity for the metrics of interest, but they also might be defined based on other factors, such as institutional demographics, similar services, or financial models. When identifying metrics and peers for benchmarking or comparison, it is essential to have good rationale for choices. Most institutional research offices have already identified or established peer groups for a specific campus as part of their annual reports. These groups would represent a good starting point when engaging in benchmarking activities. Aside from campus-based statistics collected or examined from existing records, published articles, reports, and information available from other sources also can facilitate benchmarking and comparisons.

Building Your Descriptive Statistics Skillset

Descriptive statistics are familiar to most practitioners. They provide an overview of data trends that allow for summary and comparison. Regretfully, decisions, in small and very large contexts, are often made using only frequency (percentage) or central tendency (mean) values. Variability, arguably among the most valuable statistic, is less often interpreted outside of research contexts. This chapter demonstrated that mean should never be interpreted without standard deviation. This does not suggest that practitioners must be able to calculate standard deviation by hand, but they should be able to interpret the value when it is included or know to request it when it is not. If it is necessary to calculate, most spreadsheet programs have a function for easily computing standard deviation and there are several easy to use online calculators.

Perspectives From the Field—Working With Descriptive Data

We annually use the NASPA Consortium Benchmarking survey for Campus Recreation that is endorsed by NIRSA—Leaders in Collegiate Recreation. The information we obtain from this is used in several ways once we analyze the data and further filter it using cross tabulation for specific areas of interest.

One example is that we compare our institutional data against other schools nationally (or by state or region) to find out how we are doing in multiple areas, such as students' perception of positive impact of participation in our programs, cleanliness of the facility, and the extent to which having a recreation facility impacts students' decision to stay at this university.

Statistics such as 98% either strongly (80%) or somewhat (18%) agree that "Recreation facilities are clean" compared to the national average of 92% either strongly (62%) or somewhat (30%) agree lets us know that our custodial staff is doing a great job. It also lets us share this with them as praise and a motivational tool.

Being able to report to our administration that 91% of students reported using any of our facilities, programs, or services, and that 88% of students reported that participation in campus recreation increased or improved their stress management, and that 94% reported an increase or improvement in overall health is something positive that we can use when asking for funding or even replacing positions in dire economic times.

Another way we use the data is to cross tabulate certain questions to find out specific responses from a particular subgroup. For instance, we emphasize in our staff training that we need to be welcoming and inclusive of all groups so that everyone feels safe and positive about using our facilities and programs. One such group that I wanted to ensure felt safe was those that identify as LGBT students. Using cross tabulation I was able to isolate that self-identified group of students' response to the question "Recreation facilities provide a safe environment." We learned that while 97% of our general population who answered the survey strongly or somewhat agrees with that statement, 100% of those who identify as LGBT did so. This let us know that we were doing a good job so far with our staff training and the environment we help create. We will continue to emphasize welcoming everyone and ensuring that they feel safe, but at least we now know that what we are doing is working.

Kenneth W. Morton—Director of Campus Recreation, Stephen F. Austin State University

Evaluating descriptive statistics is a critical and undervalued skill for practitioners. Being able to see through data, ask questions about what is reported and what is not, and draw conclusions based on these observations is invaluable. These skills can be built and honed by asking questions posed in this chapter while reading and evaluating statistical reports and published studies. Descriptive statistics are also taught in most introductory research courses. Beyond coursework, both Holcomb and Cox (2018) and Pryczak (2014) offer guides to interpreting statistics that also show ways to present descriptive data. Holcomb (1997) is an older but useful text with guided exercises for calculating descriptive statistics.

References

Biddix, J. P. (2010). Relational leadership and technology: A study of activist college women leaders. *NASPA Journal about Women in Higher Education, 3*(1), 25–47.

Biddix, J. P. (2011). "Stepping stones": Career paths to the SSAO for men and women at four-year institutions. *Journal of Student Affairs Research and Practice, 48*(4), 443–461.

Eagan, K., Stolzenberg, E. B., Bates, A. K., Aragon, M. C., Suchard, M. R., & Rios-Aguilar, C. (2015). *The American freshman: National norms fall 2015.* Los Angeles, CA: Higher Education Research Institute, UCLA.

Eagan, M. K., Stolzenberg, E. B., Ramirez, J. J., Aragon, M. C., Suchard, M. R., & Rios-Aguilar, C. (2016). *The American freshman: Fifty-year trends, 1966–2015.* Los Angeles, CA: Higher Education Research Institute, UCLA.

Holcomb, Z. C. (1997). *Fundamentals of descriptive statistics.* New York, NY: Routledge.

Holcomb, Z. C., & Cox, K. C. (2018). *Interpreting basic statistics: A workbook based on excerpts from journal articles* (8th ed.). New York, NY: Routledge.

National Survey of Student Engagement. (2015). *Engagement insights: Survey findings on the quality of undergraduate education—Annual results 2015.* Bloomington: Indiana University Center for Postsecondary Research.

NIRSA—Leaders in Collegiate Recreation. (2015). *NIRSA salary survey 2015: A survey of salaries in collegiate recreation.* Corvallis, OR: NIRSA.

Pryczak, F. (2014). *Making sense of statistics: A conceptual overview* (6th ed.). New York, NY: Routledge.

Reynolds, A., & Chris, S. (2008). Improving practice through outcomes based planning and assessment: A counseling center case study. *Journal of College Student Development, 49*(4), 374–387.

Silver, B. R., & Jakeman, R. C. (2014). Understanding intent to leave the field: A study of student affairs master's students' career plans. *Journal of Student Affairs Research and Practice, 51*(2), 170–182.

Statistics How To. (2017). *Misleading graphs: Real life examples.* Retrieved from http://www.statisticshowto.com/misleading-graphs/

Swecker, H. K., Fifolt, M., & Searby, L. (2013). Academic advising and first-generation college students: A quantitative study on student retention. *NACADA Journal, 33*(1), 46–53.

CHAPTER ELEVEN

TESTING DIFFERENCES

Learning Outcomes

By the end of this chapter, you should be able to:

- Understand the purpose and role of difference statistics.
- Differentiate between the major types of difference statistics.
- Read difference statistics in journal articles and reports.
- Evaluate difference statistics based on how data are collected, analyzed, and reported.
- Apply interpretations of difference statistics to student affairs practice.

Difference statistics examine change between groups, allowing researchers to make inferences (evidenced guesses) about a population, to distinguish groups, and to track changes over time. As inferential statistics, difference statistics offer generalizability, or applications beyond data that can be applied both to research and to practice. The concept of difference comes from verifying whether what is learned from a randomly drawn sample is statistically dissimilar enough to say it might be true of a population. If the sample is random and sufficiently large, the appropriate statistical (significance) test can be used to generalize findings from the sample to the population. Difference statistics also are used in combination with relationship and prediction statistics to establish strength of association (effect size) and to verify statistical assumptions (correlation, regression). Difference statistics are reported extensively in student affairs research.

Despite some variations, most difference statistics share common terminology and reporting formats, which makes reading and evaluating results straightforward with basic concept proficiency. They are used in nearly every academic field, from treatment analyses in biology to election polls in political science and intervention studies in psychology. The basic concepts related in this chapter are consistent across fields, providing a valuable, interdisciplinary research language. The chapter begins with a general overview of difference statistics and the concept of significance and then describes how to understand, read, evaluate, and apply difference results.

Understanding Difference Statistics

The concept of difference comes from verifying whether sample data is representative of the population. A researcher using difference statistics is not asking, "Is there a difference?" This can be established visually. For example, if the average satisfaction rating for campus housing options is 3.5 out of 5.0 for freshmen and 3.7 for upperclassmen, a simple conclusion is that upperclassmen are more satisfied with their housing options. A researcher using difference statistics is instead asking, "Does a difference exist in the population?" This result cannot be visually confirmed without obtaining a rating from every member of the population. Instead, the researcher would take a smaller random sample of the data and test for a statistical difference.

Words Researchers Use—Significance

When researchers evaluate differences, they use a significance test. A *significance test* evaluates differences in summary values such as mean, rank, or percentage. A significant result usually means the observed difference is also reflected in the population. Specifically, the test evaluates a null hypothesis (the sample value = the population value). A significant result (rejecting the null hypothesis) indicates that the difference observed in the sample likely mirrors a difference in the population. Alternately, a not significant result (failing to reject the null hypothesis) indicates that the difference observed in the sample is not mirrored in the population. Either result can be beneficial, depending on what is being tested. For example, a researcher may want to find a difference for learning outcomes based on attending a program (a significant result), but may not want to find a difference between how men and women experience the program (a not significant result). Understanding this basic concept is fundamental to understanding statistical significance, the primary value interpreted when reading difference statistics.

Difference statistics work by making comparisons between two or more groups sampled from a population. Two types of groups can be tested: created and established. A created group is one a researcher forms when collecting data from a random sample of a population. Returning to the example, if the researcher wanted to estimate the satisfaction rating for all students housed on campus, they would need to take two or more random samples and statistically compare them. The samples would constitute two or more created groups. An established group is based on a preexisting category defined or identified in the population. Extending the prior example, the researcher would need to randomly sample freshmen and upperclassmen for comparison. In either case, taking a random, adequately sized, and relatively equal sample from each group and then using the appropriate difference statistic allows the researcher to make an inference about students' satisfaction with their housing options.

When testing differences, created or established groups are independent variables. The measures collected about the groups are dependent variables. The scales of measurement (type, quantity, and size of the groups and measures) specify the specific difference test the researcher will use.

Testing Differences

Researchers use difference statistics to make inferences, or educated guesses about population values, to evaluate differences between two or more groups, and to evaluate differences within groups over time. Following are explanations of each function.

Reasons for Understanding Difference Statistics

- Estimate population values.
- Evaluate differences between groups.
- Evaluate differences within a group over time.

Estimate Population Values   A fundamental purpose of difference statistics is to make inferences, or evidenced guesses. Descriptive measures such as frequencies, measures of central tendency, and variability provide summary information that simplify decision making. As noted in the prior discussion about inferential statistics, it is often not possible to gather all the information needed about a population. This is especially true for understanding trends, perceptions, and experiences. Difference statistics allow researchers to learn the answers to these types of questions efficiently.

Evaluate Differences Between Groups   Student affairs researchers and practitioners often are interested in understanding how trends, perceptions, and experiences vary based on specific characteristics, demographics, or groups. For example, a published study about career fair outcomes might include difference statistics with satisfaction comparisons by major. Testing differences in ratings using a random sample of students who attended could reveal how students from different majors valued attending the event. This type of study is also referred to as a within-groups or independent samples design, because the measure is based on different (independent) groups within a population.

Perspectives From the Field—Why Significance Matters

Student affairs educators must answer the question of which programs and services that we coordinate influence student success? Additionally, what is the chance that the same or similar students would have been successful without these experiences? Knowing the difference between those who participate and those who do not, while not necessarily demonstrating causality, certainly may be a factor in making the case for continuing to provide these experiences. Conducting difference tests, such as ANOVAs, helps us to demonstrate the significance of the learning environments we are creating. Such evidence could positively influence the decision to continue these programs and services and also influence the allocation of resources (human and fiscal) or help us decide how to redirect resources if there is no significant difference between those who participate and those who do not.

Daniel A. Bureau—Executive Assistant to the Vice President for Student Affairs, University of Memphis

---

Evaluate Differences Within a Group Over Time   Sometimes it is valuable to know how trends, perceptions, and experiences change over time within the same group. For example, the same study about career fair outcomes might include a question about learning outcomes the researchers asked each student before and after they attended the event. If the surveys were given to a sufficiently large and random sample of attendees and the pre- and post-data for each student could be matched, the researcher could interpret the results as reflective of the population. This type of study is also referred to as a between-groups or dependent samples study, because the measure is based on the same (dependent) groups within a population. Other common terms are pre/post surveys or repeated measures.

Research Considerations

Four common requirements for inferential statistics were introduced in the introductory chapter on quantitative research concepts. Two of the requirements are shared by all of the difference statistics in this chapter: random sampling and sample size. The other two requirements, independence and normality, depend on the goals of the research and the influence of the test needed. Independence refers to whether the data are drawn from different individuals or measures (independent) or the same (dependent). Data from dependent samples are generally pre/post or repeated measures. Normality means that the data follow a normal curve (have high and low values but tend to group around a mean, or central number). When normality is not met (data are more grouped around high or low values), researchers testing for differences use nonparametric tests.

Main Types of Difference Statistics

This chapter introduces three main types of difference statistics, distinguished by type, use, and requirements. Two are for parametric data (normally distributed, typically interval or scale values) and one for nonparametric data (not normally distributed, typically nominal or ordinal values). Table 11.1 is a summary of the main types and uses of difference statistics, including test symbols.

Table 11.1. Main Types of Difference Statistics

Difference Test	Type	Use	Sample Requirement	Test Symbol
t-test	Parametric	*Between Groups*		t
		Tests differences between two groups using mean scores.	Two groups of at least 15 in each, preferably 30.	
		Within Groups		
		Tests differences for two mean scores within the same group.	Two scores for each member of a group of at least 15, preferably 30.	
ANOVA	Parametric	*Within Groups*		F
		Tests differences between two or more groups using mean scores.	Two or more groups of at least 15 in each, preferably 30.	
		Between Groups		
		Tests differences for two or more mean scores within the same group.	Two or more scores for each member of a group of at least 15, preferably 30.	
Chi-square	Nonparametric	Tests differences using percentages for two groups.	Two or more groups that have at least 5 in each group when combined.	χ^2

Difference tests generally all follow a basic research process that involves formulating a hypothesis, collecting random sample data from a population, testing the hypothesis, calculating the test value, and interpreting the result (significance) of the test. Variations are based on the types and formats of variables, as well as the calculations used.

A *t*-test (*t*) is a parametric test that evaluates differences between or within two groups by comparing mean scores. An *analysis of variance* (*ANOVA*; *F-test*) is a parametric test that evaluates differences between or within two or more groups by comparing mean scores. Both require numerical (interval or scale) data and need to meet minimum requirements for random sample, sample size, independence, normal distribution, and group size. Researchers use several synonymous names to describe the two main types of *t*-test and ANOVA. Table 11.2 summarizes common names for the main types and differentiates between and within groups tests.

Between Groups. A between-groups test evaluates group scores such as attitudes, perceptions, or beliefs. For example, Sax and Weintraub (2014) explored the role of parents in the emotional well-being of first-year students. They used *t*-tests to evaluate between group differences in modes of communication preferences with parents between male and female students. Similarly, Bentley-Edwards and Chapman-Hilliard (2015) examined racial cohesion and dissonance in different college contexts between groups to understand how Black college students perceived and navigated the challenge of balancing personal success and social responsibility. Specifically, they considered differences between students at historically Black

Table 11.2. Other Names for *t*-test and ANOVA

	t-test	ANOVA (*F* test)
Between Groups		
Test of Independent Means	Yes	Yes
Within Groups		
Test of Dependent Means	Yes	Yes
Pre/Post Design	Yes	Yes
Longitudinal		Yes
Paired samples	Yes	
Repeated Measures		Yes

colleges and universities (HBCUs) and predominately White institutions (PWIs). In both examples, the researchers tested differences in samples to makes generalizations about the populations of students.

Within Groups. A within-groups test evaluates individual scores over two (t) or more (F) administrations of the same test or measure. Common examples are pre- and post-treatment surveys about learning outcomes or multiple administrations of a national survey to the same students. This type of analysis is often referred to as pre/post or longitudinal design. A t-test using this design is also called a paired samples t-test. An ANOVA using this design is also referred to as a repeated measures ANOVA. Researchers use paired samples t-tests when evaluating pre- (time 1) and post- (time 2) tests or measures. This type of test is commonly used when evaluating mean learning outcomes or measures related to attitudes, values, and beliefs.

When more than one time is involved, such as a pre- (time 1), mid- (time 2), and final (time 3) test, researchers use a repeated measures ANOVA. For example, in a study of leadership practices of team captains in varsity collegiate athletics, Grandzol, Perlis, and Draina (2010) asked team captains and team members questions about their leadership characteristics pre- and postseason to examine their development during a season. In this example, the researchers tested differences within the groups to make generalizations about the population of athletes.

Chi-square (χ^2) is a nonparametric statistic that evaluates differences in two or more groups by comparing proportions, or percentages. The data tested typically are groups (nominal) and should meet the minimum requirements for random sample, sample size, and independence. In most cases, researchers use chi-square when testing differences based on percentages. For example, Dahl, Meagher, and Vander Velde (2014) tested differences in four clusters of variables (self-focused/few motivators, self and others, focus on others, and restorative/many motivators) that related to motivations and outcomes among students in a restorative justice program.

Variations of Difference Statistics

There are many variations of difference statistics, mostly distinguished by the type and format of the variables. A brief listing of common variants follows.

A one-sample t-test (t) is used to examine the mean difference between a sample and a known population mean. The name refers to only collecting one sample and comparing it to a known population. For example, if a national average for a measure of civic engagement is known, researchers might take a random sample of students on campus to compare to the known mean. No significant difference would indicate similarity.

Mann–Whitney U (U) and Kruskal–Wallis (H) are nonparametric ANOVA statistics that test for differences between two (U) or more (H) groups by evaluating the median or ranked scores. Most often, these tests are used when the responses are not normally distributed. For example, Melzer and Grant (2016) examined differences in personality traits and academic needs of prepared and underprepared college students. The researchers used Mann-Whitney U (U) tests to evaluate differences in student responses to Likert-like scales. Similarly, Glassman et al. (2013) evaluated pre- and posttest differences in perceived consequences of alcohol consumption using Kruskal–Wallis (H) tests between three groups of participants (two control and one treatment).

Extensions of ANOVA

Much of the variation in difference statistics relates to extensions of ANOVA. Although these extensions may seem complicated, researchers generally provide enough contextual information for readers to follow the analysis. Extensions of ANOVA are based on the role of additional independent and dependent variables in the study. The addition of CO, M, or both letters is an indicator of the presence and role of additional variables. Each is used regularly in student affairs research. Figure 11.1 is a graphic representation followed by brief descriptions of each extension.

Analysis of covariance (ANCOVA) is used to control for the influence of one or more independent variables on an outcome. The CO indicates the presence of one or more covariates, or controls. For example, a researcher wanting to study the effects of functional area in student affairs (independent variable) on professional job satisfaction rating (dependent variable) might control for career level (new professional, midlevel, late career).

FIGURE 11.1. EXTENSIONS OF ANOVA

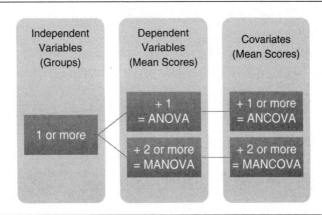

Multiple analysis of variance (MANOVA) is used to study the effect of one or more dependent variables on an outcome or assess the effects of possible relationships between outcomes. The M indicates the presence of additional dependent measures. For example, a researcher wanting to examine the effects of functional area in student affairs (independent variable) on professional job satisfaction rating (dependent variable) might also want to examine likelihood of leaving the field (dependent variable) at the same time to see if the two outcomes affect each other.

Multiple analysis of covariance (MANCOVA) is used to control for the influence of one or more independent variables on one or more additional dependent variables, or to examine possible relationships between outcomes based on independent variables and controls. The M and CO indicate the presence of additional dependent measures and covariates. For example, a researcher wanting to study the effects of functional area in student affairs (independent variable) on professional job satisfaction rating (dependent variable) might also want to examine the likelihood of leaving the field (dependent variable) at the same time, while controlling for career level (new professional, midlevel, late career).

Words Researchers Use—ANOVA Terminology

ANOVA can be confusing to read without a basic knowledge of the terminology. Following is a reference list of common terms appearing in ANOVA studies.

factor
Another name for group (for example, gender).

level
A specific characteristic or trait of a group (for example, males and females).

by
How many factors were tested; also, shown using x (for example 2 by 3 or 2 x 3 ANOVA).

way
How many groups were tested (for example a one-way or two-way ANOVA).

Reading Difference Statistics

Researchers list difference statistics in text and tables. The format can depend on the number of group differences tested. For example, if the study includes only a few groups, researchers use text. If multiple questions or measures are included, a table is more efficient. Researchers also will sometimes use figures such as line graphs to show pre/post designs, which can effectively display change within and/or between groups. This section is divided into common formats, presenting results in text and tables. Excerpts from articles and reports showing difference statistics along with general notes on interpretation follow.

Difference Statistics in Text

Reading difference statistics can be simplified by concentrating on the last part of most equations: the p, the sign, and the number that follows. Locating the comparison statistic (mean, percentage, rank) is also helpful, but it is not always reported with the result as sometimes researchers note comparisons in tables for quick review. Learning to read the other parts of the equation are important as well, but a basic understanding requires only interpretation of the significance test result. Following are examples of difference statistics from published research. When necessary for interpretation, additional explanatory notes are added in brackets.

t-*test*. Results also show that, compared to men, women describe higher quality interactions with their mothers (i.e., respectful, helpful, and supportive; and not intrusive, uninterested, or critical) ($\bar{x}_{women} = 2.53$, $\bar{x}_{men} = 2.33$, $t = -2.167$, $p < .05$) (Sax & Weintraub, 2014, p. 119).

***ANOVA*.** Students at HBCUs reported greater involvement in academic/career-based organizations, $F(1, 212)$ 5.96, $p < .02$, $\eta^2 = .03$ [As compared to students at PWIs] (Bentley-Edwards & Chapman-Hilliard, 2015, p. 51).

***Chi-Square*.** Outcome 5 identified attitude change. In Cluster 1, 45 of the students answered yes, followed by 31.5% in Cluster 2, 28.6% in Cluster 3, and 2 in Cluster 4 (see Table 5). A Pearson chi-square test showed that these differences were not statistically significant ($p = .116$), although the percentages appeared to decrease with each cluster [$\chi^2 = 5.91$] (Dahl et al., 2014, p. 374).

***Mann–Whitney U*.** Becoming an expert in a future field of study was less important to AIP (M rank = 47.3) than non-AIP students (M rank = 61.5; $U = 1010.5$, $Z = 2.51$, $p < .05$, $r = .24$) (Melzer & Grant, 2016, p. 101).

***ANCOVA*.** Results from an analysis of covariance (ANCOVA) indicated that certain fields of study are associated with higher compassion scores at the end of the participant's college career, even after taking freshman compassion scores into account. Analysis found that there was a significant effect of degree field on senior compassion scores after controlling for freshman compassion scores, $F(5) = 4.92$, $p < 0.001$. Participants studying within the social sciences displayed the highest compassion scores (Mean = 3.69), followed by those in math and the natural sciences (Mean = 3.43). Students in the School of Engineering displayed the lowest compassion scores (Mean = 3.10) (Plante & Halman, 2016, pp. 170–171).

MANOVA. With respect to psychoeducational information regarding mental health issues provided, 24% of community college participants reported receiving information related to mental health issues, compared to 40% of traditional university participants. In terms of this difference, MANOVA revealed a statistically significant difference, Wilks's lambda = .81, $F(11, 19241) = 410.6$, $p < .001$, with a modest effect size, Cohen's $d = .33$ (Katz & Davison, 2014, p. 316).

Review the statistics reported in each example. Following are interpretation notes:

- The symbols t, F, χ^2, U, and F indicate the test used. For example, F shows that ANOVA or a variation (ANCOVA, MANOVA) was used.
- The value following the = sign is the result of the calculation. For example, $t = -2.167$ is the result of the t-test. Similarly, $F(11, 19241) = 410.6$ is the result of the MANOVA.
- The df symbol in some examples is the degrees of freedom. This value is an indicator of how many groups were involved and is calculated differently for each type of test.
- The p indicates significance, or the probability that the difference in the sample is also a difference in the population. In the ANCOVA example, the p in $F(5) = 4.92$, $p < 0.001$ is the probability that there is a difference between the groups in the population.
- The sign ($< = >$) indicates that the result is less than, equal to, or greater than the probability (significance) value that follows. Using the ANOVA example, the $<$ in $F(1, 212)$ 5.96, $p < .02$, $\eta^2 = .03$ means that 98/100 times a sample is taken from this population, there will be a difference.
- The decimal that follows the sign is the significance value. Subtracting this number provides probability, or likelihood, that the result for the sample would be true of the population result. Using the ANOVA example, the .02 in $F(1, 212) = 5.96$, $p < .02$, $\eta^2 = .03$ suggests that the probability of a difference is 98/100 times.
- The final number that appears in several of the results is the effect size (ANOVA $\eta^2 = .03$, Mann–Whitney U $r = .24$, MANOVA Cohen's $d = .33$). Effect size is an indicator of the magnitude of difference and is interpreted differently based on the measure used.

Difference Statistics in Tables

The same interpretation principles apply when reading difference tests in tables, although the p, the sign, and the number often are easier to read because they are labeled.

Chi-Square Table

Dahl et al. (2014) studied which of nine individual motivators resulted in an attitude change for participants in a restorative justice program. In Table 11.3, the researchers listed two of their survey questions in columns and nine motivators in rows. The number of participants who indicated yes to both the question and the motivator (the crosstab) are labeled with (#yes) and a corresponding percentage (%). The chi-square score (χ^2) and significance (*) are also included for each crosstab. For example, 23 students (or 25.5%) indicated that M1: Pay back harmed was a motivator for Q5: Attitude toward harmed party changed. Since this result was not statistically significant (as indicated by no corresponding p value), the

Table 11.3. Individual Motivations and Outcomes (Chi-Squares)

Selected Individual Motivation	Q5: Attitude toward harmed party changed ($n=187$)			Q6: Would you participate again? ($n=187$)		
	# yes	%	χ^2	# yes	%	χ^2
M1: Pay back harmed	23	25.5	2.418	90	97.8	0.624
M2: Help harmed	19	25.3	1.89	75	98.7	1.477
M3: Direct responsibility	39	26.9	5.121*	145	99.3	13.656***
M4: Tell harmed why	13	31.2	0.216	43	95.5	0.291
M5: Apology	39	31.2	0.006	123	98.4	3.141
M6: Satisfy parents	2	40	0.194	5	100	0.17
M7: Remove offense	49	31.8	0.262	149	97.4	0.957
M8: Best option	34	30.6	0.019	107	97.3	0.199
M9: Felt pressured	2	15.4	1.596	10	76.9	17.759***

Note: *$p<.05$, **$p<.01$, ***$p<.001$
Source: From Dahl, Meagher, and Vander Velde (2014), p. 370. Reprinted by permission of NASPA—National Association of Student Personnel Administrators/Student Affairs Administrators in Higher Education.

researchers can conclude paying back the harmed party did not (consistently) change their attitude toward the harmed party. Conversely, there was a statistically significant difference between those who indicated yes for 3: Direct responsibility and Q5: Attitude toward harmed party changed, as indicated by the * corresponding to $p < .05$. The researcher can conclude that taking direct responsibility did make a difference in changing attitudes toward the harmed party. Table 11.3 shows the full results.

ANOVA Table

ANOVA results are displayed in Table 11.4. Dahl et al. (2014) combined the nine motivators into four groups (clusters) and tested differences in mean scores (rows) between groups for each question (columns). For example, the average score for Cluster 1, Question 2 was 3.23 with a standard deviation of 1.23. The ANOVA score (F) and significance ($*$) are included for each question. A difference in mean scores (significant F test) would mean there were differences between the groups. According to the results in the following table, there were significant differences for each question, as indicated by the corresponding * values. The final row (partial eta squared) is a measure of effect size.

Table 11.4. Cluster Analysis and Outcomes in M (SD)

	Q1: How satisfied were you? ($df = 3, 186$)	Q2: Do you think you have benefited? ($df = 3, 181$)	Q3: How likely to commit another violation? ($df = 3, 184$)	Q4: Participating strengthened sense of community ($df = 3, 184$)
Cluster 1	1.97 (0.78)	3.23 (1.23)	4.31 (0.95)	2.49 (1.12)
Cluster 2	1.69 (0.67)	3.42 (1.13)	4.51 (0.67)	1.98 (0.72)
Cluster 3	1.55 (1.00)	4.21 (0.78)	4.77 (0.53)	1.72 (0.73)
Cluster 4	1.49 (0.80)	4.14 (1.06)	4.72 (0.60)	1.53 (0.67)
F	3.02*	9.80***	3.94**	11.44***
Partial eta squared	.046	.140	.060	.157

Note: * $p < .05$, ** $p < .01$, *** $p < .001$
Source: From Dahl, Meagher, and Vander Velde (2014), p. 375. Reprinted by permission of NASPA—National Association of Student Personnel Administrators/Student Affairs Administrators in Higher Education.

Words Researchers Use—*Post Hoc* Test

A *post hoc* test is a follow-up test to an ANOVA. An ANOVA identifies statistically significant differences by testing groups in pairs. It does not specify which pairs of groups are different. A follow-up, or *post hoc*, test reveals these differences by testing each pair of values. In the following excerpt, Dahl et al. (2014, p. 374) described the research sequence of determining statistical difference with ANOVA, then using a *post hoc* test to specify them. These results correspond to the ANOVA results shown in the prior table.

> Outcome 1 measured satisfaction. Answers ranged from 1 = very satisfied to 5 = very dissatisfied. The means and standard deviations can be seen in Table 4. There was a statistically significant difference between groups ($p = .031$). *Post-hoc* analyses were calculated to identify the group differences. Statistical significance was found when comparing Cluster 1 (the self-focused/few motivators group) to Cluster 4 (the restorative/many motivators group), with $p = .031$. The rest of the comparisons were not statistically significant. These results show that overall satisfaction is higher for those who have restorative and multifaceted motivations for participating than those who have limited motivations that are mostly focused on the self.

Guidelines for Reading Difference Statistics

- Locate and interpret the null hypothesis.
- Focus on the direction of the sign.
- Interpret the significance value.
- Locate and interpret the comparison statistics.

Locate and Interpret the Null Hypothesis Although researchers using difference statistics are always testing hypotheses, they seldom include the actual hypothesis statements. For example, if a researcher suggests they are trying to determine differences in academic engagement levels between freshmen and sophomores, they are testing the null hypothesis that freshmen academic engagement = sophomore academic engagement. Locating the null hypotheses (stated or implied) can help interpret the test result more accurately.

Words Researchers Use—*p* and α

When reporting difference results, researchers may use *p* (significance) or α (alpha). In practice, the terms are interpreted the same way, but there is a difference.

p is the exact probability when the null hypothesis is true. In other words, *p* is an actual value, calculated from the data.

α is a chosen number above or below which the researcher evaluates the null hypothesis. In other words, α is a limit, set by the researcher.

Used together, it could be said that a researcher rejects the null hypothesis if *p* is less than α.

Focus on the Direction of the Sign   When researchers report difference statistics, they include a sign to indicate the result of the test. In most cases, a < or ≤ sign indicates the value that follows is less than or equal to *p* (the significance value). Conversely, a > or ≥ indicates the value that follows is greater than or equal to *p*. Finally, a = or ≠ indicates the value that follows is equal to or not equal to *p*. Note that when difference statistics are reported in a table, there may not be a sign to interpret. Dahl et al. (2014) reported the significance using an * in both prior tables.

Interpret the Significance Value   Researchers seldom provide the actual value of *p*. They generally choose .05 or .01 as a cutoff prior to testing, or round the actual value down when reporting to show consistency among results. Alternatively, researchers may report different values for *p* within the same paragraph or table. For example, the *p* for one item or test may be .01 while the next might be .05. In this case, the researcher is showing that within the results, there were some differences in level of significance. When researchers provide the actual value, interpret the meaning by subtraction. For example, if *p* = .03, interpret the results as likely 97/100 times. Or, if the *p* = .31, the result is likely 69/100 times. When *p* is listed as a greater value (*p* < .001 or *p* = .003), the same subtraction guidelines apply, meaning that 999/1,000 or 997/1,000 times the results are likely.

Locate and Interpret the Comparison Statistics   When reporting results from a difference test, researchers do not always display the mean, percentage, rank, or other comparison values. Sometimes, the values are provided earlier in text. This is common when comparing group differences from Likert-like questions. For example, the researcher may report that there was a difference between males and females in text, but the reader will need to search the article to find the values elsewhere such as in a summary table.

Words Researchers Use—Type I and Type II Error

Significance testing can be thought of as offering confidence. For example, a $p < .05$ result is another way of saying a researcher is confident that 95/100 times when this population is sampled, there will be a difference for these groups. But what about the 5/100 times? Sometimes there is statistical difference in a sample when there is not really one in the population. These five potential times a researcher is wrong is the rejection criterion, or the amount of error a researcher is willing to accept.

Error is a specific term in significance testing. There are two primary types. A *type I error* occurs when the results show a difference ($p < .05$) when there is not one. Conversely, a *type II error* occurs when the results show no difference ($p > .05$) when there is one. Researchers predetermine error (in other words, choose the *p* value) based on which error will be more costly or risky. It is helpful to remember that significance tests are based on probabilities. This means that even when the calculations are correct, there is still the possibility for a mistake.

Evaluating Difference Statistics

Evaluating difference statistics requires a more comprehensive understanding of the research. After reviewing the goals of a study, research question(s), and hypotheses (stated or implied), the critical reader should question the adequacy of the sample size and sampling method. This should be followed with a consideration of the difference statistic(s) chosen. Together, these components allow the reader to judge the appropriateness of the design. The researcher's responsibility is to provide sufficient information for the reader to make this judgment. Following are some critical questions for evaluating difference statistics.

Questions for Evaluating Difference Statistics

- Was the sample random and adequately large?
- Are the measures valid?
- Are the measures reliable?
- Is the difference statistic matched to the data?
- Do the results have practical significance?

Was the Sample Random and Adequately Large?   A random and adequately sized sample is essential to the basic function of difference statistics. The purpose of random sampling is to approximate the population. A nonrandom or convenience sample is unlikely to meet this purpose. When reading difference statistics, consider how the sample was obtained and be wary if it was not random. Further, the sample should be comprised of at least 15 data points per group for a *t*-test, 10 per group for ANOVA, or 5 per group for chi-square with an overall minimum sample of 30. Also, ideally the groups should be relatively equal, although ANOVA and chi-square can work with marginally unequal groups. Researchers using difference statistics typically will provide justification when the sample is inadequate.

Are the Measures Valid?   *Validity* asks the question: Does the measure accurately assess the outcome? A measure is valid when it is accurate. A related follow-up question is: Does the data directly relate to the concepts being studied? There are a several methods of establishing statistical validity that fall under two primary categories, internal and external. Internal validity concerns evidence within a study; external validity concerns generalization to outside contexts. A review of the various statistical methods for supporting validity is beyond this chapter; however, the concept can be considered using good judgment. When reviewing a measure or instrument, consider whether, conceptually, the question(s) reasonable relate to the problem. For example, questions such as preferred study locations and whether or not a student likes to study with music seem aligned with a study about academic performance. Conversely, asking the same questions in a study about alcohol use would not seem like valid measures unless the researcher established a conceptual relationship.

Are the Measures Reliable?   *Reliability* asks the question: Does the measure consistently assess the outcome? A measure is reliable when it is consistent. Two related follow-up questions are: To what extent does the measure remain consistent across repeated testing; and, To what extent do the individual measures that comprise a test or an inventory consistently assess the same concepts? The first question is directly related to repeatability. The second is a more comprehensive question about an instrument or group of concepts (sometimes referred to as a factor). Like validity, there are several statistical measures for estimating reliability. The most common of these is the reliability coefficient (also called the alpha coefficient or abbreviated as α), which is interpreted as a correlation, ranging from 0 (no consistency) to 1.0 (perfect consistency). Researchers typically report reliability when developing a new instrument or using an existing one that has not been widely adopted. Typically, readers can be confident with reliability coefficients above $\alpha = .70$.

Is the Difference Statistic Matched to the Data?   Determining which difference statistic is appropriate depends on what information is needed from the data.

Further, scales of measurement of the variables must be matched to the test. For example, an independent *t*-test is only appropriate for testing mean differences (and interval or scale dependent variable) between two groups (a nominal independent variable). The data also need to follow a normal distribution (parametric). If only percentage differences are being evaluated, then a chi-square is the correct test. In this case, the distribution of the variables is not important so long as the groups each have enough data. Unfortunately, statistical software generally does not verify the validity of a test chosen; most will calculate the test selected.

Do the Results Have Practical Significance?   In most cases, rejecting the null hypothesis indicates there is a statistical difference between groups. This result lets the researcher conclude that the finding is significant. However, a significant result does not necessarily mean the result is important. To make this determination, researchers often include a different statistic, effect size. *Effect size* quantifies statistical dissimilarity, accounting for the size (or magnitude) of the effect (or difference) rather than being influenced by the size of the sample. It is sometimes called a measure of practical significance. Restated literally, it is a measure of the size (the magnitude) of an effect (the difference). Even the most trivial test can reach significance if enough data are involved—especially at lower confidence levels. Coe (2002) noted that effect size "allows us to move beyond the simplistic, 'Does it work or not?' to, 'How well does it work in a range of contexts?'" (para. 1).

Words Researchers Use—Types of Effect Size

A major issue with effect size is that there are numerous measures for it. The ANOVA example (Bentley-Edwards & Chapman-Hilliard, 2015) included eta square (η^2), the Mann–Whitney U example (Melzer & Grant, 2016, p. 101) included Pearson's *r*. The MANOVA example (Katz & Davison, 2014) included Cohen's *d*. The ANCOVA example included partial eta squared in the table. When interpreting, it is helpful to consider effect size as a correlation measuring the strength of relationship. Although the size interpretation varies based on the measure used, researchers who include effect size generally also include an interpretation guide. For example, Bentley-Edwards and Chapman-Hilliard (2015) noted, "Eta-squared (η^2) will be used to report effect sizes of ANOVAs ($\eta^2 \leq .02$ small, $\eta^2 \leq .13$ medium, and $\eta^2 \leq .26$ large effect sizes)" (p. 50). In the MANOVA example, Katz and Davison (2014) used Cohen's *d*, which has a common interpretation ($d \leq .02$ small, $d \leq .05$ medium, and $d \leq .08$ large).

Perspectives From the Field—Statistical Significance Versus Practical Significance

As a faculty member who teaches a research and assessment course, I try to impress upon students the need to go beyond statistical significance and explore practical significance when discussing and interpreting their data analyses. And students can be challenged in fully understanding the importance of this because they don't always see practical significance mentioned or discussed in the documents (e.g., within institutional reports, textbooks, or published research articles) they are reading. For many who are newly exploring statistical analysis (and even among many seasoned practitioners who were exposed to statistics in coursework many years ago), finding something statistically significant at the $p < .05$ is akin to finding the holy grail and often leads to making inflated conclusions based on these results alone. Statistical significance in its most basic element only reports if there is a difference between groups. Since statistical significance is dependent upon sample size—a small sample may not reveal a statistically significant difference, and in a large sample, even small differences may reveal statistically significant results—it doesn't necessarily explain the effect of the difference. Or simply put, if there is any practical significance. So, once statistical significance is determined, then the next step along the path to analyzing the results is discussing the practical significance. Nonetheless, statistical significance has its importance, because without it, there is no need to discuss practical significance.

In my view, once statistical significance is established, practical significance takes on greater meaning because a researcher is now able to take the results and determine how important they are (i.e., do the differences matter, do the differences make sense). Effect size, then, is a helpful measure because it emphasizes the magnitude or the size of the difference. So, when researchers take into account the effect size, they are more likely able to view the influence of a particular cocurricular experience, living situation, or workshop to an outcome of interest (e.g., appreciation for diversity, ability to interact with others who are different from themselves, consider others' points of view before making a decision) between groups of participants. After all, knowing the magnitude of the difference is more likely (or should be more likely) to play greater importance in accountability, budgets, and understanding student learning.

Matthew Wawrzynski—Associate professor and coordinator, Higher, Adult, and Lifelong Education Program, Michigan State University

Applying Difference Statistics

In addition to their widespread use in research, an increased emphasis on quantitatively based accountability, coupled with the prevalence of national and local surveys for data collection (Schuh, Biddix, Dean, & Kinzie, 2016), underscores the need to understand and use results from difference studies. This emphasis is neither new, nor appears to be waning, as Mosier and Schwarzmueller (2002) cautioned 15 years ago, "Because of this uncertainty, student affairs and student housing have placed a strong emphasis on improving the efficiency, effectiveness, and accountability of the education that students receive at colleges and universities" (p. 103). Following are some suggestions for how to apply and use difference statistics for practice.

Opportunities for Applying Difference Statistics

- Create or expand programs, policies, and services.
- Make estimates about a population value.
- Provide the ability to evaluate programs or services.
- Allow for comparison and benchmarking.

Create or Expand Programs, Policies, and Services   Research incorporating difference statistics evaluates how students perceive, experience, and learn from programs, policies, and services. Difference statistics that generalize sample to population values can be used to consider how they may apply in similar settings and with similar groups. While descriptive statistics can provide basic summary or trends information, difference statistics permit the ability to make informed decisions based on statistical estimates. A review of related studies on programs, policies, or services showing statistical gains between or within groups can add credibility to resources requests for creating or expanding work.

Make Estimates About a Population Value   Data can be used to support decisions by collecting opinions or perspectives of all stakeholders. Unfortunately, this is rarely possible due to several factors, most notably efficiency. As accountability pressure continues to mount, requiring data to support outcomes, students are increasingly questioned about their experiences, creating survey fatigue. Difference statistics offer a way to minimize this problem. By collecting a smaller, random sample and making simple group comparisons, practitioners can estimate a population value. The data required for a difference test are relatively minimal and computed with a spreadsheet or online calculator.

Provide the Ability to Evaluate Programs or Services   As interest in evaluating learning outcomes increases, the need for data evidencing development as a result of participation in a program or service is increasingly important. When practitioners want to know the impact of a program, or change from pre- to postexperience for when the population is not accessible, a difference test based on a sample can provide an estimate of total impact for the entire group. For example, the student programming board could bring a controversial speaker to campus to discuss issues related to immigration. If very well attended, it would be difficult to administer a pre/post design to the students who attended. A randomly sampled survey of the attendees could provide insight into the experiences of all who attended.

Allow for Comparison and Benchmarking   Sometimes, practitioners want to know how their students compare to others on measures such as attitudes, beliefs, behaviors, or perceptions. For example, it may be valuable to know how student perceptions of local campus climate differ from national norms. Large-scale surveys such as the NSSE use these types of comparison measures when providing campuses with individualized reports. This form of benchmarking is valuable for evaluating performance and effective processes (Mosier & Schwarzmueller, 2002; Schuh et al., 2016). Chen et al. (2009) provided recommendations for comparing locally sampled statistical measures against published norms, using a one-sample *t*-test to compare a campus sample mean to a population mean.

Perspectives From the Field—Applying Difference Statistics

Colleges and universities that administer NSSE to assess the extent to which students engage in effective educational practices receive a collection of reports describing their students' experiences. The Frequency and Statistical Comparisons report presents about 80 item-by-item student responses and statistical comparisons to facilitate the examination of patterns of similarity and difference between students and those at comparison group institutions. For example, a look at actual data from the fictional "NSSEville University" indicates that nearly 90% of first-year students had "talked about career plans with a faculty member" versus only 78% at the comparison group institutions. Although this result clearly suggests a difference in educational practice between NSSEville University and its comparators, statistical tests of the mean scores on this item using two-tailed independent *t*-tests confirms that the difference is larger than would be expected by chance at the $p > .001$ level. In addition, NSSEville University students' average was significantly higher with a positive effect size of .3 in magnitude (calculated using Cohen's *d* for independent *t*-tests). This positive effect, which is within the "medium" range of NSSE effect sizes, demonstrates a "practically significant" and favorable result for NSSEville University. Imagine if NSSEville University had been striving to strengthen career exploration activities in its first-year seminar course and to increase the use of degree maps to guide students to majors and careers. These data about the extent to which first-year students engaged in career discussions provides one source of solid evidence of the impact of their career-related initiatives.

View the sample NSSEville University Institutional Report: http://nsse.indiana.edu/html/sample_institutional_report.cfm

Jillian Kinzie—Center for Postsecondary Research, National Survey of Student Engagement (NSSE), Indiana University Bloomington

Building Your Difference Statistics Skillset

Aside from descriptive statistics, difference measures are the most-used data analysis techniques in student affairs research. They appear as standalone measures as well as part of larger studies. In published research, the most frequently used difference statistics are ANOVA or its extensions, although *t*-tests and chi-squares appear often in national survey reports.

There are several ways enhance the ability to understand, read, evaluate, and apply difference statistics. Unfortunately, many introductory research texts make assumptions about prior knowledge (especially terminology) or software competencies that can inhibit introductory learning. Many novice and veteran researchers find Field's (2013) text logical, clear, and easily applicable and referenced. Levin and Fox (2010) also offer a user-friendly introductory and reference textbook with clear explanations including three chapters on difference statistics. More specific to student affairs, Sriram (2017) highlighted valuable and applicable ways to use significance testing for research and evaluation.

One of the most effective ways to learn to about difference statistics is to work with them. Using the section on reading as a guide, locate interesting articles and interpret the basic elements first: the hypothesis, direction of the sign, value of *p*, and comparison statistics. Build toward practical statistical skills by working with basic significance testing functions (*t*-test, ANOVA, chi-square) in Excel or using an online calculator (Graphpad or VassarStats). Extensions of ANOVA require specialized statistical programs to calculate and are taught in advanced statistics courses.

References

Bentley-Edwards, K. L., & Chapman-Hilliard, C. (2015). Doing race in different places: Black racial cohesion on Black and White college campuses. *Journal of Diversity in Higher Education, 8*(10), 43–60.

Chen, P., Gonyea, R., Sarraf, S., Brckalorenz, A., Korkmaz, A., Lambert, A. D., . . . Williams, J.M. (2009). Analyzing and interpreting NSSE data. *New Directions for Institutional Research, 141,* 35–54.

Coe, R. (2002). *It's the effect size, stupid: What "effect size" is and why it is important.* Paper presented at the 2002 Annual Conference of the British Educational Research Association, University of Exeter, Exeter, Devon, United Kingdom, September 12–14, 2002. Retrieved from http://www.leeds.ac.uk/educol/documents/00002182.htm

Dahl, M. G., Meagher, P., & Vander Velde, S. (2014). Motivation and outcome for university students in a restorative justice program. *Journal of Student Affairs Research and Practice, 51*(4), 364–379.

Field, A. (2013). *Discovering statistics using IBM SPSS statistics* (4th ed.). Thousand Oaks, CA: Sage.

Glassman, T., Haughton, N., Wohlwend, J., Roberts, S., Jordan, T., Yingling, F., & Blavos, A. (2013). A health communication intervention to reduce high-risk drinking among college students. *Journal of Student Affairs Research and Practice, 50*(4), 355–372.

Grandzol, C., Perlis, S., & Draina, L. (2010). Leadership development of team captains in collegiate varsity athletics. *Journal of College Student Development, 51*(4), 403–418.

Katz, D. S., & Davison, K. (2014). Community college student mental health: A comparative analysis. *Community College Review, 42*(4), 307–326.

Levin, J., & Fox, J. A. (2010). *Elementary statistics in social research: Essentials* (3rd ed.). New York, NY: Pearson.

Melzer, D., & Grant, R. (2016). Investigating differences in personality traits and academic needs among prepared and underprepared first-year college students. *Journal of College Student Development, 57*(1), 99–103.

Mosier, R. E., & Schwarzmueller, G. J. (2002). Benchmarking in student affairs. In B. E. Bender & J. H. Schuh (Eds.), *Using benchmarking to inform practice in higher education* (pp. 103–112). *New Directions for Higher Education, 118*. San Francisco, CA: Jossey-Bass.

Plante, T., & Halman, K. (2016). Nurturing compassion development among college students: A longitudinal study. *Journal of College and Character, 17*(3), 164–174.

Sax, L. J., & Weintraub, D. S. (2014). Exploring the parental role in first-year students' emotional well-being: Considerations by gender. *Journal of Student Affairs Research and Practice, 51*(2), 113–127.

Schuh, J. H., Biddix, J. P., Dean, L. A., & Kinzie, J. (2016). *Assessment in student affairs: A contemporary look* (2nd ed.). San Francisco, CA: Jossey-Bass.

Sriram, R. (2017). *Student affairs by the numbers.* Sterling, VA: Stylus.

CHAPTER TWELVE

ASSESSING RELATIONSHIPS

Learning Outcomes

By the end of this chapter, you should be able to:

- Understand the purpose and role of relationship statistics.
- Differentiate between the major types of relationship statistics.
- Read relationship statistics in journal articles and reports.
- Evaluate relationship statistics based on how data are collected, analyzed, and reported.
- Apply interpretations of relationship statistics to student affairs practice.

Relationship statistics evaluate associations between two or more variables. In most cases, the variables are considered associated when a change in one relates to a change in another. Unfortunately, the simplicity of interpreting relational statistics often results in readers and researchers overlooking important details. For example, notice that the prior description was one variable *relates to* and not *results in* a change in another. *Results in* is a prediction statement and while relationship statistics can be a basis for prediction, they cannot be interpreted as causation.

Relationship statistics can be either descriptive or inferential, depending on whether the sample is random and the intention is to generalize results to a broader context. They are widely used in student affairs research to evaluate relationships between variables, to quantify differences using effect size, to calculate the reliability of measures and assess factors using correlation statistics, and to consider the potential predictive ability of variables based on associations. Although the data requirements for each are slightly different, the underlying principles informing interpretation are similar. Each is evaluated based on statistical significance, and interpreted based on specific characteristics. This makes learning basic concepts for interpretation and evaluation straightforward. The chapter begins with a general overview of relationship statistics then describes how to understand, read, evaluate, and apply measures.

Understanding Relationship Statistics

The concept of relationship comes from investigating whether there is an association, connection, or correlation between two (bivariate) or more (multivariate) measures. In its most familiar form, a relationship statistic asks, "How is variable A related to variable B?" Most often, a single value describes the relationship. The value is closer to $|1|$ if the variables are related, closer to 0 if they are not. The statistic works by comparing the values, usually taken from the same source, simultaneously. Relationship statistics can be either descriptive or inferential. The distinction has to do with the sample. When data is drawn from a population or small, convenience sample, the relationship is considered to be descriptive. There would be no need to calculate the level of significance since there is no intent to make an inference about a population.

The most familiar relationship statistic is correlation (Trochim, 2006). *Correlation* evaluates the extent to which variables change together. Researchers tend to use the terms relationship and correlation interchangeably. However, other relationship statistics serve a variety of functions in quantitative research. They are used for description to show how variables affect each other. The extent and degree of relationships between and among measures can be tested to verify or support a theory. They also serve higher ordered statistical functions in regression, factor analysis, and path analysis. Further, they are used to identify predictor variables or problems in prediction equations when variables are too closely related (i.e., multi-collinearity). Finally, they are used to assess the validity or reliability of a measure when creating or evaluating a survey.

Assessing Relationships

Relationship statistics are most often reported as bivariate correlations (the relationships between pairs of variables), when researchers test theories, or as a means of categorizing or verifying classifications of variables (called factors). Following are explanations of each function.

Reasons for Understanding Relationship Statistics

- Show relationships between variables.
- Test or evaluate theory.
- Validate survey measures.
- Identify classifications or factors.

Show Relationships Between Variables   Relationship statistics evaluate how variables change in combination. For example, researchers have shown that socioeconomic status affects the likelihood of attending college. A related influence is whether or not a parent attended college. Relationship statistics have shown that these two variables, in combination, produced an even stronger effect. Often, researchers will calculate (and sometimes include) correlation statistics to demonstrate how study variables relate overall, either positively, negatively, or not at all. This is both a way of demonstrating the usefulness of a prediction model and a way to show that although variables measure different effects separately (meaning they are independent), they can affect each other.

Test or Evaluate Theory   A primary goal of statistics is to reduce data. In prediction studies, determining the least number of variables that can be used to predict an outcome is crucial. In cases where theory, based on previous research, experiences, or intuition, suggests many potential predictors, or when new potential predictors need to be evaluated, relationship statistics help to reduce the number of variables. For example, a researcher wants to understand student misuse of nonprescription drugs for academic purposes. The researcher might ask questions about their backgrounds and previous drug use experiences, types and frequencies of current drug use, involvement in other activities, and other conditions. Correlation results could reveal relationships that help create a testable theory (prediction model) to understand specific influences on nonprescription drug use.

Validate Survey Measures   When developing an instrument, it is important to know it is both valid (it measures what it is supposed to measure) and reliable (it measures what it is supposed to measure consistently). For example, a researcher develops an exit survey asking students about their advising experiences when they graduate. One of the questions asks students to rate their satisfaction with availability of their academic advisor. It is important to ensure the concepts of satisfaction and availability are interpreted accurately (valid) and consistently (reliable). To ensure this, the researcher might pilot the instrument with two groups of students and correlate responses to the question. A strong correlation is an indicator that the question is accurately worded. Similar principles apply for instrument validation, which considers the accurate and consistent measurement of all questions and uses various different relationship statistics to assess reliability.

Identify Classifications or Factors   Surveys often include multiple questions that make up one general concept. Relationship statistics can be used to verify which questions relate, or go together. Researchers sum or correlate the items to obtain a single score (called a classification or factor) for that concept. This type of statistical analysis is used widely in large-scale survey research. For example, the Community College Survey of Student Engagement (CCSSE) is a longitudinal survey intended to measure and assess the extent to which students are engaged in positive educational practices at community and technical colleges. A series of items are used to measure specific aspects of educational engagement. The following seven questions on the 2016 instrument comprise the Support for Learners score:

Item 9: How much does this college emphasize each of the following?

1 = Very little, 2 = Some, 3 = Quite a bit, 4 = Very much

    9a. Providing the support you need to help you succeed at this college.

    9b. Encouraging contact among students from different economic, social, and racial or ethnic backgrounds.

    9c. Helping you cope with your nonacademic responsibilities (work, family, etc.).

    9d. Providing the support you need to thrive socially.

    9e. Providing the financial support you need to afford your education.

Item 13.1: How often do you use the following services at this college?

1 = Rarely/Never, 2 = Sometimes, 3 = Often

    13.1a. Academic advising/planning.

    13.1b. Career counseling.

Research Considerations

Four common requirements for inferential statistics were introduced in the introductory chapter on quantitative research concepts. Adequate sample size is important for ensuring stability with relationship statistics. Researchers often use a technique called power analysis as a precise method for determining optimal sample size. As a general guide, however, bivariate correlation measures tend to function accurately with data points for 30 cases (in other words, ACT and GRE scores for 30 different people), although, as with most statistics, more data is often preferred.

Relationship statistics generally are not distinguished as independent and dependent measures. This is referred to as interdependence. A bivariate correlation coefficient considers the interdependence of two variables (how they relate to each other) while a *t*-test considers how one variable changes (dependent) based on manipulating one of its influences (independent).

With ratings and other types of numerical data, the measures should be normally distributed (grouped around a central mean and tending to have few high and low values as in a bell curve). The data also should be linearly distributed. This refers to the trend of the relationship between the two variables—whether the data points occur in a pattern (line or curve) when plotted. Outliers, or data points that are dissimilar to others in a dataset, can seriously affect correlation statistics.

Words Researchers Use—Pearson and Cohen

An important name in statistical measurement is Karl Pearson (1857–1936); the namesake of Pearson's *r*. Pearson is considered by some to be the founder of statistics as a discipline and acknowledged as a forefather to statistics as its own discipline. Pearson was a professor at University College in London in the early 20th century. He is credited as developing correlation, regression, and the chi-square contingency table. The impact of his work was widespread and found specific applications in the early student personnel work initiated by Walter Dill Scott.

Researchers using relationship statistics often cite Cohen when referring to specific methods or guidelines. Jacob Cohen (1923–1988) was a psychologist who developed many of the standardized techniques for estimation statistics. For example, Cohen (1988, 1992) provided basic guidelines that researchers frequently cite for assessing power analysis or magnitudes of relationships (effect size interpretation). Cohen, Cohen, West, and Aiken (2002) are the authoritatively cited source for applied uses of correlation and regression.

Main Types of Relationship Statistics

When researchers assess relationships, they typically use a correlation coefficient. A *correlation coefficient* measures the strength of association of two variables (as an absolute value), ranging from −1 (perfect negative correlation) to +1 (perfect positive correlation), with 0 indicating no association. Because the variables influence each other, they are sometimes called interdependency measures. This distinguishes them from dependency measures, such as difference statistics, where change in one variable (dependent) depends on change in another (independent).

Table 12.1. Main Types of Relationship Statistics

Relationship Test	Use	Requirement	Test Symbol
Pearson Correlation	Measures the degree of the relationship between two numerical variables. It is considered a parametric test.	Numerical (interval or scale) data. The sample size required depends on the desired (potential) strength of association.	r
Spearman rho	Measures the degree of the relationship between two ordinal, or ranked, variables. It is considered a nonparametric test.	Ordinal or ranked data.	ρ

This chapter describes two main types, Pearson correlation (r) and Spearman rho (ρ). The test, use, requirement, and symbols for both are summarized in Table 12.1.

Pearson correlation (r) assesses the degree of relationship between (generally) numerical variables. The complete but seldom used name of the measure is the Pearson product-moment correlation coefficient, although it is often abbreviated as simply Pearson's r. In most cases, Pearson's r requires that data be normally distributed (parametric), but it is sometimes used with all scales of measure. Pearson's r is the most common measure of association.

Spearman's rho (ρ) considers the degree of association between nonnumerical variables. The complete name of the measure is the Spearman rank-order correlation coefficient. Spearman's rho is used frequently in student affairs research involving Likert scale, satisfaction, or ranked data when the responses are not normally distributed (nonparametric).

Both statistics work by plotting all pairs of values in a graph (x–y axis), measuring the distance from each intersection of pairs to a perfect correlation line, and averaging the distances. When used as inferential statistics, they also have a significance test associated with interpretation. A significant result with a random sample indicates the relationship is reflected in the population.

Variations of Relationship Statistics

Three additional correlation measures are occasionally used in student affairs research. The first two are nonparametric measures based on contingency tables (crosstabs). Partial correlations are parametric measures that allow researchers to consider subsets of data using a Pearson statistic.

Words Researchers Use—Correlation Terminology

Coefficient

A *coefficient* is the result of a statistical calculation. For example, if a researcher tested the relationship between gender (male/female) and group involvement (yes/no) the result of the test would be a correlation coefficient.

Correlation Matrix

A *correlation matrix* is a display format for correlation results, or coefficients. It is shown as a table with correlation coefficients displayed where variable pairs intersect at rows and columns.

Factor Analysis

Factor analysis is a method of statistically combining several variables into a single measure. The combination of variables is based on correlations. It is commonly used in survey research. Factor analysis has the benefit of letting a researcher use multiple questions to evaluate a complex concept, such as self-efficacy. It is also useful for reducing the number of questions on a survey by identifying questions unrelated to a phenomenon of interest.

Cronbach's Alpha

Cronbach's alpha is a reliability measure that assesses relationships (correlations) between several items in a survey to identify factors. It is used to evaluate internal consistency.

Phi coefficient (Φ) and Cramer's V are nonparametric measures that evaluate the degree of relationship between nominal variables. The Phi coefficient works with discrete nominal variables, such as gender (male/female) and group membership (yes/no). Cramer's V evaluates nominal variables with more than two categories, such as gender (yes/no) and class standing (freshmen, sophomore, junior, senior). Both are typically used as effect size measures for chi-square. Chi-square tests the null hypothesis that two or more groups are different (statistical significance), while Phi coefficient (Φ) or Cramer's V provides an estimate of the magnitude of that difference (practical significance).

Partial correlation is a variation of Pearson's r where the researcher hypothesizes additional factors (covariates) that affect the association between variables. Researchers statistically control for the effects of the covariates to consider how the pair of variables they are interested in behave without the influence of the additional variable(s). For example, Palmer et al. (Palmer, McMahon, Moreggi, Rounsaville, & Ball, 2012) studied the effects of marijuana use among college students. The researchers were interested in negative consequences of using marijuana, but recognized that alcohol and marijuana are often used together. They used partial correlations to control for past-month alcohol use when examining the association between days of past-month marijuana use and negative consequences.

Reading Relationship Statistics

Researchers show relationship statistics in text or tables, depending on how many measures were involved in the study or the role of measures in the overall results (primary or precursor). For example, when displaying scores for a few variables researchers tend to show the statistics in text. A study that has a primary focus on understanding relationships between multiple variables would more likely include a table (correlation matrix) to show all variables. Researchers also show relationship measures in tables when they are precursors to additional multivariate analysis, or when displaying factor analysis scores. The reporting format (text or tables) is fairly standardized across the different measures, regardless of how the measures are displayed.

When used as an inferential statistic, relationship statistics also have a level of significance. A significant result (for example, $p < .05$) indicates there is an association between the variables and that the association is likely mirrored in the population. Understanding direction, strength, and significance and recognizing form is essential to reading relationship statistics, in all their variations. Following are excerpts from articles, followed by general notes on interpretation.

Relationship Statistics in Text

Following are examples of the basic format for how various types of relationship statistics appear in text. Recalling that researchers choose different statistical measures based on the variables tested, note the different types used in the Spanierman et al. (2013) excerpts.

Pearson's r. The variables with significant correlations with procrastination were perceived discrimination ($r = 0.19$, $p < 0.05$), CC ($r = -0.17$, $p < 0.05$), and academic self-efficacy ($r = -0.14$, $p < 0.05$) (Lowinger et al., 2016, p. 96).

Phi Coefficient Φ. To assess whether significant demographic differences existed between LLC and non-LLC participants, we performed a chi-square analysis. Results indicated that both gender, $\chi^2 (1) = 52.24$, $p < .001$, $\Phi = .39$; and U.S. citizenship, $\chi^2 (1) = 5.70$, $p < .05$, $\Phi = .13$; differed significantly between LLC and non-LLC groups with more females and international students in the LLC sample (Spanierman et al., 2013, p. 314).

***Cramer's* V.** Race was distributed equally across groups, χ^2 (6) = 9.63, $p > .05$, Cramer's $V = .15$ (Spanierman et al., 2013, p. 314).

Partial Correlation. Partial correlations (controlling for past month alcohol frequency) were conducted for students who were past-month marijuana or medication misusers. As predicted, significant positive associations were found between days of past month marijuana use and past-month medication misuse, $r(160) = .16$, $p < .05$ (Palmer et al., 2012, p. 130).

Examine the statistics reported in each example. Following are some interpretation notes:

- The symbol (r, p, Φ, or V) shows what type of test was used. In most cases, it only shows the test was a correlation. Specific types of tests used are generally listed in the methods section. In the examples, Pearson, Spearman, and partial correlations are all listed as r.
- The number following the equal sign (=) is the strength of the relationship. A 1 is a perfect relationship, meaning that the values are identical. A 0 represents the absence of a linear relationship, meaning that the values are very different. For the purposes of correlation, 1 is an absolute value $|1|$. In other words, a -1 or 1 is still a perfect relationship. The closer to 1, the stronger the relationship (the higher the correlation). In the partial correlation example, $r = .16$ indicates a small strength of relationship.
- The sign in front of the number indicates the direction, shown as positive or negative. Researchers rarely use a + (instead just leaving the value as is) but will almost always show a − sign. A positive correlation reveals that as one value goes up, the other goes up. A negative value reveals that as one value goes down, the other goes up, or vice versa. For example, the negative Pearson correlation ($r = -0.14$) indicates that the lower the academic self-efficacy, the higher the procrastination level.
- The p or P indicates significance, or the probability of a relationship in the population, based on the sample. When significance is listed, interpret the result as an inferential statistic. For example, the Cramer's V example tested significance at .05.
- The sign ($<$ $=$ $>$) reveals that the result is less than, equal to, or greater than the significance that follows. For example, the Cramer's V example sign was $>$, indicating in this case that race was similar across groups.
- The final number is the significance value (0.05, .05, .05, .01). Recalling the interpretation guide, this is the number subtracted (generally from 100) to indicate probability, or likelihood, that the sample result would mirror a population result.
- Sometimes the result will include a number in parenthesis. This is the degrees of freedom and tells how many data points (e.g., participants, responses) were involved.

Relationship Statistics in Tables

When displayed in a table, relationship statistics are generally shown in a correlation matrix. This format is useful for efficiently showing how pairs of variables relate by viewing row and column intersections. There is some variation on how a matrix is displayed. Researchers may list all variables on the rows and columns, use names on the rows with corresponding numbers on the columns to save space (see Lowinger et al., 2016, following), or may not repeat variable names on columns. Sometimes, half of the matrix values are missing (as in the example). This is because the matrix is an inverse, meaning that all pairings are repeated twice. Factor analysis scores are also typically displayed in tables. They are interpreted in the same way as correlations.

Correlation Matrix. To read a matrix, look for the intersection of variables. For example, in Table 12.2, the correlation between row 8, English ability, and column 7 (which corresponds to English ability) is **−0.235**. According to the key, the bold text corresponds to a significance level of 0.05. Values that are not bolded are not considered to be correlated.

Factor Scores Table. Table 12.3 shows the results of a factor analysis intended to identify relationship between student–faculty interaction and cognitive skills development among college students. Displayed in the table are the individual factors and items (labeled as Factor/item), scores for each item that make up each factor (labeled as Factor loadings), and scores among all items in a factor (labeled as α). The factor loadings are Cronbach's alpha (α) scores. They are measures of internal consistency, or the relationship between multiple items (respondents tended to answer these in a similar pattern—the closer to 1, the better the relationship). The Cronbach's alpha scores are interpreted as the strength of the relationship between the items in a factor. For example, the four items that make up student–faculty interaction factor were correlated at .80.

Guidelines for Reading Difference Statistics

- Interpret the test result (strength of association).
- Review the sign in front of the test result (direction).
- Identify and evaluate significance (*p*).

Interpret the Test Result (Strength of Association) The result of a relationship test should be interpreted as an indicator of the strength of association between the variables. In most cases, the closer the value is to $|1|$, the stronger the correlation; the closer to 0, the weaker the linear relationship. However, a correlation of 0 does not mean there is no relationship between variables—just

Table 12.2. Pearson Correlation Between Key Variables (*N* = 212)

	1	2	3	4	5	6	7	8	9	10	11	12
1. Gender	1											
2. Length of stay in the U.S.	0.085	1										
3. Academic self-efficacy	−0.086	0.127	1									
4. Perceived discrimination	−0.052	**0.177**	**−0.193**	1								
5. Homesickness	**0.173**	0.078	−0.105	0.319	1							
6. Perceived fear	−0.067	0.016	**−0.280**	**0.645**	**0.396**	1						
7. Culture shock and stress	0.002	−0.077	**−0.219**	**0.453**	**0.552**	**0.509**	1					
8. English ability	−0.050	−0.228	**0.499**	**−0.128**	**−0.145**	**−0.295**	**−0.235**	1				
9. Collective coping (CC)	0.077	−0.011	**0.144**	−0.092	0.076	0.017	−0.020	−0.011	1			
10. Engagement coping (EC)	0.050	−0.059	**0.458**	**−0.192**	−0.025	**−0.237**	**−0.209**	**0.261**	**0.343**	1		
11. Avoidance coping (AC)	0.039	−0.043	−0.037	0.089	−0.026	**0.148**	−0.020	−0.129	**0.582**	**0.202**	1	
12. Procrastination	0.021	0.125	**−0.142**	**0.189**	0.107	0.107	0.083	0.085	**−0.167**	−0.103	0.009	1

Note: Bold numbers indicate statistical significance at the .05 level.

Source: From Lowinger et al. (2016), p. 98. Reprinted by permission of NASPA—National Association of Student Personnel Administrators/Student Affairs Administrators in Higher Education.

Table 12.3. Factor Loadings and Internal Consistencies for Confirmatory Factor Analyses ($n = 5,169$)

Factor/item	Factor loading	α
Cognitive skills time 1		.84
Analytical and critical thinking skills time 1	.80	
Ability to write clearly and effectively time 1	.78	
Ability to read and comprehend academic material time 1	.78	
Ability to understand a specific field of study time 1	.64	
Ability to prepare and make a presentation time 1	.56	
Other research skills time 1	.49	
Student-faculty interaction		.80
Talked with faculty outside of class about course material	.87	
Communicated with a faculty member by email or in person	.77	
Interacted with faculty during lecture class sessions	.69	
Worked with a faculty on an activity other than coursework	.51	
Classroom engagement in critical reasoning		.88
Examined and assessed other methods and conclusions	.84	
Reconsidered own position after assessing other arguments	.75	
Incorporated ideas from different courses	.74	
Evaluated methods and conclusions	.72	
Generated new ideas or products	.66	
Used facts or examples to support viewpoint	.65	
Cognitive skills time 2		.84
Ability to read and comprehend academic material time 2	.78	
Analytical and critical thinking skills time 2	.77	
Ability to write clearly and effectively time 2	.74	
Ability to understand a specific field of study time 2	.69	
Other research skills time 2	.57	
Ability to prepare and make a presentation time 2	.56	

Source: Reprinted with permission of Springer, from Kim and Lundberg (2016), p. 295; permission conveyed through Copyright Clearance Center, Inc.

that the relationship does not follow a linear trend (as a value increases or decreases, the other increases or decreases). Another way a relationship test result can be interpreted differently is when the measures are used for effect size. In this case, researchers generally also include an interpretation guide. For example, Pittman and Foubert (2016) noted, "Effects sizes were calculated to quantify the size of the difference between the two groups being studied. Cohen (1988) outlined parameters for what consists of a small, medium, and large effect size" (p. 19).

Review the Sign in Front of the Test Result (Direction)   The sign in front of the test result indicates the direction of the relationship. Researchers generally only include a sign if the direction of the association is negative. A positive value (no sign) suggests that as one variable increases, the other also increases. A negative value (−) suggests an inverse relationship, or as one variable decreases, the other variable increases.

Identify and Evaluate Significance (*p*)   If the results include a *p* value, the researcher is suggesting that the relationship is reflected in the population. The direction of the sign ($< = >$) shows whether the result is significant. The value of *p* shows the level of confidence in the result. For example, $p < .05$ indicates a significant relationship 95/100 times a random sample is drawn from the population. When reported in text, the *p* value generally follows the test result. When reported in a table, significance often is denoted with an * referring to a footnote or indicated with bolded text.

Evaluating Relationship Statistics

There are several initial questions to ask when evaluating relationship statistics. As with any quantitative measure, the first questions should concern the appropriateness of the sample. This is especially important if the statistics are being used to make inferences. The next question should concern the intended functions of the statistics chosen and how they are interpreted. Finally, there is consideration of the form of the relationship as nonlinear, linear, or curvilinear. Following is an overview of these general considerations for evaluating relationship statistics. Afterward is a more specific discussion of considerations for evaluating correlation.

Questions for Evaluating Relationship Statistics

- Was the sample appropriate for the study?
- What is the function and interpretation of the test statistic?
- Is there sufficient information about the form of the relationship?

Was the Sample Appropriate for the Study?   With regard to how the sample is collected, if the researcher is making an inference or generalization about a population, the sample should be randomly selected. Otherwise, relationship statistics have less rigid requirements for sample size than many other types of inferential statistics. Correlations in particular are relatively stable for smaller groups (less than 30) and most of the forms of effect size are based off nonparametric measures, which have less rigid minimum sample standards. As with any statistic, however, small samples are less likely to reach statistical significance, even when there is a difference (Cohen, 1992). Researchers concerned with ensuring adequate samples for evaluating significance often use power analysis, a procedure that estimates the minimum sample needed to reach a potential level of significance.

What Is the Function and Interpretation of the Test Statistic?   Relationship statistics serve several primary and numerous foundational functions in quantitative research. Several common functions in student affairs research include evaluating relationships between variables, quantifying differences between variables using effect size, calculating the reliability of measures and assessing relationships between factors using correlation statistics, and considering the potential predictive ability of variables based on associations. While the interpretation of relationship statistics generally involves evaluating the direction and strength of association, the threshold, or lower limit, of test values can vary depending on the statistic used. For example, correlation coefficients are generally interpreted as strong the closer they are to $|1|$. Effect size can be considered strong at .50 (Cohen, 1992). Reliability measures, factors, and predictors are often considered strong at or above .70 (Sriram, 2017; Tabachnick & Fidell, 2012). However, readers should interpret strength of association for any measure in the context of the study. Durlak (2009) related the following caution:

> Unfortunately, too many authors have applied [Cohen's] suggested conventions as iron-clad criteria without reference to the measurements taken, the study design, or the practical or clinical importance of the findings . . . Moreover, assuming that "large" effects are always more important than "small" or "medium" ones is unjustified. It is not only the magnitude of effect that is important, but also its practical or clinical value that must be considered. (p. 923)

Is There Sufficient Information About the Form of the Relationship?   Correlation coefficients are based on linear trends; therefore, a linear trend is more distinct the farther away it gets from 0. However, a value close to 0 doesn't necessarily mean there is no correlation. It could indicate a curvilinear trend in the data. If the researcher included scatterplots in the results or appendix, this can be easy to notice. If not, the research question must be considered conceptually. Based on the statistical result provided, if there is little or no relationship between the variables when a relationship is expected, the trend may not be linear. The relationship between student involvement and GPA is an example. A correlation test may show only a small relationship, but a scatterplot could reveal a curvilinear trend. Sometimes, researchers do not examine scatterplots when interpreting results and miss curvilinear trends.

FIGURE 12.1. LINEAR RELATIONSHIPS

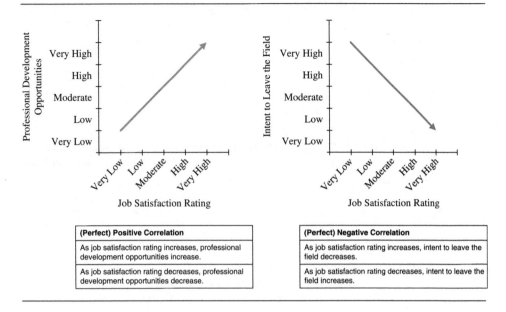

(Perfect) Positive Correlation
As job satisfaction rating increases, professional development opportunities increase.
As job satisfaction rating decreases, professional development opportunities decrease.

(Perfect) Negative Correlation
As job satisfaction rating increases, intent to leave the field decreases.
As job satisfaction rating decreases, intent to leave the field increases.

Additional Considerations for Evaluating Correlation

Evaluating correlation statistics requires additional considerations. These include understanding direction, strength, and form as well as the ability to read scatterplots.

Evaluating Direction. Direction reveals whether a correlation result is positive or negative. Figure 12.1 displays a positive linear relationship on the left and a negative linear relationship on the right. These are considered perfect correlations because each value intersects at the same rate.

Evaluating Strength. The strength of association refers to the degree of the linear relationship between the variables, as indicated by how close the test result is to $|1|$. Strength is expressed numerically as the correlation coefficient. A perfect relationship is a -1 or 1. No linear relationship at all is a 0. Following is a commonly accepted interpretation guide for strength (Cohen, 1992).

> **General Guide (absolute values)**
>
> .00—no correlation
>
> .10—weak correlation
>
> .30—moderate correlation
>
> .60—strong correlation
>
> 1.00—perfect correlation

Evaluating Form. The form of a correlation refers to the shape of the line formed when the variables are plotted. The three basic forms are nonlinear, linear, and curvilinear. A nonlinear relationship means there is no relationship between the variables. A linear relationship suggests that two or more variables are related in an upward or downward trend. The prior examples showed linear relationships. Sometimes, the relationships are curvilinear. Figure 12.2 displays a positive curvilinear relationship on the left and a negative curvilinear relationship on the right.

Reading Scatterplots. Correlation measures plot the intersection of two or more values to assess a relationship. A *scatterplot* is a graphical representation of associations between variables. Each data point (or value) on a scatterplot has two coordinates. One goes left to right (*x* coordinate) and the other up or down (the *y* coordinate). When all values are plotted on the same chart, they form a scatterplot. Statistical

FIGURE 12.2. CURVILINEAR RELATIONSHIPS

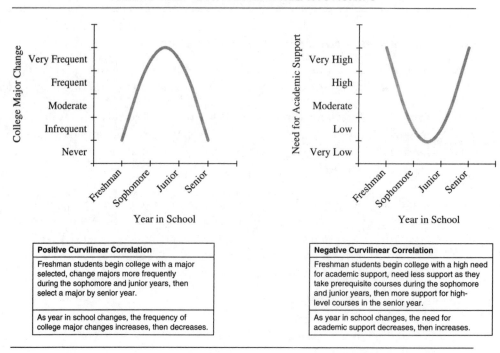

Positive Curvilinear Correlation
Freshman students begin college with a major selected, change majors more frequently during the sophomore and junior years, then select a major by senior year.
As year in school changes, the frequency of college major changes increases, then decreases.

Negative Curvilinear Correlation
Freshman students begin college with a high need for academic support, need less support as they take prerequisite courses during the sophomore and junior years, then more support for high-level courses in the senior year.
As year in school changes, the need for academic support decreases, then increases.

software fits an imaginary line representing a perfect linear or curvilinear (if specified) relationship to the graph to see how close the plots lie to the line. When the plots form a linear shape, such as in the prior examples for direction, the statistical value increases the closer the plots are to the perfect line. The farther away the plotted pair, the weaker the relationship. When the plots form a curvilinear shape, as in the prior examples for form, there is still a relationship, but there is no commonly agreed on value for the strength of the relationship.

It is difficult to see the form of a correlation simply by looking at the value of the coefficient. Knowing whether the relationship is linear or curvilinear (or even partially linear with a curvilinear form at one of the ends) can have implications for interpreting results. Further, a substantial benefit of examining scatterplots is the ability to identify outliers, which can be difficult to detect with larger datasets. An *outlier* is an errant data point that does not seem consistent with the others, pointing to potential problems (or opportunities) with the findings. Acknowledging outliers lets researchers develop a rationale for removing them, which results in a higher correlation between data points (in other words, a tighter fit for the data).

Being able to read scatterplots is a valuable skill for evaluating relationship statistics, but is deceptively difficult. It requires some abstract thinking, which can be challenging. When viewing a scatterplot, look for a pattern in the plotted values. The pattern can indicate an approximate direction, strength, and form of the relationships between variables. Figure 12.3 shows several example scatterplots. Notes for interpretation follow.

Applying Relationship Statistics

Student affairs practitioners seldom use relationship statistics; however, many of the questions they ask in practice are associational in nature. Descriptive statistics reveal summary characteristics and generally are easy to collect, analyze, and interpret. Inferential statistics can suggest how an effect may or may not be reflected in the larger population and add efficiency to decision making. A well-designed relationship study can be valuable for both these cases. Beyond implementing methods for practice, reviewing research that includes relationship results can be beneficial for similar reasons. This is particularly true for interpreting effect size, which can reveal whether or not a program or service would be valuable to implement based on its potential impact. Following are some considerations for using correlation statistics as well as suggestions for how to apply results from relationship studies to practice.

FIGURE 12.3. EXAMPLE SCATTERPLOTS

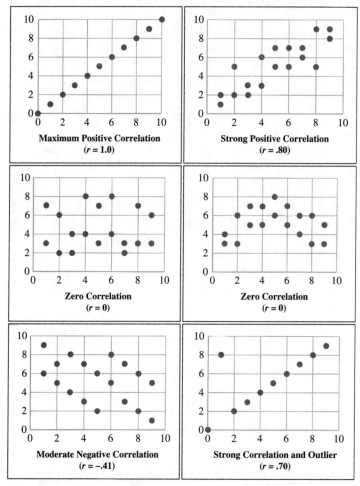

- To interpret direction, view the data from left to right. If the data show an upward trend, there is likely a positive linear relationship. Conversely, if the data show a downward trend from left to right, there is likely a negative linear relationship. If there does not seem be a pattern, or if the data have upward or downward trends at the two ends (curvilinear), there is not likely a linear relationship between the two variables. The *r* values listed below each of the scatterplots also indicate direction.
- To interpret form, look for the pattern the plots seem to make. Trace an imaginary line on the scatterplot. If the data indicate a pattern that moves up or down or from left to right, there is likely a linear relationship. A peak at the left and right with a drop in the middle or low points at left and right with a rise in the middle indicates a curvilinear relationship. Data scattered all over the graph indicates no relationship.
- To interpret strength, look for how closely the data gather around the imaginary line. The closer the plots fall to the line, the stronger the relationship. The *r* values listed below each of the scatterplots also indicate strength of association.

Opportunities for Applying Relationship Statistics

- Describe relationships between variables.
- Infer the relationship between variables.
- Understand potential impact.
- Consider the validity of measures.

Describe Relationships Between Variables   The basic descriptive function of relationship statistics is to reveal relationships between variables, which can provide support for decisions. This function lets practitioners consider how one variable affects or influences another. This does not reveal causation, but can provide a sense of the associations between two or more measures. For example, a conduct officer might consider the potential connection between alcohol violations and living on campus, using nonrandom data about the number of occurrences. Using a correlation statistic, she might find alcohol violations are moderately correlated with living on campus. This information could inform several resource decisions including revisions to resident assistant training, the need for campus police officers, the need for additional sanctioning support, and consideration of how on-campus students obtain alcohol. The problem with this approach, which is a limitation of most correlation studies, is what is not modeled. In this case, while the data show living on campus results in more alcohol violations, they don't take into account that the majority of students on campus are under 21, most violations related to living on campus occur in the first two weeks of the semester, and other factors that can affect why students drink on campus rather than off.

Infer the Relationship Between Variables   When it is possible to collect random data, relationship statistics can support inferences, or evidenced guesses, about the phenomenon. Like the descriptive function, this allows practitioners to consider how measures are related. For example, if the same conduct officer wanted to learn more about nonprescription drug use on campus, she might survey a random sample of students about different types of drugs and reasons they take them. She might include a category for stimulant drugs and academic enhancement. A correlation statistic might reveal a weak, nonsignificant relationship between using drugs for this specific purpose and would allow her to shift resources from preventive efforts focused on this area to another. While this function also provides some helpful data about how data are related, it also cannot account for other factors that are unmeasured, such as access to drugs, previous experience taking them, or peer effects.

Perspectives From the Field—How Relationship Statistics Inform Student Affairs Practice

Relationship statistics help us start thinking about not just the causes and effects in teaching and learning, but all the variables that affect the interchange. It is easy to make the mistake of reading correlation as causal. However, we know that influence works in multiple directions in education, and may not be uniform over time. Having the sophistication to ask what else may be at play matters.

For example, in studying first-generation students, many report higher levels of confidence than do students with college-graduate parents. At first, one may read a correlation as implying that these students do not feel a need for help. Indeed, there is less help seeking behavior (office-hour attendance, workshop participation, peer tutors, and other similar elements) among first-generation students. Perhaps what affected the answer to the confidence question was a desire to project readiness to others and not appear in need.

Another key question I ask is whether there are curvilinear relationships, which tend to flatten a correlation result. For example, faculty often invest substantially in teaching at early career (when they are investing in building their practices) and at late career (as they are particularly mindful of retirement and leaving a legacy within students). However, at midcareer, faculty also confront the pressures at the height of their research careers and institutional demand for their service to department, university, and/or disciplinary field. Reading correlational data on its face would suggest that faculty invest less in teaching as their career unfolds, rather than revealing the nuance of beginning, mid, and late career.

Relationship statistics are exciting because they do not end a conversation. Rather, they start many rich discussions.

Malinda M. Matney—Director of Assessment, Center for Research on Learning and Teaching, University of Michigan

Understand Potential Impact   Relationship statistics are used widely in published research as well as in large-scale surveys and institutional reports. They are common in studies focused on engagement, persistence, and retention and are frequently displayed in research that includes a survey data collection or factor analysis. Being literate in relationship statistics provides the ability to understand and evaluate the potential impact of research-based decisions in practice. For example, knowing that there is a statistical difference is often less important to practice than knowing how much more effective the difference actually is (effect size). Pittman and Foubert (2016) provided an example:

The three predictor variables (role of mentors, supervision style received, and professional involvement) together significantly predicted the professional identity of new student affairs professionals with an $R^2 = 0.13$, $F(3, 91) = 4.668$, $p < 0.01$. Effect sizes were calculated using a Cohen's f ($f^2 = 0.159$) showing a small effect (Cohen, 1988). Although these results are statistically significant, other variables likely affect the prediction of professional identity for new student affairs professionals. (p. 21)

Consider the Validity of Measures   Published research, national survey reports, and benchmarking studies frequently include statistics indicating the validity of measures and associated factors. While evaluating a new instrument using correlation for reliability or for identifying factors is beyond introductory research skills, being able to read and evaluate these measures as reported can lend insight to practice. For example, if an institutional or division goal is to increase student engagement, viewing statistical reports that list a factor for engagement can help identify activities and behaviors that contribute to increasing engagement scores. This type of data can support resource decisions contributing to new or expanded programs, policies, and services.

Building Your Relationship Methods Skillset

Practitioners can build skills by reviewing relationship statistics in published studies, questioning both what is included in text and what research and experience suggest might not appear, such as interpreting form (linear versus curvilinear) and accounting for effect size. An applied way to build skills is learning to read, evaluate, and create scatterplots. As noted previously, although reading scatterplots is an inexact skill, visualizing relationships can reveal how measures work together as well as identify outliers that need to be addressed. Showing scatterplots as part of a report at a planning meeting can also be an engaging way to discuss statistical results.

Pragmatically, working with the correlation function in spreadsheet programs or statistical software can help in skill building. Excel offers some basic tools for calculating correlation as well as the ability to create scatterplots. For formal instruction, correlation statistics and effect size are generally taught in introductory applied statistics classes. Reliability statistics and factor analysis are advanced concepts that be offered as part of advanced coursework or specialized conference workshops and trainings. Recommended textbooks include Mertler and Vanetta (2013) and Sriram (2017).

References

Cohen, J. (1988). *Statistical power analysis for the behavioral sciences* (2nd ed.). Hillsdale, NJ: Erlbaum.

Cohen, J. (1992). A power primer. *Psychological Bulletin, 112*(1), 155–159.

Cohen, J., Cohen, P., West, S. G., & Aiken, L. S. (2002). *Applied multiple regression/correlation analysis for the behavioral sciences* (3rd ed.). New York, NY: Routledge.

Durlak, J. A. (2009). How to select, calculate, and interpret effect sizes. *Journal of Pediatric Psychology, 34*(9), 917–928.

Kim, Y. K., & Lundberg, C. A. (2016). A structural model of the relationship between student-faculty interaction and cognitive skills development among college students. *Research in Higher Education, 57*(3), 288–309.

Lowinger, R. J., Kuo, B. C. H., Song, H.-A., Mahadevan, L., Kim, E., Yu-Hsin Liao, K., . . . Han, S. (2016). Predictors of academic procrastination in Asian international college students. *Journal of Student Affairs Research and Practice, 53*(1), 90–104.

Mertler, C. A., & Vanetta, R. A. (2013). *Advanced and multivariate statistics statistical methods: Practical application and interpretation* (5th ed.). Glendale, AZ: Pyrczak.

Palmer, R. S., McMahon, T. J., Moreggi, D. I., Rounsaville, B. J., & Ball, S. A. (2012). College student drug use: Patterns, concerns, consequences, and interest in intervention. *Journal of College Student Development, 53*(1), 124–132.

Pittman, E. C., & Foubert, J. D. (2016). Predictors of professional identity development for student affairs professionals. *Journal of Student Affairs Research and Practice, 53*(1), 13–25.

Spanierman, L. B., Soble, J. R., Mayfield, J. B., Neville, H. A., Aber, M., Khuri, L., & De La Rosa, B. (2013). Living learning communities and students' sense of community and belonging. *Journal of Student Affairs Research and Practice, 50*(3), 308–325.

Sriram, R. (2017). *Student affairs by the numbers.* Sterling, VA: Stylus.

Tabachnick, B. G., & Fidell, L. S. (2012). *Using multivariate statistics* (5th ed.). Upper Saddle River, NJ: Pearson.

Trochim, W. M. K. (2006). *Research methods knowledge base: Correlation.* Retrieved from http://www.socialresearchmethods.net/kb/statcorr.php

CHAPTER THIRTEEN

MAKING PREDICTIONS

Learning Outcomes

By the end of this chapter, you should be able to:

- Understand the purpose and role of prediction statistics.
- Differentiate between the major types of prediction statistics.
- Read prediction statistics in journal articles and reports.
- Evaluate prediction statics based on how data are collected, analyzed, and reported.
- Apply interpretations of prediction statistics to student affairs practice.

Prediction statistics estimate the influence of one or more measures on an outcome. Following the reductionist purpose of quantitative research, a fundamental goal is to identify the least number of measures that accurately predict an outcome. Prediction research yields important implications for student affairs practice. Many of the effects of student services on graduation, job placement, and other college outcomes can be indirect. Measuring and modeling student services–related influences on student success has been an invaluable contribution to the field. Prediction studies gave student affairs the ability to demonstrate how the profession measurably affects students on a large scale. For example, Astin (1977, 1993), Tinto (1975; Tinto & Pusser, 2006), Kuh (2009), and others have shown that social integration, often operationalized as involvement, positively and significantly affects persistence, retention, and graduation rates.

Prediction statistics are difficult to learn and conduct because they require an understanding of all prior statistics (description, difference, and relationship) in addition to new terminology. Prediction is used most effectively when researchers have an expertise about a topic formed through familiarity with prior research and theory in combination with intuition informed by research and/or practice. Building statistical models is a highly conceptual activity that consists of carefully selecting predictors and outcomes, specifying their order, correctly measuring variables, and intuiting what is missing or not indicated in the results. While learning how to conduct prediction research may be a less practical skill, learning to interpret (and question) results is increasingly essential as the use of forecasting becomes a more prominent approach for demonstrating accountability, evaluating effectiveness, and projecting outcomes based on resource allocation (Schuh, Biddix, Dean, & Kinzie, 2016).

This chapter focuses on two main types of prediction statistics and introduces prominent variations used in student affairs research. Included is a basic interpretation guide for reading prediction statistics, focusing on regression analysis. Understanding prediction results relies on many of the similar principles as other forms of quantitative research. Evaluating prediction results can be more challenging due to the new terminology associated with requirements. To the extent possible, the necessary information is distilled into essential components, skimming some of the deeper technical discussions and nuances. The chapter begins with a general overview of prediction statistics then describes how to understand, read, evaluate, and apply measures.

Understanding Prediction Statistics

The concept of prediction comes from estimating how one or more variables affect, or predict, an outcome. In its most familiar form, a prediction question asks, "How does variable A affect variable B?" The researcher determines an outcome of interest and collects or analyzes existing data measuring that outcome and potential predictors. Potential predictors are identified either by previous research, experience, intuition, or a combination that constitutes a researcher's belief for how the outcome can be influenced. The goal is to identify one or more potential predictors (less is usually better) that produce a change in an outcome. In prediction studies, the predictors are independent variables and outcomes are dependent variables.

Potential predictors and outcome variables generally are collected with survey research or from existing datasets. Often, data are comprised of multiple measures taken from individuals. For example, a practitioner wanting to know how student involvement affects student engagement might administer a survey to a random sample of students asking about their involvement experiences and an overall rating of engagement. It is important to note that an outcome like engagement does not have to be a single variable. It may be a factor comprised of scores from multiple measures. Either way, the results of the analysis would show which of the questions measured on the survey regarding involvement best influence engagement.

Words Researchers Use—Synonyms for Prediction

When researchers write about regression, they use several verbs synonymously. Following is a listing of the most commonly used words, along with some minor distinctions worth noting.

Prediction
One or more variables will be used to estimate an outcome.

Impact
The influence of a program or intervention is assessed to understand its effect on an outcome.

Influence
One or more variables will be used to measure their influence on an outcome.

Cause
One or more variables will be used to determine causes (independent variables) and resultant effect (dependent variable).

Affect
One or more variables will be used to measure change on an outcome.

Making Predictions

Prediction statistics and in particular regression are commonly used in student affairs studies to evaluate the effect, impact, or influence of student services on cognitive (academic engagement, motivation), educational (GPA, graduation, persistence, retention), or psychosocial (identity development, social integration) outcomes. Other uses of prediction statistics include assessing campus environment or policy, predicting group membership, testing casual theories, and to a lesser extent in research, forecasting outcomes. Following are explanations of each function.

Reasons for Making Predictions

- Understand how variables affect outcomes.
- Assess environmental effects on student success.
- Predict group membership.
- Refine or extend theory.
- Forecast outcomes based on trends.

Understand How Variables Affect Outcomes Prediction statistics offer the ability to test how variables, individually and in combination, can affect an outcome. Examples of commonly used predictors directly related to student affairs practice include campus residence, involvement in campus organizations, and participation in service or leadership programs. These influences often are used in combination with demographic characteristics such as gender and race/ ethnicity or precollege variables such as high school entering GPA or parental income to predict academic success outcomes such as retention, persistence, and graduation (Reason, 2003, 2009). The ability to link student services to academic success outcomes through prediction studies has been a significant benefit for student affairs practice, adding measurable legitimacy in an increasing era of accountability. Tinto's (1975; Tinto & Pusser, 2006) work on student departure is a prominent example.

Prediction studies also focus on broader outcomes. Examples include the effects of community service on student development (Cruce & Moore, 2007), the relationship between student interactions with student affairs professionals and cognitive outcomes (Martin & Seifert, 2011), learning and moral reasoning in the first year (Mayhew, Seifert, Pascarella, Nelson Laird, & Blaich, 2012), gender differences and academic performance (Zacherman & Foubert, 2014), involvement influences on leadership development (Carter, Ro, Alcott, & Lattuca, 2016; Dugan & Komives, 2010), the relationship between student and institutional characteristics on civic outcomes (Ishitani & McKitrick, 2013), and predictors of professional identity development in student affairs (Pittman & Foubert, 2016).

Assess Environmental Effects on Student Success An important function of prediction research for student affairs is the ability to assess the impact of environmental effects on student success. These can include alcohol and other drug use (Manning, Pring, & Glider, 2012), civic engagement (Bowman, 2011), living arrangement (Long, 2014), racial climate and inclusivity (Harper & Hurtado, 2007; Milem, Chang, & Antonio, 2005), religious and spiritual climate (Bryant, Wickliff, Mayhew, & Berringer, 2009), or sexual assault and sexual misconduct (Cantor et al., 2015). Other factors that influence climate and culture including personnel, policy, and practice. Prediction studies assessing the influence of these and other effects on student success are generally created using large-scale campus climate or culture surveys. Outcomes measures most often relate to competency or skill development as well as education outcomes.

Predict Group Membership   Researchers use prediction to classify students or predict behavior based on group membership. In this case, membership is treated as a discrete (retained–not retained, member–nonmember) outcome. Retention and persistence studies often fall into this category, as students are classified as either staying or leaving, based on precollege characteristics, academic performance, or involvement. Aside from the discrete characteristics of outcomes, a major difference between these types of studies and research assessing individual influences on outcomes is that a goal is to classify groups, rather than identify effects (Dugan, 2013). With retention and persistence outcomes, for example, researchers include risk factors and may add other influences to gain a more accurate classification. For example, Ishitani (2016) examined how academic and social integration affected persistence outcomes. The results of the study emphasized the need for helping students integrate in the first year, but these effects largely disappeared by the second.

Refine or Extend Theory   Student development theories often are initially conceptualized and evidenced with qualitative research (Patton, Renn, Guido, & Quaye, 2016; Torres, Jones, & Renn, 2009) and later refined or extended with prediction models. For example, much of the initial moral development theory conceptualized by Piaget then Kohlberg and later Gilligan was evidenced using qualitative methods. Mayhew et al. (2012) added nuances to the theory using prediction with large-scale datasets. Komives' Leadership Identity Model initially was derived from grounded theory and later assessed using regression-based factors (Dugan & Komives, 2010). Another example is Tovar's (2013) work to operationalize sense of belonging and mattering among community college students based on theories developed by Schlossberg and Josselson. Researchers also extended King and Baxter Magolda's (2005) interview-derived framework for intercultural maturity by applying regression results to study first-year students' development of a global perspective (Engberg & Davidson, 2016) and to examine the potentially inhibiting role of fraternity/sorority involvement on intercultural competence (Martin, Parker, Pascarella, & Blechschmidt, 2015). An example of new theory development is Bryant, Gayles, and Davis's (2012) model of civic development that suggested the role of social activism goals in fostering sense of responsibility.

Forecast Outcomes Based on Trends　Prediction is a powerful tool for forecasting outcomes at the national level as well as for estimating admissions, advising, enrollment, housing, and outcomes data on campus. For example, researchers at the National Center for Education Statistics (NCES) publish an annual report projecting college attendance and degrees awarded based on regression methods (Hussar & Bailey, 2016). Adelman's influential reports for the Department of Education, *Answers in the Toolbox* (1999) and the *Toolbox Revisited* (2006), provided the academic and conceptual foundation for numerous studies on college completion. While Adelman's work was not predictive in intent (emphasizing instead association and contribution), its operationalization of academic intensity (inclusive of effort and commitment) led to a clearer understanding of student success. Subsequent researchers have added these considerations to social and psychosocial factors, such as Ishitani's (2006) study of attrition and degree completion behavior among first-year students.

At the campus level, institutional researchers engage in enrollment management practices to examine the combination of activities that effect student enrollment such as student college choice, transition to college, student attrition and retention, and student outcomes (Hossler & Bontrager, 2014). The approach builds information sharing and, ultimately, prediction models incorporating data from recruitment and financial aid, student support services, curriculum development and other academic areas, persistence, and student outcomes. In addition, although few published studies outline ways to use forecasting in student housing, Kelly, Demonte, and Jones (n.d.) described ways to use predictive analysis to understand student satisfaction, learning experiences, enrollment, persistence, and retention related to living on campus. Recently, in a pragmatic article targeting chief enrollment officers, Langston, Wyant, and Scheid (2016) described several ways to calculate and use regression models for enrollment projections.

Research Considerations

Designing and conducting prediction studies require that data meet conditions that even large-scale, very rigorous survey projects have a difficult time attaining. The four requirements for inferential statistics (random sampling, adequate sample size, independence, and normality) are important for most prediction statistics. Regression adds that predictor variables should not be too highly correlated. Some of the requirements are more problematic than others when not met. For example, minimum data requirements are essential, but alternative random sampling methods can be justified in some cases. Normality is critical for some prediction statistics (such as multiple regression), but not problematic for others (such as logistic regression).

Perspectives From the Field—Choosing Predictors for Regression

The initial challenge in choosing multiple regression as an analytical tool is how to select effective predictor variables to maximize the R-square, the proportion of the outcome variance associated with the predictor variables. While it is ideal to create a set of predictor variables that are highly correlated with the outcome variable, predictor variables must have low correlations among themselves. This is necessary to identify distinct contributions of each predictor variable to the outcome variable. Furthermore, the selection of predictor variables should be built on empirical evidence from existent theories to underpin the conceptual framework. Additionally, the inclusion of certain items unique to individual institutions may be considered for institutional effectiveness and evaluation purposes.

Terry T. Ishitani—Associate Professor of Higher Education, the University of Tennessee

Researchers conducting prediction studies learn that dataset preparation (inclusive of checking that requirements are met, identifying outliers, and addressing missing data) can take longer than actually collecting data and completing the analysis. Also, perhaps more than any other method, prediction statistics are theory-driven. Prediction equations should be informed by an understanding of prior research to create a working theory (prediction model) that is testable using obtainable data. In other words, prediction models have to be theorized as well as justified—making those choices can be difficult without a good knowledge of the literature.

Main Types of Prediction Statistics

When researchers test for prediction, they typically use regression. *Regression* is an inferential statistic that examines the relationship between one or more predictor (independent) and outcome (dependent) variables. This chapter covers two types used in student affairs research, multiple and logistic. The test, use, requirement, and symbols for both are summarized in Table 13.1.

Multiple regression is used to predict the relationship between one or more numerical variables and a single numerical outcome. The term multiple comes from the ability to use more than one predictor. This lets researchers account for the singular as well as simultaneous effects of multiple variables. Note that nonnumerical predictors (such as year in school) can be used for multiple regression, but must be recoded (statistically changed) to function accurately.

Table 13.1. Main Types of Prediction Statistics

Prediction Test	Use	Requirement	Test Symbols
Multiple Regression	Predicts a numerical outcome using one or more numeric predictors.	Normally distributed predictors and a numerical (interval or scale) outcome.	b or β
Logistic Regression	Predicts a discrete outcome using one or more of any form of predictors.	Any type of predictors and a discrete (nominal or ordinal) outcome.	b or β OR

Note: OR = odds ratio

Logistic regression is used to predict the relationship between one or more variables (any type) and a single discrete outcome. There are two types of logistic regression: binary (only two possible outcomes—yes–no) and ordinal (the outcome is ordered—low–middle–high group). The term logistic comes from the calculation behind the equation, which uses the log of the outcome variable as a way to test the linear contribution of predictors. The main advantages of this approach are the flexibility it allows for predictors and the relative ease of interpretation.

Astin's IEO Model and Regression

Alexander Astin conceptualized his Input–Environment–Outcome (IEO) (1970a, 1970b) as a theory-to-practice model using prediction statistics to understand college outcomes. Later (1977, 1993), he applied the model to large-scale datasets and was able to empirically demonstrate various college effects based on precollege and college environment influences and experiences. The IEO model uses a variation of regression called block modeling to control for the effects of inputs (predictors) and aspects of the college environment (also predictors) on outcomes (Astin & Dey, 1997). The number of predictors in each block can vary based on the size of the dataset. Researchers using the IEO model employ both multiple and logistic regression.

Variations of Prediction Statistics

Four other forms of prediction are less often used in student affairs, but important to be able to identify: path analysis, multilevel modeling, discriminant function analysis (DFA), and structural equation modeling (SEM). Path analysis predicts an outcome based on a hypothesized sequence, or path. Multilevel modeling is a form of regression that specifically accounts for levels or classifications that may influence a study. It is sometimes called hierarchical linear modeling (HLM) for the software program used to analyze data. Discriminant function analysis (DFA) is a technique that sorts or differentiates variables based on the groups (as outcomes) they most likely belong to. Structural equation modeling (SEM) identifies missing, or latent, effects of variables.

Words Researchers Use—Regression Terminology

Regression Model or Equation
A *regression model* (or equation) is a combination of variables hypothesized to predict an outcome. The actual equation is typically shown with mathematical operators. In practice, however, the terms are used interchangeably to refer to the combination of variables.

Blocked Regression
Blocked regression is a form of regression in which predictors are put into sets or blocks specified by the researcher and added to the analysis in a sequence. Researchers using the IEO model often use blocked regression for sets of input and environment predictors.

Stepwise Regression
Stepwise regression is a form of regression in which the predictors are added or removed based on a significance level (*p* value) set by the researcher. Predictors that meet this criterion are kept in the final model, comprising the regression equation.

Beta Coefficient (*B, b*)
A coefficient is another word for predictor in regression. Specifically, a *beta coefficient (B, b)*, also referred to as a beta weight, is the value a predictor contributes to the prediction equation.

Odds Ratio (*OR*)
An *odds ratio (OR or Exp(B))* is a value representing a predictor variable that represents the odds an outcome will occur given the presence of that predictor.

R^2
R^2 is a statistical measure that suggests how well the regression model (with all predictors) fits, or predicts, the outcome. It can be considered an indicator of accuracy. A 0 indicates the model does not predict the outcome. A 1 is a perfect prediction. Squaring R provides can be interpreted as the percentage of the outcome explained by the model. For example, $R^2 = .42$ means 42% of outcome can be explained by the predictors in the model. Researchers sometimes report Adjusted R^2 instead, which accounts for how many predictors are in the model.

Reading Prediction Statistics

Researchers generally list prediction variables in text and, in the case of regression, identify the independent (predictor) variables and dependent (outcome) variable(s) with separate headings or paragraphs following the research questions. A typical reporting format includes demographic characteristics or descriptive measures of study variables in a methods section with either a correlation matrix or text about variable correlations prior to a results section. Results often are displayed in tables to show various statistics relevant to interpreting each variable. This approach efficiently allows readers to see how individual variables affect outcomes. In text, results often are limited to a final model equation or beta coefficients for significant predictors. Key symbols in regression results are the beta coefficients (B, b), significance for predictors (p), model fit (R^2 and Adjusted R^2), and, in the case of logistic regression, odds ratio (OR).

Following are excerpts from articles, followed by general notes on interpretation. The section is organized by type of regression rather than reporting format as in other chapters to help with learning how to read individual results and to serve as an efficient reference.

Reading Multiple Regression

Vianden and Barlow (2014) sought to understand (predict) undergraduate student loyalty to the institution, citing Bean's (2005) belief that loyalty is a significant predictor of persistence. The researchers developed the following question to guide the study, which lists the study variables:

> What factors predict student loyalty to the university, specifically how do precollege characteristics (e.g., race, gender, first-generation student status), student behaviors or attitudes (e.g., intent to leave, satisfaction, fit), and institutional conditions (e.g., quality of teaching, quality of student services, quality of staff) affect the development of student loyalty? (p. 17)

After hypothesizing a conceptual model based on prior literature, the researchers adapted and administered an existing survey and used factor analysis to reduce the number of questions into several variables. Following are the results in summary text format, followed by interpretation notes.

Multiple Regression in Text

> The multiple regression analyses indicated that the full prediction model including student college attitudes and behaviors, along with precollege characteristics and institutional conditions explained 69% of the variance in loyalty scores ($R^2 = .691$, $F(18, 1109) = 137.947$, $p < .001$). (Vianden & Barlow, 2014, p. 23)

Since prediction is an inferential statistic, reading results begins with evaluating significance. The $p < .001$, reveals the regression result is significant (or an improvement over no predictors). The primary focus for most readers is $R^2 = .691$, which indicates that 69% of the change in loyalty score is explained by the predictors. F and the value afterward (137.947) is an ANOVA result testing whether the model predicted the outcome.

Multiple Regression in a Table. Following the abbreviated text results, researchers typically include information about each predictor in a table. After the results reported previously, Vianden and Barlow (2014) noted that "Specifically, seven SULI subscales and three demographic variables were statistically significant predictors of student loyalty (Table 4)" (p. 23). The results shown in Table 13.2 illustrate multiple regression reporting in table format, followed by interpretation notes.

Most regression tables are displayed with predictors listed along rows and their values relative to the outcome in the adjacent columns. Following College Choice Rank to Column 1 reveals three values: $.509^{**}$, .111, and .083. These are the values for College Choice Rank after it was used to predict the outcome of Student Loyalty. Note that some values are missing in the table, Model 3 scores for Student Attitudes and Behaviors and Model 2 and 3 scores for Institutional Conditions. This shows that the researchers conducted three regressions, one with all sets of predictors (Model 1), one with only two (Model 2), and one with only one set (Model 3). Since prediction is an inferential statistic, reading results begins with evaluating significance. A significant result (*) for an independent variable (predictor) can be interpreted as affecting the dependent variable (outcome). The larger the value (B or β), the larger the contribution:

- B (also sometimes b) is the unstandardized coefficient. This means that the regression coefficient is in the original measurement unit.
- β is the standardized coefficient. This means that the regression coefficient is in a different (standardized) measurement unit. Specifically, β is a standard deviation.

Standard error (*SE*) B is a measure of variability. It can be interpreted as the standard deviation of B. R^2 values are listed at the bottom of the table, showing the overall predictive accuracy of each model.

Reading Logistic Regression

Swecker, Fifolt, and Searby (2013) examined the influence of the number academic advisor meetings on first-generation student retention. The following research question guided the study:

> What is the relationship between academic advising and the retention of first-generation students at a 4-year, public, research institution in the southeastern United States? (p. 47)

Table 13.2. Regression Coefficients for Three Models Predicting Student Loyalty ($n = 1,207$)

Clusters	Model 1			Model 2			Model 3		
	B	SE B	β	B	SE B	β	B	SE B	β
Precollege Characteristics									
College Choice Rank	.509**	.111	.083	.507**	.111	.083	1.843**	.175	.302
International Student	2.627	1.355	.036	2.686*	1.354	0.36	1.813	2.240	.025
Race	−1.589*	.544	−.053	−1.631*	.542	−.055	−1.348	.902	−.045
Sex	.703*	.296	.041	.796*	.294	.046	.875	.490	.051
Father's Education	−.166	.087	−.038	−.167	.088	−.038	−.214	.147	−.049
Mother's Education	−.106	.090	−.024	−.106	.90	−.023	.054	.150	.012
Distance From Home	.170	.104	.029	.185	.103	.031	.733**	.168	.125
Classification	.037	.115	.006	.039	.114	.006	.292	.186	.045
Student Attitudes and Behaviors									
Freq. Student Engagement	.098**	.030	.064	.102**	.029	.068			
Intent to Leave	−.331**	.052	−.118	−.321**	.052	−.114			
Satisfaction	.642**	.054	.269	.641**	.055	.262			
Institutional Fit	.581**	.043	.311	.578**	.042	.309			
Initial Impressions	.197**	.028	.170	.184**	.027	.159			
Perceived Skill Devt.	.187**	.024	.194	.173**	.022	.180			
Institutional Conditions									
Quality of Facilities	−.005	.048	−.002						
Quality of Teaching	−.071*	.026	−.059						
Quality of Student Svcs.	−.024	.029	−.019						
Quality of Staff	.042	.031	.032						

Notes: Dependent Variable = Loyalty, Model 1 $R^2 = .691$ $\Delta R^2 = .691$**, Model 2 $R^2 = .689$ $\Delta R^2 = −.002$, Model 3 $R^2 = .119$, $\Delta R^2 = −.570$**

* $=p \leq .05$, ** $= p \leq .001$

Source: From Vianden and Barlow (2014), p. 24. Reprinted by permission of NASPA—National Association of Student Personnel Administrators/Student Affairs Administrators in Higher Education.

The researchers used historical data from institutional records to create a dataset. Following are results from the final model in summary text format, followed by notes on interpretation.

Logistic Regression in Text

> Data show a significant relationship between the number of meetings and the retention of first-generation college students. While the variables of gender, race, and major showed no significance in relation to retention, the variable of number of advisor meetings proved to be a reliable indicator of student retention. The significance value for number of advisor meetings for the year was .000 with a Wald value of 13.28. (Swecker, Fifolt, & Searby, 2013, p. 49)

Logistic regression results (binary and ordinal) follow the same basic principles as multiple regression. Look for significance first, which the researchers report as .000. Instead of an *F* test, logistic regression uses a Wald statistic, but the results are interpreted similarly.

Logistic Regression in a Table. Following the abbreviated text results, researchers typically include information about each predictor in a table. After the results reported previously, Swecker et al. (2013) noted that "With log linear transformation, the odds ratio of Exp(B) for the number of advisor meetings was 13.557 with the 95% confidence interval (CI) [3.336, 55.090]" (p. 49). The results shown in Table 13.3 illustrate logistic regression reporting in table format, followed by interpretation notes.

Table 13.3. Regression of Variables

Variable	B	Wald	*p*	Exp(B)	95% CI
Gender	.216	.611	.435	1.242	[.722, 2.131]
Race (White)		5.246	.073		
Race 1 (Black)	−.329	.709	.400	.720	[.335, 1.547]
Race 2 (other)	−.930	4.382	.036	.394	[.165, .942]
Major		1.727	.631		
Major 1	.318	.605	.437	1.374	[.617, 3.058]
Major 2	.033	.005	.942	1.034	[.427, 2.500]
Major 3	−.112	.063	.802	.894	[.375, 2.135]
Log number of advisor meetings	2.607	13.281	.000	13.557	[3.336, 55.090]
Constant	−2.611	12.096	.001	.073	

Source: From Swecker, Fifolt, and Searby (2013), p. 50. Reprinted with permission from the *NACADA Journal.* Copyright 2013 by the NACADA: The Global Community for Academic Advising. Article available at http://www.nacadajournal.org/doi/pdf/10.12930/NACADA-13-192

Predictors are listed along rows and their values relative to the outcome in the adjacent columns.

The major difference from multiple regression is that in addition to beta coefficients, logistic regression results can be reported as odds ratios, abbreviated as *OR* or Exp(B). Interpret this value with the following guide:

- Check the significance for the variable. Significant values are interpreted as predictors.
- If the variable value is greater than 1, interpret it to mean increasing odds (with each 1 unit change). Conversely, if the value is less than 1, the odds decrease.
- Exp(B) can be interpreted as a multiplier. For example, 1.13 Exp(B) suggests the chances of the outcome occurring increase by 1.13 times with each increase in the predictor. So, the odds of retaining students are 1.13 times higher for every additional advisor meeting.
- Exp(B) also can be interpreted as a percentage by multiplying the tenths and hundredths places by 100. For example, an Exp(B) of 1.13 is $13 \times 100 = 13\%$. So, the odds of retaining students increased by 13% for every additional meeting with an advisor.

The researchers also included confidence interval (CI) results, which is similar to *SE* B as an indicator of variance. Specifically, CI is the range within which we can expect the odds to fall 95% of the time we sample from this population.

Guidelines for Reading Prediction Statistics

- Interpret the significance of the model.
- Cautiously interpret model fit.
- For multiple regression, review the beta coefficient values.
- For logistic regression, review the Exp(B) or odds ratios.

Interpret the Significance of the Model   Regression results have one or more significance tests shown in text after an equation, or at the bottom of a table. The value should be interpreted to mean that the variables (in the model) predicted the outcome. Researchers sometimes distinguish different types of models. Following are some additional details on interpretation that are applicable to most reported regression results.

- Full model indicates that this model contained all the predictors.
- Reduced model indicates this model has fewer predictors.
- Models 1, 2, 3, etc. indicate there were multiple models and this is the order tested.
- Final model refers to the finished version of the regression, used to interpret results.

Cautiously Interpret Model Fit   Researchers using multiple regression generally include an R^2 statistic as an indicator of model fit, or how well the model predicted the outcome. While this should not be overinterpreted (see Evaluating in the following section), it can serve as an indicator of the predictive value of the model. Logistic regression does not use R^2, but some commonly used approximations in student affairs research are McFadden's R^2, Nagelkerke's, and Cox and Snell. Each are similarly interpreted as an estimate of how much variance in the outcome the model explains.

For Multiple Regression, Review the Beta Coefficient Values   When reading the detailed results of a multiple regression analysis, review the beta coefficients, which are most often displayed in text. If the variable is significant, interpret a positive value to mean the predictor contributed to the outcome. The higher the number, the stronger the predictor. More specifically, for each one-unit increase in the predictor, the dependent variable goes up. This also applies to variations of prediction that use beta coefficients, such as path analysis, multilevel modeling, DFA, and SEM.

For Logistic Regression, Review the Exp(B) and/or Odds Ratios   When reading the detailed results of a logistic regression analysis, review the Exp(B) or odds ratios, which may be displayed in text or a table. If the variable is significant, interpret the value as positive or negative and then either as a multiplier or convert to a percentage. If the variable value is greater than 1, interpret it to mean increasing odds with each 1 unit change. Conversely, if the value is less than 1, interpret it to mean the odds decrease.

Evaluating Prediction Statistics

Evaluating prediction statistics is a complex task due to the different methods and multifaceted measures used for assessing results. However, some basic questions can be helpful for evaluating findings in most published student affairs studies. These relate to the sample, plausibility of the model, and the influence of the predictors. Following is an overview of these considerations.

Perspectives From the Field—Reading Regression as Units of Change

Researchers using regression analysis typically report change as units. It is common to see this written as follows: "For every one unit of change in the predictor, expect a change in the outcome." To make sense of this practically, you need to understand what a one-unit change looks like for your predictor (or independent variable of interest). In multiple regression, for example, if the outcome measure (dependent variable) is a composite score such as critical thinking from 0 to 25, the regression coefficient for a given predictor would tell you that critical thinking scores on the dependent outcome measure would go up (or down if it is a negative number) by the value of the predictor each time you increase it. Interpreting regression coefficients can be further complicated if you are trying to interpret models where predictors have different scales (name, rank, and/or number). Standardized coefficients (and outcome measures if you are using multiple regression) fix this problem by converting all values to standard deviation units so both the predictors and the outcome measures can be thought of in terms of standard deviations. In other words, your unit of change when you have standardized variables in a multiple regression is a standard deviation.

In my own research using multiple regression, I typically standardize coefficients and all dependent outcome measures to make interpreting results straightforward and practically applicable. So, for example, in a study my colleague and I conducted, we found that as students' scores on the interactions with student affairs professionals scale increased by one standard deviation (one unit), their score on a measure of academic motivation increased by .137 of a standard deviation or about 1/7 of a standard deviation (Martin & Seifert, 2011). This may not sound like much, but given that we were able to determine this statistically by controlling for a host of potentially confounding variables including a pretest of our dependent outcome measure, this finding holds both practical and statistical significance.

Georgianna L. Martin—Assistant Professor, College Student Affairs Administration, University of Georgia

Questions for Evaluating Prediction Results

- Is the sample size adequate?
- Is the model plausible?
- How much do the predictors influence the outcome?

Is the Sample Size Adequate?   While very large samples are not essential for prediction statistics, they can help offset problems when other method requirements are difficult to meet. A smaller, representative sample is generally preferred over a larger sample that may not be reflective of the population. It is also important to note that regression statistics have minimum requirements for the number of cases (or data points) to predictors. This is referred to as a case-to-variable ratio. A common recommendation is 30:1 (Mertler & Vannatta, 2013). So, a researcher studying how being an international student (predictor) affects academic engagement (outcome) would need demographic data for at least 30 students for a 1 predictor study. Adding an additional predictor (such as social integration) would require 30 more students. Smaller case-to-variable ratio studies are possible, but the researcher should provide good rationale to support nonconformity.

Is the Model Plausible?   An overlooked consideration for prediction statistics is whether or not the proposed model is plausible, or "makes sense." Critical readers should consider the following questions:

1. Is the proposed model reasonable?
2. Do the variables make sense as predictors for the outcome?
3. Are any of the predictors problematic when used together?
4. What predictors are missing that should be included?

Before making a determination about the plausibility of a model, read the review of literature and methodology closely. The researchers should include rationale for all variables, details about model specification, and a listing of limitations that address potential concerns. Model plausibility can be a challenging assumption to evaluate because it requires some knowledge about the topic. In many cases, however, intuition can be a good guide.

How Much Do the Predictors Influence the Outcome?   Individual predictor scores (beta coefficients or OR) show how predictors change an outcome; however, they do not reveal how much of the change is attributable to the model, or conversely how much is unexplained. Individual predictor scores also do not indicate change in the outcome as each new variable or variable group is added to an analysis. In addition to model fit, researchers use R^2 or pseudo-R^2 measures to track the improvement in regression results from block to block (within a model) or model to model.

For example, the prior table from Vianden and Barlow (2014) showed results for three regression models, each adding a new group (or block) of predictors. The researchers reported R^2 for each model in a table footnote. In the text after the table, the researchers noted that "Removing the student attitudes and behaviors variables from the regression in the third model resulted in a significant change in the amount of variance predicted (Model 3 $R^2 = .119$, $\Delta R^2 = -.570$, F-change (6, 1113) = 339.635, $p < .001$) indicating that critical predictors were within this cluster. The greatest amount of variance in student loyalty appears attributable to student attitude and behaviors variables" (p. 24). In other words, the researchers tracked the R^2 scores after each time they computed the regression (Models 1, 2, and 3). They listed these changes as ΔR^2.

Plante and Halman (2016) studied factors associated with undergraduate student compassion from the time of admittance to the time of graduation. They tracked regression results using R^2 to show how much the compassion score changed each time predictors were added. Table 13.4 displays the results. The R^2 Change column shows that each time a new predictor was added (Models 2–5), the overall R^2 value improved (from .252 in Model 1 to .345 in Model 6).

Table 13.4. Multiple Regression Model Summary

Model Change	R	R^2	Adjusted R^2	Std. Error of the Estimate	R^2 Change	F Change	df_1	df_2	Sig. F
1	0.502[a]	0.252	0.251	0.85950	0.252	164.230	1	487	0.0002
2	0.530[b]	0.281	0.278	0.84392	0.028	19.145	1	486	0.000
3	0.546[c]	0.298	0.294	0.83455	0.017	11.973	1	485	0.001
4	0.568[d]	0.322	0.317	0.82063	0.025	17.602	1	484	0.000
5	0.580[e]	0.337	0.330	0.81289	0.014	10.257	1	483	0.001
6	0.587	0.345	0.337	0.80876	0.008	5.949	1	482	0.015

[a]Predictors: (Constant), Freshman Compassion Scale Score
[b]Predictors: (Constant), Freshman Compassion Scale Score, Diversity Workshop Attendance
[c]Predictors: (Constant), Freshman Compassion Scale Score, Diversity Workshop Attendance, Senior Political Views
[d]Predictors: (Constant), Freshman Compassion Scale Score, Diversity Workshop Attendance, Senior Political Views, Religious Service Attendance
[e]Predictors: Predictors (Constant), Freshman Compassion Scale Score, Diversity Workshop Attendance, Senior Political Views, Religious Service Attendance, Connection to University Community
Source: From Plante and Halman (2016), pp. 164–174. Reprinted by permission of NASPA—National Association of Student Personnel Administrators/Student Affairs Administrators in Higher Education.

Applying Prediction Statistics

Aside from functional areas directly related to enrollment management such as admissions or institutional research, most student affairs practitioners seldom use prediction statistics. However, many campus-based, as well as professional, decisions are informed or influenced by prediction-based projections or forecasts. For entry- to mid-level practitioners, the ability to read, evaluate, and incorporate prediction results into practice demonstrates higher ordered research literacy and application. By mid- to late career as responsibilities grow, critical decisions about programs and services impacting admissions, engagement, retention, and persistence are often informed by prediction data. Following are some considerations for using prediction statistics as well as suggestions for how to apply results from prediction studies to practice.

Opportunities for Applying Prediction Results

- Evidence policy or support programs.
- Advocate for programs and services.
- Take responsibility for persistence and graduation.

Evidence Policy or Support Programs   Learning to read and evaluate prediction statistics is a valuable skill for practitioners evidencing policy changes or supporting programs. Results from statistically representative prediction studies can be used to suggest that a similar effect from a new or revised policy might be attained based on its implementation in a similar setting. For example, much of the research related to student success in the first year is based on multiple large-scale studies that have demonstrated the importance of student-faculty interaction and forms of student engagement (Mayhew et al., 2016). As a way to increase interaction and to provide opportunities for promoting involvement, practitioners used these results to evidence the need for first-year studies (FYS) programs.

Another example is the infusion of service into academic and cocurricular programming on campus. While engaging in service has been a historical part of student involvement, evidence from Cooperative Institutional Research Program (CIRP) survey results two decades ago (Astin & Sax, 1998) provided evidence for broadening programs. Other initiatives supported by prediction research include leadership development (Dugan & Komives, 2007) and identification and sustainability of diverse learning environments (Hurtado & Guillermo-Wann, 2013).

Advocate for Programs and Services   Increasingly, quantitative measures drive decision making in higher education. It is critical that student affairs practitioners are able to evaluate results for strengths, weaknesses, and opportunities. A highly applicable skill is being able to recognize trends in prediction data. While part of interpreting data is understanding what is reported, knowing what is missing is an invaluable data literacy skill. Being able to look at results and identify and advocate for ways student affairs could address problems or enhance existing solutions is critical. For example, institutional data showing that students who commute to campus tend to be less engaged is an opportunity to advocate for additional resources for commuter students. Conversely, results from the college of engineering's annual advising survey showing students who participated in tutoring were more likely to be retained might be viewed as an opportunity to initiate a peer tutoring program. Interpreting results in this way does not require high level statistical knowledge; however, being able to recognize trends and potential influences in prediction statistics could enhance opportunities for student affairs involvement across the institution.

Perspectives From the Field—Using Prediction Research for Student Affairs Practice

The area of student affairs research has become more complex and expansive in recent years. At the very least, student affairs professionals need to be able to interpret quantitative studies in refereed journals to determine if the results and conclusions might be applicable to their own campuses. Additionally, with the increased focus on retention and persistence, student affairs must be able to develop models that include variables (i.e., living on campus, going to the recreation center, joining a student organization) that demonstrate the impact of our work on student success. This effort provides an opportunity to partner with institutional research offices to create an overall student success model. Throughout the process of data analysis and predictive modeling, as student affairs professionals, we cannot forget individual students and their unique needs and opportunities for growth.

Darby M. Roberts—Director of Student Life Studies, Texas A & M University

Take Responsibility for Persistence and Graduation   A significant opportunity for student affairs in demonstrating its value on campus is to be directly involved with persistence and graduation research. Prediction statistics are most frequently used on campus to project academic outcomes such as retention, persistence, graduation, and in some cases GPA. Prediction studies offer the ability to understand how one or more influences, such as joining a student organization or participating in additional service hours, could influence these outcomes. The office of institutional research or an equivalent office (for example, enrollment management) may be in charge or these functions. While retention and persistence results are generally widely distributed on campus, the equations used to determine these outcomes may be less visible. Partnering with the individuals responsible for assessing trends and advocating for adding measures related to student services and programs into academic outcomes projections are good practices for evidencing student affairs work.

Building Your Prediction Methods Skillset

Learning to read prediction statistics, and in particular regression results, requires knowledge of the basic concepts reviewed in this chapter—understanding what a prediction model is and how it is developed, identifying variables, reading beta coefficients and odds ratios, and evaluating R^2 and pseudo-R^2 values as related to model fit and predictor contributions. Practicing by reading text and table results in various articles and reports while referencing the relevant sections of this text is an effective way to learn to quickly recognize and interpret results. Another effective means of building skills is by working with institutional research staff. Asking questions about summary reports and the data and/or equations that informed them provides a deeper look at the metrics used to generate answers to several important campus questions.

Most practitioners looking to move beyond reading and evaluating prediction research likely will need to take an applied statistics class. Further, since regression is a methodology that relies on understanding and using descriptive, difference, and relationship statistics, it is typically taught as the second part of a two-course sequence. Moving from a basic understanding of prediction statistics to being able to use them in practice can be challenging. However, learning how to use prediction statistics becomes an increasingly valuable skill as practitioners progress in their careers and most will find the time spent learning will yield longer term benefits.

References

Adelman, C. (1999). *Answers in the toolbox: Academic intensity, attendance patterns, and bachelor's degree attainment.* Washington, DC: U.S. Department of Education.

Adelman, C. (2006). *The toolbox revisited: Paths to degree completion from high school through college.* Washington, DC: U.S. Department of Education.

Astin, A. W. (1970a). College influence: A comprehensive view. *Contemporary Psychology, 15*(9), 543–546.

Astin, A. W. (1970b). The methodology of research on college impact. *Sociology of Education, 43*, 223–254.

Astin, A. W. (1977). *Four critical years*. San Francisco, CA: Jossey-Bass.

Astin, A. W. (1993). *What matters in college? Four critical years revisited*. San Francisco, CA: Jossey-Bass.

Astin, A. W., & Dey, E. L. (1997). *Causal analytical modeling via blocked regression analysis (CAMBRA): An introduction with examples*. Los Angeles: University of California, Los Angeles, Higher Education Research Institute.

Astin, A. W., & Sax, L. J. (1998). How undergraduates are affected by service participation. *Journal of College Student Development, 39*(3), 251–263.

Bean, J. P. (2005). Nine themes of college student retention. In A. Seidman (Ed.), *College student retention: Formula for student success* (pp. 215–244). Westport, CT: Praeger.

Bowman, N. A. (2011). Promoting participation in a diverse democracy: A meta-analysis of college diversity experiences and civic engagement. *Review of Educational Research, 81*(1), 29–68.

Bryant, A. N., Gayles, J. G., & Davis, H. A. (2012). The relationship between civic behavior and civic values: A conceptual model. *Research in Higher Education, 53*(1), 76–93.

Bryant, A. N., Wickliff, K., Mayhew, M. J., & Berringer, L. B. (2009). Developing an assessment of college students' spiritual experiences: The collegiate religious and spiritual climate survey. *Journal of College and Character, 10*(6), 1–10.

Cantor, D., Fisher, B., Chibnall, S., Townsend, R., Lee, H., Bruce, C., & Thomas, G. (2015, September 21). Report on the AAU Campus Climate Survey on Sexual Assault and Sexual Misconduct. Retrieved from https://www.aau.edu/sites/default/files/%40%20Files/Climate%20Survey/AAU_Campus_Climate_Survey_12_14_15.pdf

Carter, D. F., Ro, H. K., Alcott, B., & Lattuca, L. R. (2016). Co-curricular connections: The role of undergraduate research experiences in promoting engineering students' communication, teamwork, and leadership skills. *Research in Higher Education, 57*(3), 363–393.

Cruce, T. M., & Moore, J. V. (2007). First-year students' plans to volunteer: An examination of the predictors of community service participation. *Journal of College Student Development, 48*, 655–673.

Dugan, J. P. (2013). Patterns in group involvement experiences during college: Identifying a taxonomy. *Journal of College Student Development, 54*, 229–246.

Dugan, J. P., & Komives, S. R. (2007). *Developing leadership capacity in college students: Findings from a national study*. A Report from the Multi-Institutional Study of Leadership. College Park, MD: National Clearinghouse for Leadership Programs.

Dugan, J. P., & Komives, S. R. (2010). Influences on college students' capacities for socially responsible leadership. *Journal of College Student Development, 51*(5), 525–549.

Engberg, M. E., & Davidson, L. M. (2016). Students' precollege engagement and the development of a global perspective. *Journal of The First-Year Experience & Students in Transition, 28*(1), 49–70.

Harper, S., & Hurtado, S. (2007). Nine themes in campus racial climates and implications for institutional transformation. In S. R. Harper & L. D. Patton (Eds.), *Responding to the realities of race on campus* (New Directions for Student Services, no. 120). San Francisco, CA: Jossey-Bass.

Hossler, D., & Bontrager, B. (2014). *Handbook of strategic enrollment management*. San Francisco, CA: Jossey-Bass.

Hurtado, S., & Guillermo-Wann, C. (2013). *Diverse learning environments: Assessing and creating conditions for student success—Final report to the Ford Foundation*. University of California, Los Angeles: Higher Education Research Institute. Retrieved from https://www.heri.ucla.edu/ford/DiverseLearningEnvironments.pdf

Hussar, W. J., & Bailey, T. M. (2016). *Projections of education statistics to 2024* (43rd ed.). Washington, DC: National Center for Education Statistics. Retrieved from https://nces.ed.gov/pubs2016/2016013.pdf

Ishitani, T. T. (2006). Studying attrition and degree completion behavior among first-generation college students in the United States. *Journal of Higher Education, 77*(5), 861–885.

Ishitani, T. T. (2016). Time-varying effects of academic and social integration on student persistence for first and second years in college. *Journal of College Student Retention, 18*(3), 263–286.

Ishitani, T. T., & McKitrick, S. A. (2013). The effects of academic programs and institutional characteristics on postgraduate civic engagement behavior. *Journal of College Student Development, 54*(4), 379–396.

Kelly, H., Demonte, K., & Jones, D. (n.d.). *Using predictive analytics to understand housing enrollments.* Retrieved from http://www1.udel.edu/IR/presentations/HousingRetention.pdf

King, P. M., & Baxter Magolda, M. B. (2005). A developmental model of intercultural maturity. *Journal of College Student Development, 46*(6), 571–592.

Kuh, G. D. (2009). Understanding campus environments. In G. S. McClellan & J. Stringer (Eds.), *The handbook of student affairs administration* (3rd ed., pp. 59–80). San Francisco, CA: Jossey-Bass.

Langston, R., Wyant, R., & Scheid, J. (2016). Strategic enrollment management for chief enrollment officers: Practical use of statistical and mathematical data in forecasting first year and transfer college enrollment. *Strategic Enrollment Management Quarterly, 4*(2), 74–89.

Long, L. D. (2014). Does it matter where college students live? Differences in satisfaction and outcomes as a function of students' living arrangement and gender. *The Journal of College and University Student Housing, 40*(2), 66–85.

Manning, P., Pring, L., & Glider, P. (2012). Relevance of campus climate for alcohol and other drug use among LGBTQ community college students: A statewide qualitative assessment. *Community College Journal of Research and Practice, 36*(7), 494–503.

Martin, G. L., Parker, G., Pascarella, E. T., & Blechschmidt, S. (2015). Do fraternities and sororities inhibit intercultural competence? *Journal of College Student Development, 56*(1), 66–72.

Martin, G., & Seifert, T. (2011). The relationship between students' interactions with student affairs professionals and cognitive outcomes in the first year of college. *Journal of Student Affairs Research and Practice, 48*(4), 389–410.

Mayhew, M. J., Rockenbach, A. N., Bowman, N. A., Seifert, T. A. D., Wolniak, G. C., Pascarella, E. T., & Terenzini, P. T. (2016). *How college affects students: 21st century evidence that higher education works* (Vol. 3). San Francisco, CA: Jossey-Bass.

Mayhew, M. J., Seifert, T. A., Pascarella, E. T., Nelson Laird, T. F., & Blaich, C. F. (2012). Going deep into mechanisms for moral reasoning growth: How deep learning approaches affect moral reasoning development for first-year students. *Research in Higher Education, 53*, 26–46.

Mertler, C. A., & Vannatta, R. A. (2013). *Advanced and multivariate statistical methods: Practical application and interpretation* (5th ed.). Glendale, AZ: Pyrczak.

Milem, J. F., Chang, M. J., & Antonio, A. L. (2005). *Making diversity work on campus: A research-based perspective.* Washington, DC: Association of American Colleges and Universities.

Patton, L. D., Renn, K. A., Guido, F. M., & Quaye, S. J. (2016). *Student development in college: Theory, research, and practice* (3rd ed.). San Francisco, CA: Jossey-Bass.

Pittman, E. C., & Foubert, J. D. (2016). Predictors of professional identity development for student affairs professionals. *Journal of Student Affairs Research and Practice, 53*(1), 13–25.

Plante, T., & Halman, K. (2016). Nurturing compassion development among college students: A longitudinal study. *Journal of College and Character, 17*(3), 164–174.

Reason, R. D. (2003). Student variables that predict retention: Recent research and new developments. *NASPA Journal, 40*(4), 172–191.

Reason, R. D. (2009). An examination of persistence research through the lens of a comprehensive conceptual framework. *Journal of College Student Development, 50*(6), 659–682.

Schuh, J. H., Biddix, J. P., Dean, L. A., & Kinzie, J. (2016). *Assessment in student affairs: A contemporary look* (2nd ed.). San Francisco, CA: Jossey-Bass.

Swecker, H. K., Fifolt, M., & Searby, L. (2013). Academic advising and first-generation college students: A quantitative study on student retention. *NACADA Journal, 33*(1), 46–53.

Tinto, V. (1975). Dropout from higher education. *Review of Educational Research, 45*, 89–125.

Tinto, V., & Pusser, B. (2006). *Moving from theory to action: Building a model of institutional action for student success.* Washington, DC: National Postsecondary Education Cooperative.

Torres, V., Jones, S. R., & Renn, K. A. (2009). Identity development theories in student affairs: Origins, current status, and new approaches. *Journal of College Student Development, 50*(6), 577–596.

Tovar, E. (2013). *A conceptual model on the impact of mattering, sense of belonging, engagement/involvement, and socio-academic integrative experiences on community college students' intent to persist* (Unpublished doctoral dissertation). Claremont Graduate University, Claremont, CA.

Vianden, J., & Barlow, P. J. (2014). Showing the love: Predictors of student loyalty to undergraduate institutions. *Journal of Student Affairs Research and Practice, 51*(1), 16–29.

Zacherman, A., & Foubert, J. (2014). The relationship between engagement in cocurricular activities and academic performance: Exploring gender differences. *Journal of Student Affairs Research and Practice, 51*(2), 157–169.

CHAPTER FOURTEEN

EXPLORING MIXED METHODS

Learning Outcomes

By the end of this chapter, you should be able to:

- Understand the purpose and role of mixed methods in research.
- Differentiate between the major mixed methods designs.
- Know answers to basic questions about mixed methods in research.
- Relate mixed methods research to student affairs practice.

Many research problems can be studied with a single method. Qualitative research offers the opportunity to explore, while quantitative research offers the opportunity to explain. Each has the capability to contribute to knowledge and improve practice, although the process, outcomes, and findings can vary considerably. A third type of research, mixed methods, offers the opportunity to benefit from the strengths of both exploration and explanation in the same study and presents a more holistic study of a research problem. However, mixed methods studies have seldom appeared in student affairs published research.

The purpose of the chapter is to serve as an introduction and reference guide for understanding, reading, evaluating, and using mixed methods. This chapter includes a broad overview and introduction to key authors, reviews the current and potential use of mixed methods for student affairs, and highlights key questions and essential concepts. The chapter was written with a single question in mind:

What essential concepts do student affairs practitioners and researchers need to know to understand mixed methods?

The question is addressed with a series of questions and answers, derived from common challenges and difficulties for new learners. The chapter overviews key terms in mixed methods research to provide a foundational understanding of what is meant by mixing methods, why and how researchers use mixed methods designs, and how findings are presented. Also included is an overview of how to evaluate mixed methods research. The chapter begins with a historical overview to provide context about the development of mixed methods research and closes with suggestions for developing foundational skills.

Understanding Mixed Methods

Mixed methods integrates multiple, different methods in the same study to explain, explore, or inform a research topic. Depending on the sequence and timing of the data collection, the priority of the methods used, and the outcomes a researcher intends to accomplish, the mixing points of the study can vary. These points of convergence are referred to as integration, which is a fundamental and defining characteristic of mixed methods research.

One of the first and primary texts for mixed methods is Tashakkori and Teddlie's (1998) *Mixed Methodology: Combining Qualitative and Quantitative Approaches.* The authors traced the history of mixed methods research through the paradigm wars opposing quantitative and qualitative research before proposing its initial terminology and methods. Jick's (1979) article outlining the basic tenets of triangulation, Greene, Caracelli, and Graham's (1989) review of mixed and multiple methods in evaluation studies, Morse's (1991) concept of diagramming as a way to design mixed methods studies, and Bryman's (2006) emphasis and review of integration each helped to codify mixed methods research as a field. A major development in the dissemination of mixed methods research was the launch of the *Journal of Mixed Methods* in 2007. The journal included an editorial staff and board comprised of major contributors to the field across multiple academic disciplines.

Tashakkori and Teddlie have since contributed a discussion of design typologies (2006), considerations of quality (2008), an edited volume including additional methodologists as well as research examples (2010), and an ongoing discussion of contemporary issues (2011). Greene (2007, 2008) further contributed to the development of a conceptual framework by identifying different purposes for mixing methods from published literature and exploring design characteristics. Mertens (2003, 2007) has been influential in developing pragmatism as the major theoretical framework.

Creswell has been a leading authority in mixed methods research, beginning with his inclusion of mixed methods design in his widely-used research design textbook (2002). Creswell and Plano Clark's (2017) *Designing and Conducting Mixed Methods Research* (third edition) has been a standard text for both novice and expert mixed methods researchers. With each new edition, the authors have incorporated broad perspectives, clarified terminology, and collated and expanded knowledge about how to design, conduct, and evaluate mixed methods research.

The Pragmatist Perspective

Mixed methods research is generally associated with a pragmatist perspective. *Pragmatism* is a problem-centered and solution-oriented research perspective that uses multiple methods to address a research problem. Plano Clark and Ivankova (2016) identified pragmatism as both a philosophy and a set of techniques. Creswell (2013) stressed that a pragmatic perspective focuses on the research problem and questions and uses the designs or methods best suited for providing an answer. Mixed methods researchers view this approach as a more comprehensive look at a problem that sets aside arguments over truth inherent in constructivist and postpositivist studies to focus instead on the pragmatic resolution of a problem. According to Morgan (2007), pragmatism "rejects the need to choose between a pair of extremes where research results are either completely specific to a particular context or an instance of some more generalized set of principles" (p. 72). As a result of this focus, pragmatic research may seem similar to assessment or evaluation, which tends to centralize the problem to identify and present a solution.

Words Researchers Use—Transformative or Social Justice Perspective

Mixed methods researchers sometimes advocate for direct involvement in the research, extending the pragmatic focus by taking a stance toward making a positive social change (Sweetman, Badiee, & Creswell, 2010). Transformative design, also referred to as social justice (McCoy, 2016) or advocacy design (Mertens, 2007), incorporates a theoretical framework, such as feminism or critical theory, to conduct change-oriented research (Greene, 2007). Theory is used to advance causes and to identify and address needs, particularly among historically underrepresented or marginalized populations. It provides a scaffold to the project that includes political action, empowerment, collaboration, and a commitment to change. The researcher takes a position, remains sensitive to the needs of the population being studied, and then recommends specific changes to improve social justice for the population.

McCoy (2016) used the example of studying Queer Students' of Color experiences at a historically Black college and university (HBCU). Using a transformative design, the researcher first selects one of the common designs (concurrent, sequential, or embedded) and employs queer theory to frame the study including research questions, data collection and analysis, interpretations, and inferences. The study's inferences offer recommendations for creating inclusive campus communities for Queer Students of Color attending HBCUs.

Overview of Mixed Methods

Perspective: Pragmatism

- Problem-centered: The primary focus of the research is on addressing the problem, which requires a multifaceted approach and openness to research methodology.
- Oriented to real-world practice: Results, discussion, and implications generally offer direct and specific solutions to problems.
- Operationalizing theory (sometimes): Depending on the methods used, design can be used to create and then to test a theory or test, revise, and (re)test a revised theory.

Type: Mixed Methods

- Integrated methods: Two or more qualitative or quantitative methods are integrated at one or more phases of the study.
- Holistic interpretation: Interpretation is based on or influenced by different forms of data.
- Pragmatic focus: Research is typically focused on solving or addressing a problem.

Design: Concurrent, Sequential, Embedded

- Concurrent: Data collection and analysis occurs independently in similar time frames.
- Sequential (explanatory or exploratory): Data collection and analysis of one method precedes and influences the next.
- Embedded: Using secondary data within a larger primary method study to answer questions at a different level.

Method(s): Multiple

- Combined methods: Methods used can be any combination of two or more qualitative or quantitative methods.

Mixed Methods in Student Affairs Research

Published mixed methods research in student affairs has been sparse and, as a result, difficult to categorize broadly in a way to suggest how it is used in the field. An overview of several published studies follows in this chapter to show specific ways methods are mixed. Currently, there are too few published studies to highlight trends based on specific topics. However, mixed methods researchers in student affairs have found the use of both methods helpful in presenting a more holistic picture of findings. For example, Garcia, Huerta, Ramirez, and Patrón (2017) identified specific ways practitioners could work to enhance leadership development, capacity, and experiences of Latino male undergraduates using mixed methods:

> What is highlighted by this study's findings, however, is that the opportunity structure must be available to Latino students interested in getting involved in various activities on campus. It is not enough to recommend that practitioners encourage students to get involved in fraternities, ethnic student organizations, or internships as a way to enhance their leadership; instead, practitioners must recognize their role in supporting the creation and founding of these types of experiences, particularly on campuses with small populations of racialized students. (p. 16)

Table 14.1 shows some functions mixed methods research serves in student affairs practice. The first four are taken from the student affairs–related considerations McCoy (2016) outlined. The others are more speculative, but were influenced by methodological writings in other fields. None are mutually exclusive, meaning that mixed methods can serve multiple functions in a study.

Perspectives From the Field—The Value of Mixed Methods for Student Affairs

Mixed methods provide a powerful way for student affairs educators to tell the amazing stories of how the programs and services they provide support student learning and success. Student affairs educators are humble and hardworking people who are called to do hard work that is heart work. We roll up our sleeves, focus on the problem, and get things done. Too rarely do we tell the stories of how we recognized and responded to a need that led to remarkable results. Yet, in an era of data-driven decision making and program prioritization, we have no choice but tell our story to stakeholders in the languages they understand. Everyone knows stakeholders who crave metrics and predictive relationships, wanting to know the efficacy of a program from the numbers. Then, there are stakeholders who want to know how the program was implemented and the stories of the students who participated in it. The savvy student affairs educator integrates these data collection methods in order to tell the whole story to both sets of stakeholders. Ryerson University in Toronto, Canada, has created a position within their student affairs division specifically to tell the story of their programs to stakeholders. The manager of Student Affairs Storytelling mixes methods in order to articulate more fulsome conclusions and more nuanced implications and recommendations. I suggest we owe our students nothing less.

Tricia Seifert—Department head and assistant professor, Adult & Higher Education, Montana State University

Table 14.1. Functions of Mixed Methods in Student Affairs

Function	Application and Explanation
To overcome the weaknesses of a single design.	Single method studies, even when using multiple types of data and forms of data collection, have prominent weaknesses. Generally, qualitative data analysis is difficult to replicate and apply while quantitative data tend to limit examination of meaning. Using multiple methods provides a way to offset those weaknesses. McCoy (2016) used the example of conducting interviews to explain survey-based data on why Latino males complete their undergraduate degrees at rates lower than their White peers.
To explore a topic more holistically.	Mixed methods let researchers view problems from multiple angles and at multiple levels to consider individual, group, institution, and process considerations. McCoy (2016) referred to this function as "(providing) alternative perspectives" and gave the example of exploring policy using both numbers and stories to explain an issue. McCoy (2016) regarded this as the primary reason for conducting a mixed methods study.
To provide stronger inferences.	According to McCoy (2016), mixed methods can be used to promote better interpretations and conclusions in a student affairs context. Findings from multifaceted studies can enlighten results from a single method, strengthening confidence in making data-informed decisions. This is a complementary approach related to addressing the limitations of using a single method.
To explore divergent or complementary views.	McCoy (2016) noted that divergent findings can suggest the need to transform data (such as quantifying qualitative data to show the prevalence of trends), can lead to questions about how well the findings from single method represent the nature of the problem, and can influence the need for a second phase of a study to investigate the problem further.
To construct and evaluate a new instrument.	An initial appeal for mixed methods research was the ability to create and test a new instrument. An example is using data from focus groups to identify measures for a larger scale survey. This process also works well for adapting or refining an existing instrument. Crede and Borrego (2013) used this approach in their study of engineering graduate school retention to identify factors and then to create a survey evaluating retention among graduate students in engineering.
To create, implement, or test a theory.	Similar to qualitative and quantitative design, theory is also used in mixed methods research to influence the research design, sample selection, data integration, results integration, and discussion of results. Mixed methods extend these capabilities in two additional ways. First, a researcher might identify a working theory and then test the applicability of its core concepts more broadly. Second, a researcher could apply a theory to a problem and then evaluate its application.

Table 14.1. (*Continued*)

Function	Application and Explanation
To address a question at different levels.	Educational research problems are seldom simple, often because stakeholders operate within multiple layers and communities. For example, changing policy related to speech on campus may not address student perception and behavior, administrative response, or potential legislative involvement. Mixed methods research is better positioned to examine problems from these multiple layers, by providing multiple lenses through multifaceted data collection and analysis. For example, Seifert, Goodman, King, and Baxter Magolda's (2010) results revealed how contextual factors at the student and institutional levels influenced learning outcomes among first-year students.

Essential Concepts in Mixed Methods

Mixed methods is still a relatively new research methodology. Similar to qualitative methods, some of the terminology and core concepts are not commonly agreed upon; however, in the past few years, several methodologists have begun to use some terms and practices more consistently. This section introduces essential, foundational concepts as frequently asked questions. Table 14.2 is a summary list of key questions along with associated concepts that comprise the primary features of mixed methods encountered when reading, reviewing, or conducting research. Each question and associated concept examined in subsequent sections.

Table 14.2. Key Questions and Associated Essential Concepts

Key Question	Essential Concepts
What is meant by mixed methods?	Multiple methods and data, integration
What are advantages and challenges to mixed methods?	Research depth vs. researcher skill
How do researchers choose a mixed methods design?	Interaction, priority, timing, procedures
What are some specific ways methods are mixed?	Method combination examples
How do researchers analyze mixed methods data?	Independent analysis, merged analysis
How are mixed methods results presented?	Diagramming, side-by-side displays
How are mixed methods studies evaluated?	Key components, rigor

Table 14.3. What Mixed Methods Is and Is Not

What Mixed Methods Is	What Mixed Methods Is Not
Integrating two or more different research types (qualitative and quantitative) in the same study	Collecting multiple forms of the same type of data (for example, interview and observation)
Using distinct research methods (such as interview and survey) to explore a problem	Collecting multiple forms of different types of data (for example, interview and survey) without integrating the data at one or more points (for example, data collection, interpretation, discussion)
Collecting (and sometimes analyzing) data systematically at the same time (concurrent), in a set order (sequential), or at multiple levels (embedded)	Adding a second data collection method to a study, such as open-ended questions at the end of a survey
Interpreting both types of data to more holistically address a research problem	Labeling a study mixed methods without rationale

What Is Meant by Mixed Methods?

The term mixed refers to the idea that two or more methods are mixed, or blended in some way. This is in contrast to multiple methods, which is characterized as using multiple data sources within a single study. In describing the utility of mixed methods, Jick (1979) noted that "one begins to view the researcher as builder and creator, piecing together many pieces of a complex puzzle into a coherent whole" (p. 608). Table 14.3 is a chart contrasting some characteristics of mixed methods, influenced by Creswell (2015, pp. 2–3).

Initially, mixed methods referred to triangulation methods, similar in concept to the qualitative technique of validating findings with multiple sources. Triangulation in this context refers to collecting different data within the same research type (for example, interviews and documents). The fundamental difference is the mixing of two different methods, which is not accomplished with two of the same type. The concept of integration is key in distinguishing multiple and mixed methods studies. Crede and Borrego (2013) discussed both triangulation (as a strategy) and integration (as a fundamental design component) in their survey creation process.

> Finally, we were able to triangulate the qualitative data from the ethnography and the final survey results to draw additional conclusions about how international diversity contributes to the graduate student experience in engineering research groups. By integrating the data at several levels we were able to fully realize the value of such an in-depth qualitative component to this research, and offer recommendations to mixed methods researchers considering this approach. (p. 74)

Words Researchers Use—Triangulation

Triangulation can be a confusing research term because it has two different meanings. The more commonly used definition comes from qualitative research. Denzin (1978) described one aspect of triangulation as way of confirming results in a study by combining methods. Subsequent qualitative researchers took this characterization to mean using multiple forms of data such as interviews with observation and document analysis to corroborate or support findings. One image often used is a three-legged stool, with the seat representing findings, and the legs representing multiple supporting methods (Hall & Rist, 1999).

Triangulation was also an early name for mixed methods studies, when the concept was in a developmental phase of identifying terminology. Jick (1979) was among the first to suggest that triangulation could be a separate design, rather than a validation strategy. Greene et al. (1989) argued that triangulation was more of a purpose, or function of mixed methods, than an umbrella term for overall design. Citing Mathison (1988), they noted, "such practice muddles the concept of triangulation as originally construed and remains insensitive to other possible benefits of mixed-method designs" (p. 255). Since then, triangulation has been regarded as more of a function of mixed methods than its primary description (Morgan, 2013).

What Are Advantages and Challenges to Mixed Methods?

Researchers have detailed numerous advantages and challenges associated with conducting mixed methods research (Creswell & Plano Clark, 2010, 2017; Tashakkori & Teddlie, 2008). These include researcher skill, time, and resources, and resolving discrepancies between two methods. Creswell (2015) advocated that mixed methods studies must contain a rationale for mixed methods to inform the reader of its purpose and intent. This section describes some of the major advantages and challenges associated with mixed methods research beneficial for reading and evaluating studies.

There are several notable advantages to using a mixed methods approach. Including a secondary method can be valuable when unexpected results arise, especially in a sequential design in which the researcher can explore an unexpected finding in more depth (qualitative) or with more breadth (quantitative). Also, mixed methods can provide generalizability to qualitative results by adding a broader sample. Similarly, it can be used to add context and meaning to quantitative results. Finally, although mentioned as a primary function, the ability to create and validate an instrument or theory is a major advantage mixed methods offers.

Researchers using mixed methods also experience challenges. Primarily, researchers need to be proficient in each form of data collection and analysis. Mixed method researchers sometimes offset this challenge by working in teams. Seifert et al. (2010) used this approach, noting each research team member was "responsible for the method for which they had the greatest expertise, thus avoiding the challenge of insufficient expertise in one of the data collection and analysis methods" (p. 251). Another challenge is the time and resources needed to conduct a mixed methods study, which can be prolonged if data collection is sequential and one method is dependent on results from the prior method. Morse (1991) stressed that "each method must be complete in itself . . . This standard allows each component to be published independently" (p. 121).

In addition, mixed methods studies offer numerous decision points. Beyond initial design, data collection, and analysis, mixed methods researchers need to consider balance between multiple forms of evidence, when and how to integrate methods, and how to handle discrepancies and outliers. Further, some designs generate unequal evidence or are not easily comparable. An example is Garcia et al.'s (2017) use of longitudinal dataset (Cooperative Institutional Research Program, 2007, 2011) in conjunction with individual interviews. The quantitative data were comprised of 222 individuals from 69 institutions in an existing dataset; the 24 interview participants were drawn from 4 of the study institutions. Also, because the dataset was longitudinal (conducted over time), interviews were conducted several years after the survey data collection so that survey and interview participants were not from the same sample.

How Do Researchers Choose a Specific Mixed Methods Design?

The selection of any research design (qualitative, qualitative, or mixed) typically begins by specifying the research problem and questions and selecting the method that best fits. The basic procedure for choosing a mixed methods design (concurrent, sequential, or embedded), according to Creswell and Plano Clark (2010), is to start simple by identifying a clear reason for the study (purpose), drawing a basic diagram of the procedures to help determine the methods and sequence, and focusing on what the design intends to accomplish (the practical outcomes). Mixed methods researchers have specified several key decisions that help choose a specific design.

Identifying the Interactions or Integration Between the Methods. *Integration* is the point in which the design, data collection, analysis, results, and/or interpretation of data in a study interact. The level of interaction is influenced by the extent to which the methods are kept independent. Independent methods are only mixed during interpretation. Interacted methods are mixed at different points in the study in different ways. Greene (2007) argued that this decision is among the "most salient and critical" (p. 120) dimensions in a mixed methods design.

Considering the Priority of the Methods. Priority refers to the importance or weighting of the methods in the study. There are three possibilities: equal priority, quantitative priority (qualitative secondary), and qualitative priority (quantitative secondary). The researcher's skill, access to participants and data, and available resources influence the priority of the methods. The priority should be consistent with the research problem, purpose, and question(s) (Creswell & Plano Clark, 2010).

Sequencing the Timing of the Methods. Timing refers to the order of data collection and interpretation in a study. Creswell and Plano Clark (2010) described this as the "temporal relationship between the quantitative and qualitative strands" (p. 65). Timing also differentiates the major designs as concurrent (both methods occurring at the same time) or sequential (one method following the other). Concurrent timing often is used to provide a more complete understanding of influential factors by interpreting methods together. Sequential timing allows for exploration or explanation of results from the first method. Embedded studies may follow either approach.

What Are Some Specific Ways Methods Are Mixed?

The three basic designs specify four ways methods can be mixed (concurrent, sequential exploratory, sequential explanatory, and nested). Following are some specific examples. An arrow (>) indicates a sequential design and a plus (+) indicates concurrent design.

Focus Groups > Survey (Sequential Exploratory Design). Baker and Sgoutas-Emch (2014) examined sources of financial stress on college students to identify programs that could address concerns using a sequential exploratory (qualitative followed by quantitative) design. Data collection involved focus groups followed by a survey. The survey data supported and expanded knowledge gained from the focus groups by revealing stress frequency related to the financial stressors and severity of experiences and allowing for group comparisons. The researchers noted that "By asking distinct questions and using different methods, we gathered data that give an authentic view of student financial stress" (p. 120).

Focus Groups and Individual Interviews > Survey (Sequential Exploratory Design). Chesbrough (2011) studied motivations toward service among college students, finding differences based on gender, hours and service, and year in college regarding how students described service and learning outcomes. The researcher used a sequential exploratory (qualitative followed by quantitative) design to collect focus group and individual interview data followed by a survey. Chesbrough (2011) found differences between men in women in terms of how they described factors contributing to their involvement in service and their learning. For example, men were more likely to describe outcomes and limited time commitment as reasons for their involvement and choice of projects. Women more often described being motivated internally by subjective desires to contribute and were also more likely to become involved in an ongoing service commitment.

Observations and Interviews > Survey (Sequential Exploratory Design). Crede and Borrego (2013) examined engineering graduate school retention, also using a sequential exploratory (qualitative followed by quantitative) design involving 9 months of ethnographically guided observations and interviews they used to develop a survey. The article is focused on the process of survey development and details advantages, challenges, and considerations for researchers using this approach.

Survey Data + Document Analysis (Concurrent Design). Taub, Johnson, and Reynolds (2016) studied implementation of gender-neutral housing. The researchers surveyed chief housing officers regarding housing arrangements. Qualitative data were gender-neutral housing policies ($n = 107$) solicited from survey participants. Survey data revealed the extent to which institutions had considered gender-neutral housing, obstacles encountered, and types of facilities designated as gender neutral. Qualitative analysis of policies revealed descriptions of eligibility, specific designated facilities, information to parents who may not approve of the living arrangement, and problems related to roommate departure. Integrated results revealed barriers to implementation and the general status of gender-neutral housing options.

National Dataset + Individual Interviews (Concurrent Design). Seifert et al. (2010) examined first-year college impact on liberal arts outcomes. The researchers used a concurrent design (large scale quantitative survey data in conjunction with interviews). Results revealed three practices in the survey data that aligned with emergent themes from the interviews: academic challenges, diversity experiences, and supportive relationships. The researchers regarded data integration as contributing to a more comprehensive understanding of the findings.

Garcia et al. (2017) studied contributors to Latino male undergraduate students' leadership development, capacity, and experiences. The researchers used a convergent parallel (simultaneous method) design consisting of national survey data from the Cooperative Institutional Research Program (CIRP) (2007 initial and 2011 follow-up) in conjunction with one-on-one interviews (three per participant) with

24 Latino males attending four institutions in two regions. Results revealed the importance of fraternities, ethnic student organizations, and internships as well as peer contexts. The dual findings highlighted the need for these structures, but provided the authors with more direct recommendations.

Presurvey > Document Analysis > Postsurvey and Comparative Survey (Embedded Design). Kovtun (2011) assessed first-year courses for international students to determine academic and cultural adaptation. Data collection involved two rounds of surveys (pre–post and between subjects with a control of nonclass participants) with analysis of final term papers describing lessons learned. Although the author did not articulate a specific mixed methods design, the study could be considered nested, as the qualitative results were embedded in the quantitative pre–post and comparative surveys. Results suggested that participation in the course led to improvements in academic skills and enhancement of psychosocial development.

How Do Researchers Analyze Mixed Methods Data?

Mixed methods data typically are analyzed using standard data analysis techniques specific to the types of data collected. For example, quantitative research questions involving differences would use significance testing techniques while qualitative research questions involving existing codes would use an *a priori* coding approach. Researchers analyze mixed methods data independently or by merging the raw data into a central dataset. Independent analysis is the more common approach. When analyzed this way, results are typically presented separately and then discussed together.

Merging data requires transformation. The most common way this done is by quantifying (using counts of) qualitative codes or themes and adding those statistics to a quantitative dataset. Bryman (2006) cautioned that depending on the qualitative data source and/or how it is analyzed and used, merging data in this way may not constitute actual mixed methods. He noted, "this does not represent a genuine form of quantitative research since the data have not been gathered in line with its underlying principles" (p. 103). In his review of integration in mixed methods studies, Bryman did not include instances where this was the only form of qualitative analysis, stating, "There is clearly some confusion concerning whether the quantification of qualitative, unstructured data is indicative of a quantitative or a qualitative research approach" (p. 100).

How Are Mixed Methods Results Presented?

Mixed methods results are presented based on the design of the study and priority of the methods used. For example, a concurrent study where both methods are given equal priority typically will include results separately for each method. Conversely, a sequential study would present the results in the order of the study. Depending on the priority, results from the first method may be summarized or not included to highlight the importance of the second, more prominent method. Otherwise, results are presented using standard reporting formats for statistics (for example, tables or figures) and qualitative data (for example, themes with representative quotations).

Mixed methods researchers also often use diagrams and side-by-side displays to showcase the design or results. A *methods diagram* is a drawing with specific notations showing the research methods and procedures. It may be very simple or complex, depending on the study. Morse (1991) is credited with providing the first system of notations. She used a plus sign (+) to indicate concurrent methods, an arrow (>) to indicate sequential design, and capitalization to indicate the priority of the method (QUAL, qual, QUAN, quan). Creswell and Plano Clark (2010) added additional notations, such as notes beside or below boxes to show products. Following is a list of commonly used symbols and shapes, followed by a few examples.

Seifert et al. (2010, Figure 1, p. 252) included a concurrent design diagram with equal priority methods (QUAN and QUAL). Instead of plus signs, they used arrows to show a sequenced flow of the procedures and a rectangle to show the final phase of interpretation (see Figure 14.1). The figure does not show integration with a separate notation, but the authors noted it occurred at the sampling (selecting institutions), results (compare and contrast), and discussion (interpretation) phases.

Figure 14.2 is from Baker and Sgoutas-Emch (2014, Figure 1, p. 116). The researchers displayed a modified sequential design (qualitative > quantitative > quantitative > qualitative). Instead of using boxes with arrows, they identified the data collection methods as boxes with triangular borders. The figure does not show the integration, which happened at each phase and then again during interpretation.

FIGURE 14.1. A CONCURRENT DESIGN DIAGRAM WITH EQUAL PRIORITY METHODS

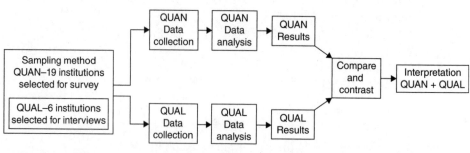

Source: Republished with permission of Sage Publications, from Seifert, Goodman, King, and Baxter Magolda (2010), Figure 1, p. 252; permission conveyed through Copyright Clearance Center, Inc.

FIGURE 14.2. MODIFIED SEQUENTIAL DESIGN

Study Design	8 Focus Groups	Student Stress Survey	ACHA-NCHA	4 More Focus Groups
• Mixed methods	• Qualitative & quantitative	• Quantitative	• Quantitative	• Qualitative & quantitative
• Analyses	• In vivo & descriptive coding, content analysis, frequency counts, descriptive statistics	• Descriptive statistics, correlations, one-way ANOVA	• Descriptive statistics, correlations, cross-tabulations with chi square analysis	• In vivo & descriptive coding, content analysis, frequency counts, descriptive statistics
• Uses	• Derive categories & contextual statements that represent students' perceptions of stress • Generate questions for further study • Compare quantified data to survey findings • Enrich & explain survey findings	• Identify frequency & severity of specific types & impacts of stress & stressors using large sample • Provide comprehensive analysis of students; expand, compare, & contrast with findings from other components of study	• Use routinely (every 2 years) to assess health issues using large student sample at university • Add stress-related questions to expand, compare, & contrast with data from other components of study • Provide baseline & evaluate change due to strategic plan	• Include student cohorts missed in prior study components • Derive additional categories & contextual statements on stress • Compare quantified data to survey findings • Enrich & explain survey findings

Source: From Baker and Sgoutas-Emch (2014), Figure 1, p. 116. Reprinted with permission of the *College Student Affairs Journal.*

Baker and Sgoutas-Emch also included bullets below each box to show the research process and associated products.

Another way mixed methods researchers display results is by using a side-by-side comparison graphic. This is a useful tool for interpreting data as well as for displaying results. It can be an effective strategy for confirming results or exploring divergence. In Table 14.4, Seifert et al. (2010, Table 2, p. 262) presented the integrated results from the qualitative themes and quantitatively developed scales demonstrating congruence between data sources.

Table 14.5 is from Baker and Sgoutas-Emch (2014, Table 2, p. 121). The researchers showed alignment in data collection (sample questions), displaying how each data point relates to the next method in sequence, and including a listing of sample findings. They noted:

> By asking distinct questions and using different methods, we gathered data that give an authentic view of student financial stress. In the focus groups, students identified specific financial stressors such as lack of financial aid, lack of flexibility in financial aid during personal crises, lack of financial advice, necessity of working while going to college, and most distressing of all for students, encumbering debt and the emotional distress associated with it. As a result of coding and content analysis of the focus group transcripts, we derived the six key issues underlying financial stress. (p. 120)

Table 14.4. Side-by-Side Comparison Graphic

Qualitative Themes	Good Practice Scales
Challenging courses theme identified	**Academic challenge and high expectations**
Delving into ideas in meaningful way	Rigor of assignments
Exploring new and multiple perspectives	Exams/assignment require higher order thinking
Learning to support ideas with evidence	Faculty asking challenging questions
Resulted in increased interest in learning	Resulted in inclination to inquire and lifelong learning
Interactions with diverse peers	**Diversity experiences/Influential interactions with peers**
Challenged students to consider multiple perspectives	Serious conversations with diverse peers
Unsure how to respond	Attend diversity programming
Yielded interest in learning more	Associated with inclination to inquire and lifelong learning and intercultural effectiveness
Transition to college intellectual and community life	**Good teaching and high-quality interactions with faculty/Influential interactions with peers**
Culture of caring faculty	Faculty care about students and have positive out-of-class interactions
Faculty and staff helping students learn the skills needed to meet academic challenges	Faculty provide feedback promptly and are clear and organized in their teaching
Facilitated greater comfort in managing the campus environment	Students experience positive peer relationships that help navigate the college environment
	Associated with increased student well-being

Source: Republished with permission of Sage Publications, from Seifert, Goodman, King, and Baxter Magolda (2010), Table 2, p. 262; permission conveyed through Copyright Clearance Center, Inc.

Reading a diagram is a valuable way to understand and evaluate mixed methods research. It is also useful to diagram the study if a researcher has not included one. Diagramming is helpful for understanding the researcher's logic for using mixed methods, the contribution of the research design and methods to the study, and for understanding how interpretation relates to the data.

How Are Mixed Methods Studies Evaluated?

When describing the precursor to mixed methods (methodological triangulation), Jick (1979) as well as Denzin (1978) and later Morse (1991) highlighted a significant strength of using two methods as serving as its own a validation check. This approach assumed each method produced complementary results. As mixed methods developed, researchers recognized the value of divergent findings and began to include information about each method separately as well as details about the overall rigor of the design. Following is an overview of each approach.

Table 14.5. Alignment in Data Collection

Sources of Data	Focus Groups	Student Stress Survey	ACHA-NCHA
Sample questions	What stressors do students like you experience?	How often have you experienced stress due to finances in the past month?	Did you find finances difficult to handle in last 12 months?
Sample findings	Financial stress was rated as 2nd most frequent and severe out of 8 types of stress. Issues underlying financial stress: • Lack of personal finance management knowledge & skills[a] • Insufficient funds for daily needs[b] • High costs & limited financial aid[c] • Unrealistic expectations • Lack of efficient & clear financial aid processes • Postuniversity debt burden	20% of students reported stress due to finances on most days in past month. Significantly more stress due to finances related to: • More hours of work for pay[d] • Lower levels of parental education[e] • Lower overall health[f]	30.5% of men and 39.3% of women had difficulty handling finances in the last 12 months. Higher rates reported by: • Females • Students of color • Students who work more than 20 hours per week

Note: [a,b,c]Table 3 presents excerpts from the Financial Stress Strategic Plan that addresses these two key financial stress issues. [d]$r_s(1,623) = .201$, $p < .001$. [e]$r_s(1,575) = -.15$, $p < .0001$. [f]$r_s(1,622) = -.18$, $p < .0001$.

Source: From Baker and Sgoutas-Emch (2014), Table 2, p. 121. Reprinted with permission of the *College Student Affairs Journal.*

When mixed methods researchers describe the rigor of their study in separate sections, they typically use concepts traditionally associated with each method (validity and reliability for quantitative data and trustworthiness and dependability for qualitative data). Morse, Barrett, Mayan, Olson, and Spiers (2002) noted, "Whether quantitative or qualitative methods are used, rigor is a desired goal that is met through specific verification strategies. While different strategies are used for each paradigm, the term validity is the most pertinent term for these processes" (p. 19). Chesbrough (2011, pp. 696–697) used this approach to describe rigor for the qualitative and quantitative aspects of the sequential exploratory design separately (see Table 14.6).

Table 14.6. Approaches to Validity Testing

Qualitative Validity	Quantitative Validity
Triangulation of data collection using single and mixed-gender focus groups and individual interviews. Member checking by asking participants to review draft findings and emerging themes from the research to assess accuracy of the interpretations. Peer debriefing by asking an external evaluator to review and ask questions about the research to establish clarity and plausible interpretations. External audit of the study involving a full review of all files and records of the study as well as of data analysis and interpretation strategies and outcomes of the study.	Validation of the survey instrument using content validity by two external experts and faculty colleagues at the research site as well as a review by participants in the qualitative phase. Established statistical reliability and internal consistency of the survey instrument using factor analysis and coefficient alphas for all questions as well as the instrument (factor scores were included in the article).

When researchers describe the overall rigor of their study, they address specific aspects of the methodology. Following is an overview of considerations for evaluating mixed methods designs.

- In convergent design, readers should consider whether the variables and/or themes are comparable. For example, if both large-scale survey data are collected alongside individual interviews, are the data equivalent? Greene et al. (1989) further asked if the results serve the purpose of triangulation or complementarity?

- For sequential designs, readers should question the rationale for transitioning from one method to the next. If an additional sample is used, is the procedure clear and easily traced back to the former method? For example, if interviews are used to suggest a group demographic for a larger survey follow-up, is the rationale for selection and the sampling procedure clear and adequate? If an instrument was created as part of the first method, are there sufficient details about its construction, both the items and the full instrument? Greene et al. (1989) referred to this as developing a more effective and refined conclusion by using results from one method to inform or shape the use of another.

- For transformative design, readers should consider how the results, and in particular the implications, build credibility across stakeholders (those affected as well as policy makers). For example, were community members involved as research partners? Does the researcher discuss their ideology and values in relation to the study (McCoy, 2016)?

Ideally, researchers include information for each method and the full design, but space and other considerations are often prohibitive. Creswell (2015) and Plano Clark and Ivankova (2016) emphasized that researchers must include the rationale for using multiple types of research. This can give insight to design rigor. Teddlie and Tashakkori (2009) offered a comprehensive approach to evaluating both methods and designs, recommending that readers should focus on the design's quality and interpretive rigor when evaluating mixed methods research. Design quality includes the suitability and overall fidelity of the design, within-design consistency, and analytical adequacy. Interpretive rigor includes interpretive and theoretical consistency, interpretive agreement as well as distinctness, and the efficacy of the integration.

Perspectives From the Field—What Mixed Methods Has to Offer

Student affairs professionals regularly use quantitative and qualitative thinking in their practice. We track numbers all the time, such as evaluation ratings, graduation rates, and campus rankings. We also capture words all the time, such as student experiences, program reports, and staff perceptions. Mixed methods research provides a formalized way for student affairs professionals to have their questions answered and improve their practices by combining what they learn from both numbers and words—something we already do in our everyday work! However, mixed methods thinking means that we actively consider what new ideas emerge by integrating the numbers and words together. For example, mixed methods can offer a more complete and holistic understanding of a program's impacts by combining measures of outcomes with interviews about student experiences. Mixed methods can also offer a more in-depth explanation of an issue by using numbers to identify individuals engaged in risky behaviors and then talking with those individuals to explain why the behaviors are occurring and how they might be prevented. Furthermore, mixed methods can offer more contextualized assessment of a problem by talking to key students about their perceptions and then using that information to design a survey to assess how prevalent the perceptions are among all students. As these examples show, mixed methods offers us ways to use both numbers and words to examine and inform our practices as student affairs professionals.

Vicki L. Plano Clark—Associate professor, School of Education, University of Cincinnati

Building Your Mixed Methods Research Skillset

The ten competency areas for practitioners (ACPA/NASPA, 2015), as well as the standards for master's level preparation in the field (CAS, 2015), relate foundational outcomes for research. Specifically applicable to mixed methods research, ACPA/NASPA's (2015) Foundational Intermediate Competencies relate the following:

> Foundational Outcomes
>
> Select AER methods, methodologies, designs, and tools that fit with research and evaluation questions and with assessment and review purposes.
>
> Assess the legitimacy, trustworthiness, and/or validity of studies of various methods and methodological designs (e.g., qualitative versus quantitative, theoretical perspective, epistemological approach).
>
> Intermediate Outcomes
>
> Demonstrate a working knowledge of additional methodological approaches to AER (e.g., mixed methods, historical or literary analysis, or comparative study) including elements of design, data collection, analysis, and reporting as well as strategies for ensuring the quality.

A basic knowledge of mixed methods research includes knowing the data collection and reporting strategies of both qualitative and quantitative research. This leads to an understanding of how the methods were used together (and integrated) to address a problem. Further, learning to read and create diagrams based on research descriptions is a valuable skill in evaluating all types of research. Beyond these foundational skills, exposure to published mixed methods research can help suggest ways problems in practice might be addressed more holistically to support assessment efforts.

Creswell (2015) recommended that researchers wanting to learn more about mixed methods should have a general understanding of the research design process. Beyond this, having the skills necessary for designing separate studies for each method, rationalizing their use together, working with both congruence and discrepancies, and intentionally seeking integration points are important. Adding additional data collection to an existing assessment effort (such as interviewing individuals who are surveyed about program learning outcomes) is a helpful way to start thinking about how methods might be used in combination.

References

American College Personnel Association & National Association of Student Personnel Administrators. (2015). *Professional competency areas for student affairs practitioners.* Washington, DC: Authors.

Baker, M. A., & Sgoutas-Emch, S. A. (2014). Evidence-based strategic planning using mixed methods and the social ecological model to target student financial stress. *College Student Affairs Journal, 32*(1), 113–128.

Bryman, A. (2006). Integrating quantitative and qualitative research: How is it done? *Qualitative Research, 6*(1), 97–113.

Chesbrough, R. D. (2011). College students and service: A mixed methods exploration of motivations, choices, and learning outcomes. *Journal of College Student Development, 52*(6), 687–705.

Council for the Advancement of Standards in Higher Education. (2015). *CAS professional standards for higher education* (9th ed.). Washington, DC: Author.

Crede, E., & Borrego, M. (2013). From ethnography to items: A mixed methods approach to developing a survey to examine graduate engineering student retention. *Journal of Mixed Methods Research, 7*(1), 62–80.

Creswell, J. W. (2002). *Educational research: Planning, conducting, and evaluating quantitative and qualitative research.* Upper Saddle River, NJ: Merrill.

Creswell, J. W. (2013). *Research design: Qualitative, quantitative and mixed methods approaches* (4th ed.). Thousand Oaks, CA: Sage.

Creswell, J. W. (2015). *A concise introduction to mixed methods research.* Thousand Oaks, CA: Sage.

Creswell, J. W., & Plano Clark, V. (2010). *Designing and conducting mixed methods research* (2nd ed.). Thousand Oaks, CA: Sage.

Creswell, J. W., & Plano Clark, V. (2017). *Designing and conducting mixed methods research* (3rd ed.). Thousand Oaks, CA: Sage.

Denzin, N. K. (1978). *The research act: A theoretical introduction to sociological methods.* New York, NY: Praeger.

Garcia, G. A., Huerta, A. H., Ramirez, J. J., & Patrón, O. E. (2017). Contexts that matter to the leadership development of Latino male college students: A mixed methods perspective. *Journal of College Student Development, 58*(1), 1–18.

Greene, J. C. (2007). *Mixed methods in social inquiry.* San Francisco, CA: Jossey-Bass.

Greene, J. C. (2008). Is mixed methods social inquiry a distinctive methodology? *Journal of Mixed Methods Research, 2*(1), 7–22.

Greene, J. C., Caracelli, V. J., & Graham, W. F. (1989). Toward a conceptual framework for mixed-method evaluation designs. *Educational Evaluation and Policy Analysis, 11*(3), 255–274.

Hall, A. L., & Rist, R. C. (1999). Integrating multiple qualitative research methods (or avoiding the precariousness of a one-legged stool). *Psychology & Marketing, 16*(4), 291–304.

Jick, T. (1979). Mixing qualitative and quantitative methods: Triangulation in action. *Administrative Science Quarterly, 24*(4), 602–611.

Kovtun, O. (2011). International student adaptation to a U.S. college: A mixed methods exploration of the impact of a specialized first-year course at a large Midwestern institution. *Journal of Student Affairs Research and Practice, 48*(3), 349–366.

Mathison, S. (1988). Why triangulate? *Educational Researcher, 77*(2), 13–17.

McCoy, D. L. (2016). Mixed methodology research. In F. Stage & K. Manning (Eds.), *Research in the college context: Approaches and methods* (2nd ed., pp. 95–108). New York, NY: Routledge.

Mertens, D. M. (2003). Mixed methods and the politics of human research: The transformative-emancipatory perspective. In A. Tashakkori & C. Teddlie (Eds.), *Handbook of mixed methods in social and behavioral research* (pp. 135–164). Thousand Oaks, CA: Sage.

Mertens, D. M. (2007). Transformative paradigm: Mixed methods and social justice. *Journal of Mixed Methods Research, 1*, 212–225.

Morgan, D. L. (2007). Paradigms lost and pragmatism regained: Methodological implications of combining qualitative and quantitative methods. *Journal of Mixed Methods Research, 1*(1), 48–76.

Morgan, D. L. (2013). *Integrating qualitative and quantitative methods: A pragmatic approach.* Thousand Oaks, CA: Sage.

Morse, J. M. (1991). Approaches to qualitative-quantitative methodological triangulation. *Nursing Research, 40,* 120–123.

Morse, J. M., Barrett, M., Mayan, M., Olson, K., & Spiers, J. (2002). Verification strategies for establishing reliability and validity in qualitative research. *International Journal of Qualitative Methods, 1*(2), 13–22.

Plano Clark, V., & Ivankova, N. V. (2016). *Mixed methods research: A guide to the field.* Thousand Oaks, CA: Sage.

Seifert, T. A., Goodman, K., King, P. M., & Baxter Magolda, M. B. (2010). Using mixed methods to study first-year college impact on liberal arts learning outcomes. *Journal of Mixed Methods Research, 4*(3), 248–267.

Sweetman, D., Badiee, M., & Creswell, J. W. (2010). Use of the transformative framework in mixed methods studies. *Qualitative Inquiry, 16*(6), 441–454.

Tashakkori, A., & Teddlie, C. (1998). *Mixed methodology: Combining qualitative and quantitative approaches.* Thousand Oaks, CA: Sage.

Tashakkori, A., & Teddlie, C. (2008). Quality of inferences in mixed methods research: Calling for an integrative framework. In M. Bergman (Ed.), *Advances in mixed methods research: Theories and applications.* Thousand Oaks, CA: Sage.

Tashakkori, A., & Teddlie, C. (2010). *Handbook of mixed methods in social and behavioral research* (2nd ed.). Thousand Oaks, CA: Sage.

Taub, D. J., Johnson, R., & Reynolds, B. (2016). The implementation of gender-neutral housing: A mixed-methods study across ACUHO-I member institutions. *Journal of College and University Student Housing, 42*(2), 76–93.

Teddlie, C., & Tashakkori, A. (2006). A general typology of research designs featuring mixed methods. *Research in the Schools, 13*(1), 12–28.

Teddlie, C., & Tashakkori, A. (2009). *Foundations of mixed methods research: Integrating quantitative and qualitative approaches in the social and behavioral sciences.* Thousand Oaks, CA: Sage.

Teddlie, C., & Tashakkori, A. (2011). Mixed methods: Contemporary issues in an emerging field. In N. K. Denzin & Y. S. Lincoln (Eds.), *Handbook of qualitative research* (4th ed.). Thousand Oaks, CA: Sage.

GLOSSARY

analysis of variance (ANOVA) (*F*-test)   A parametric test that evaluates differences between or within two or more groups by comparing mean scores.

assessment   The collection, analysis, and interpretation of context-specific data to inform the effectiveness of programs and services.

authenticity   An expression of the genuineness of interview data; concerned with data collection.

basic interview   An in-depth individual or focus group interview that does not follow a specific theoretical framework beyond basic constructivism. The general purpose is to elicit perspective and meaning.

basic qualitative design   A research design that uses primary methods for data collection and a generalized approach to data analysis.

Belmont Report   A document detailing the basic rights and provisions for the protection of human participants in research.

benchmarking   A method for locating and evaluating existing data to make comparisons. Benchmarking also can include generating data locally for comparison to external trends.

beta coefficient (*B*, *b*)   The value a predictor contributes to the prediction equation; also referred to as a beta weight.

case study   A form of qualitative research that involves the collection and analysis of multiple forms of data to build understanding about an individual, site, or process.

central tendency   The central or most typical value in a group of numbers. The three most common types are mean (the arithmetic average), median (the midpoint of the data), and mode (the most frequently occurring value).

chi-square (χ^2)   A nonparametric statistic that evaluates differences in two or more groups by comparing percentages. Data tested typically are groups (nominal).

class interval   A grouping of numerical data into categories based on a range.

code   A category or unit of analysis used to describe a singular aspect of data.

coding   A process of data analysis that involves identifying patterns and themes in qualitative data to represent findings.

coefficient   The result of a statistical calculation.

conceptual framework   An initial framework the researcher develops from existing theory.

concurrent mixed methods   A research method that involves collecting both qualitative and quantitative data simultaneously.

constructivism   A philosophical perspective that seeks to understand reality from individual interpretations (multiple meanings), accounting for culture, context, or other factors that affect those realities.

contrived observation   An observation in which the researcher deliberately varies the setting in some way.

correlation   A quantifiable relationship between variables; the extent to which variables are interdependent or change together.

correlation coefficient   A factor that measures the strength of association of two variables (as an absolute value), ranging from –1 (perfect negative correlation) to +1 (perfect positive correlation), with 0 indicating no association.

correlation matrix   A display format for correlation results, shown as a table with correlation coefficients displayed where variable pairs intersect at rows and columns.

criterion sampling   A sampling method used to specify a phenomenon, experience, or event and locate participants that meet the criteria.

critical discourse analysis   An extension of discourse analysis that uses critical theory to study the use and meaning of documents. This method has three properties: relational (the focus is not on individuals or entities, but social relations), dialectical (relations between objects are different but not discrete), and transdisciplinary.

Cronbach's alpha   A reliability measure that assesses relationships (correlations) between several items in a survey to identify factors. It is used to evaluate internal consistency.

cross tabulation, or "crosstab"   A grouping of numerical data into categories by combining two or more variables.

dependent variable   An outcome affected by one or more independent variables. Dependent variables can be directly collected as a question or measure on a survey or derived by summing or statistically combining several questions into one measure (called a factor).

descriptive statistics   A set of quantitative data analysis techniques used to condense numerical information into interpretable, manageable, and useful summary measures to examine trends and tendencies.

design   The foundational framework of a study that influences decisions researchers make before, during, and after data collection.

difference statistics   Inferential statistics that examine change between groups, allowing researchers to make inferences (evidenced guesses) about a population, to distinguish groups, or to track changes over time.

discourse analysis   The study of how language is used in text and other contexts.

document   A text or image data source.

document analysis   The process of analyzing text-based data.

document review   A form of qualitative data analysis that involves examining existing information, inclusive of documents, records, or artifacts in text, visual, or mixed formats. In addition to analyzing words or images, researchers also are concerned with the presentation of materials, which can include authorship, context, medium, and format.

effect size   A statistical measure that quantifies the difference between two or more measures. Restated literally, it is a measure of the size (the magnitude) of an effect (the difference). It is sometimes called a measure of practical significance.

embedded design   A mixed methods research design that involves using one type of data to answer a secondary research question within a predominant method. It is sometimes referred to as nested design.

empirical   Data collected directly from a source (such as survey or interview) or obtained from an existing dataset consisting of directly collected data.

existing dataset   An organized collection of numerical or document data.

experimental design   A quantitative research design that typically involves a treatment or condition that has been manipulated by the researcher. Experimental design is seldom used in student affairs because it requires randomly assigning participants to a control and an experimental group.

explanatory sequential design   A mixed methods research design in which the researcher collects and analyzes quantitative data and then collects qualitative data to explain the quantitative findings.

exploratory interview   A focus group interview that broadly explores an issue or topic to develop a more specific research question or agenda. Typically, a group is asked open-ended questions as a way to develop a focus on a specific topic or issue.

exploratory sequential design   A mixed methods research design in which the researcher collects and analyzes qualitative data and then collects quantitative data to explore the qualitative findings.

factor analysis   A method of statistically combining several variables into a single measure, commonly used in survey research. The combination of variables is based on correlations.

focus group   An approach to qualitative data collection using using open-ended questions or prompts to gain perspectives from a group.

frequency   A summarized count of values.

grounded theory   A systematic qualitative data analysis procedure used to create an explanation or theory of a process, issue, or action.

independent variable   A measured or manipulated quantity or trait that is believed to affect an outcome.

individual interview   An approach to qualitative data collection using open-ended questions or prompts to gain perspectives from an individual.

inferential statistics   A set of quantitative data analysis techniques used to make an informed guess, or inference, about a value in a population based data collected from a sample.

informed consent   The process of gaining an individual's approval for participation in a study.

Institutional Review Board (IRB)   A committee comprised of faculty, staff, and community members who review ethical considerations of research.

instrument   A tool used to record data. An instrument can be quantitative, such as a survey, or qualitative, such as an observation checklist or interview guide. It can be highly structured (all questions are listed), loosely structured (some questions or prompts are listed), or completely unstructured (few or no questions are listed).

integration   The point in a mixed methods study in which the design, data collection, analysis, results, and/or interpretation of data in a study interact.

interval variable   A numerical variable derived from an ordered rating like the Likert scale (strongly disagree, disagree, agree, strongly agree), in which the difference between values is meaningful.

interviewing   The process of identifying key informants, determining questions to ask, recording responses, and (often) seeking others who can confirm, contradict, or otherwise provide additional perspectives on a topic. See also *basic interview, narrative interview.*

literature review   A synthesis of research on a topic.

location sampling   The researcher chooses a specific location and observes the location one (or ideally more) days during different times.

logistic regression   A method used to predict the relationship between one or more variables (any type) and a single discrete outcome. There are two types of logistic regression: binary (only two possible outcomes—yes–no) and ordinal (the outcome is ordered—low–middle–high group).

methodology   A research plan that serves initially as scaffolding and later as a framework for a study.

methods diagram   A drawing with specific notations showing the research methods and procedures. Depending on the design of the study, it may be simple or complex.

minimal risk   The least possible harm that a researcher anticipates could result from involvement in a study. It is generally thought of as being not greater than risk encountered in ordinary circumstances or situations in daily life or during participation in routine physical or physiological tests.

mixed methods   A research method that integrates multiple different methods in the same study to explain, explore, or inform a research topic. Depending on the sequence and timing of the data collection, the priority of the methods used, and the outcomes a researcher intends to accomplish, the mixing points of the study can vary.

multimodal analysis   The study of both images and text in documents.

multiple regression   A statistical technique used to predict the relationship between one or more numerical variables and a single numerical outcome.

narrative design   A research design that uses descriptions or accounts of events to enlighten experiences and perspectives.

narrative interview   An in-depth interview with an individual aimed at understanding an experience as narrated by the person who experienced it. This type of interview is typically conducted in multiple sessions to relate the story of a single individual (referred to as a life-history) or to identify themes from several individuals that converge across stories describing a common experience.

nominal variable   A variable that is a qualitative designation rather than a numerical value, such as gender, or a characteristic, such as sorority membership. Also sometimes called a categorical variable.

nonexperimental design   A quantitative research design that typically involves a treatment or condition that has not been manipulated, such as the distribution of a survey.

nonparametric   The term used for nonnumeric variables (typically nominal or ordinal) that do not follow a normal distribution. It would not be appropriate to calculate mean with a nonparametric variable, such as class standing.

nonparticipant observation   The practice of collecting data in a location while avoiding interaction with the individuals present and without otherwise affecting the site or setting.

observation   The practice of selecting a person or group, or a time and location, and recording data about the environment or the interactions and activities that take place.

odds ratio (*OR* or Exp(*B*))   A value representing a predictor variable that represents the odds an outcome will occur given the presence of that predictor. Typically associated with logistic regression.

ordinal variable   A numerical variable derived from a list of categories, such as class standing (freshman, sophomore, junior, senior) in which the order is meaningful.

outlier   A data point that does not seem consistent with the others, pointing to potential problems (or possible opportunities) with the findings.

parameter   A value that exists in a population.

parametric   The term used for numeric variables (interval or scale) that follow a normal distribution. It would be appropriate to calculate a mean with a parametric value, such as age.

participant-observation   The practice of collecting data while intentionally being a noticeable part of (or participant in) the observed activity or setting. The observer typically interacts with others, although the level of interaction can vary.

Pearson correlation (*r*)   A correlation coefficient used to assess the degree of relationship between (generally) numerical variables. The complete but seldom used name of the measure is the Pearson product-moment correlation coefficient, although it is often abbreviated as simply Pearson's *r*.

peer review   The process by which a group of experts makes a determination about a study before it is published, critiquing both the methodology and data sources, as well as its potential contribution to a specific aspect of the field.

person sampling   Data collection concerned with how an individual or group behaves. Time and location may be considerations, but not the central focus.

perspective   A point of view; the lens through which a person sees and makes sense of the world around them.

phenomenological interview   A method of collecting data that focuses on capturing perspectives from lived-through moments, experiences, and remembered stories with the goal of describing a phenomenon.

phenomenology   A qualitative research design concerned with how individuals experience, conceptualize, perceive, and/or understand (or make meaning of) phenomena.

population   All members of a specific group selected based on the goals of a study.

post hoc **test**   A follow-up test to analysis of variance (ANOVA). An ANOVA identifies statistical significant differences by testing pairs, but it does not specify which pairs are different. A follow-up, or *post hoc*, test reveals these differences by testing each pair of values.

postpositivism   A philosophical perspective that views truth as a discoverable reality and seeks to determine causes that influence outcomes through objective reductionist methods.

pragmatism   A problem-centered and solution-oriented research perspective that uses multiple methods to address a research problem according to which designs and methods are best suited to providing an answer.

prediction statistics   Inferential statistics that estimate the influence of one or more measures on an outcome.

problem statement   A statement that specifies the need and value of a study by answering three questions: What is known about the topic? What is not known about the topic? and Why do we need to know what is not known about the topic?

qualitative research   A set of research methods that seek to explore and represent reality as it exists in context and to enlighten the ways in which individuals experience that reality. Qualitative methods answer "how" and "why" questions by focusing on understanding and exploring the qualities of a person, place, process, or phenomenon.

quantitative research   A set of research methods that seek to identify and explain reality as it exists empirically. Quantitative research is characterized by the use of numerical data.

quasi-experimental design   A quantitative research design that typically involves a pre–post measure that evaluates a treatment, condition, or effect of time. It is differentiated from experimental design because it does not require randomly assigning participants to a control and an experimental group.

R^2 A statistical measure that suggests how well a regression model (with all predictors) fits, or predicts, an outcome. It can be considered an indicator of accuracy.

regression   An inferential statistic that examines the relationship between one or more predictor (independent) and outcome (dependent) variables.

regression model (or equation)   A combination of variables hypothesized to predict an outcome.

relationship statistics   Inferential statistics that evaluate associations between two or more variables. In most cases, the variables are considered related when a change in one relates to a change in another.

reliability   A determination of how consistently a measure assesses an outcome. A measure is reliable when it is consistent.

research   A systematic approach to learning that involves asking and answering questions.

research ethics   A set of principles concerned with the responsible treatment of individuals and their data. Ethics encompass the responsibilities researchers have to participants and their data before, during, and after a study.

research proposal   A written justification for conducting a study, based on identification of a clear problem statement, well-evidenced literature review, viable research questions, accessible data sources, and feasibility of data collection and analysis.

research questions   The specified areas of interest of a study, guiding how a research problem will be researched and addressed. Good research questions reveal the data sources (such as variables or people), methods, and analysis.

sample   A set of data collected and/or selected from a population. See also *criterion sampling; location sampling; person sampling; snowball sampling; time sampling; time-and-location sampling.*

saturation   The point in data collection and analysis after which no new information is discovered.

scale variable   A numerical variable derived from continuous numbers such as service hours (0–infinity).

scales of measurement   A classification system used to differentiate variables. Scales of measurement include nominal, ordinal, interval, and scale. See also *interval variable, nominal variable, ordinal variable, scale variable.*

scatterplot   A graphical representation of associations between variables. Each data point (or value) on a scatterplot has two coordinates. One goes left to right (*x* coordinate) and the other up or down (the *y* coordinate). When all values are plotted on the same chart, they form a scatterplot.

sequential mixed methods   A mixed method research design that involves collecting qualitative and quantitative data in distinct, sequenced phases.

significance test   An evaluation of differences in summary values such as mean, rank, or percentage. A significant result usually means the observed difference is also reflected in the population.

simple observation   An observation in which the researcher has no control over the setting or participants.

snowball sampling   A sampling method that involves locating information-rich sources based on recommendations. The process continues, or snowballs, until the researcher is satisfied with the richness of the data (or until *saturation* is reached).

Spearman's rho (ρ)   A correlation coefficient that considers the degree of association between nonnumerical variables. The complete name of the measure is the Spearman rank-order correlation coefficient. Spearman's rho is used frequently with Likert-like ratings or ranked data when the responses are not normally distributed (nonparametric).

standard deviation   The average variability (or deviation) in a set of numbers. Range reveals how far apart the data are in total; standard deviation reveals how far apart the responses are on average.

statistic   A value calculated from a sample. Another word for statistic is parameter estimate, which suggests the researcher is estimating the true value (parameter) based on a sample.

survey   A data collection tool, or instrument, that researchers use to collect numerical data.

theme   A central classification of codes. Themes are generally presented in the results section of a study with explanations and illustrative excerpts from the data.

theoretical framework One or more theories a researcher uses to guide aspects of the study, ranging from selection of literature to review to design considerations such as data sources or instruments.

time sampling Observation at a chosen time of a given location for one (or ideally more) day.

time-and-location sampling Observation of phenomena or events at multiple locations at different times.

transferability The extent to which research findings are relatable to a similar context.

trustworthiness The extent to which qualitative data and analysis are credible, transferable, dependable, and confirmable.

***t*-test (*t*)** A parametric test that evaluates differences between or within two groups by comparing mean scores.

type I error An error that occurs when the results show a difference (for example, $p < .05$) when there is not one; a false positive.

type II error An error that occurs when the results show no difference (for example, $p > .05$) when there is one; a false negative.

validity The degree to which a measure accurately assesses an outcome. A measure is valid when it is accurate. Internal validity concerns evidence within a study; external validity concerns generalization to outside contexts.

variability The spread of data. It is also sometimes referred to as dispersion.

variable A measured or manipulated quantity or trait. Variables broadly are classified into two types, independent and dependent. Variables also have a distribution, or shape, classified as nonparametric or parametric.

visual analysis The process of analyzing image-based data.

INDEX